Barbara from Jane + Eddie
August

Malraux
LIFE AND WORK

Malraux

LIFE AND WORK

*

EDITED BY

Martine de Courcel

WEIDENFELD AND NICOLSON
LONDON

ISBN 0 297 77177 9

Printed and bound by Morrison and Gibb Ltd
London and Edinburgh

CONTENTS

II THE TEMPTATIONS OF THE EAST

III THE ETHICS OF IMAGINATION

CONTRIBUTORS

WALTER G. LANGLOIS: Professor of French literature and head of the Department of Modern and Classical Languages, University of Wyoming; editor of *Malraux Miscellany* (USA) and *La Série André Malraux* (France); owner of the most extensive collection of documents and photographs concerning Malraux

SIR ISAIAH BERLIN: President of the British Academy and President of Wolfson College, Oxford (1966–75)

HUGH THOMAS: Professor of History and Chairman of the Graduate School of Contemporary European Studies, University of Reading

SIR A. J. AYER: Wykeman Professor of Logic, University of Oxford, and Fellow of New College, Oxford

PIERRE BOCKEL: Dean of Strasbourg Cathedral and chaplain of the Brigade Alsace Lorraine during the Resistance

GASTON PALEWSKI: French politician and diplomat; Membre de l'Institut; Directeur du Cabinet with General de Gaulle; ex-President du Conseil constitutionnel

ANDRÉ HOLLEAUX: Conseiller d'Etat; Directeur du cabinet at Ministry of Cultural Affairs with Malraux for four years

NICOLE ALPHAND: Wife of Hervé Alphand who was French Ambassador to Washington, DC (1956–65) and head of the French Foreign Office (1965–72)

CHANG MEI YUAN: Chinese scholar; author of thesis on Malraux, Confucianism and Taoism

GIRIJA MOOKERJEE: Indian poet and scholar; political fighter; diplomat

TADAO TAKEMOTO: Japanese poet and essayist; Secretary-General of the National Federation of Unesco associations in Japan; translated Malraux's work into Japanese

FRANÇOISE DORENLOT: Professor of French Literature at City College, New York; author of *Malraux, ou l'Unite de Pensée*

JOHN LEHMANN: Writer and literary critic

MANÈS SPERBER: Writer and journalist; disciple of Adler with whom he worked in Vienna for ten years; involved in anti-fascist activities in Europe during the 1930s

SIR E. H. GOMBRICH: Art historian and Director of the Warburg Institute; Professor of the History of Classical Tradition, University of London

JEAN LEYMARIE: Conservateur en chef des musées nationaux; Directeur de l'Ecole du Louvre

C. L. SULZBERGER: American Journalist and writer; columnist for the New York Times

VICTORIA OCAMPO: Eminence grise of modern South American Literature; founder and editor of the literary magazine, *Sur*

ILLUSTRATIONS

Between pages 150 and 151

INTRODUCTION

by Martine de Courcel

Seldom does one start a book at the beginning. In this case, such behaviour, usually reprehensible, is undoubtedly justified and even to be encouraged, the reader going straight to the best part: the *Anti-critique* by André Malraux. In this *Anti-critique* he describes at greater length than ever before the process of metamorphosis in literature and opens up new vistas on the subject of biography. If the reader has been orderly, what follows will enlighten him as to the purpose of this work; if not, he may nonetheless find it useful to be told how this book has become what it is.

For Malraux, as always, goes straight to the core without lingering over the intermediate strata, and while he traces the origins of the Colloquy which he believes to be a new form of literature and to which *Malraux: Life and Work* belongs, we, on the other hand, may be well advised to take a slower, longer, less striking, more logical path and to explain its make-up.

I

The main ambition of this book was to knock down the wall of rhetoric which appears to bar, for the Anglo-Saxons and particularly the British, the access to Malraux's work. Rhetoric being for them an object of disapproval and a cause of embarrassment. So it seemed at first that the contributors should be British or American. But it soon became obvious that certain aspects of Malraux's work – in so far as they were too exclusively related to the context of French national life – should be studied by French authors. Also, as the choice of subjects to be dealt with became clearer, it seemed to me that Malraux's world-wide stature demanded that authors from the countries whose art and culture had influenced him, and who in turn had been influenced by his thinking, should contribute to the book: hence the chapters by Chang Mei Yuan, Girija Mookerjee and Tadao Takemoto.

I set out, therefore, to match authors and subjects without any very clear plan, knowing simply *where* I was starting from and *where* I wanted to get. The purpose, as Malraux was to write in his *Anti-critique* was not 'to make a work intelligible, but to give the feeling of its quality'. The structure of the book stemmed from its very existence, and it was only later that the different chapters fell into place and that a table of contents emerged with a logic of its own in which themes and chronology blended. I think a very real and immediate Malraux is revealed through the relatively abstract essays such as 'Malraux and Chinese Thinking', 'Malraux and the Creative Process', 'The Administration of Culture', and that the austerity of such essays is counterbalanced by the more factual contributions, namely the recollections of Victoria Ocampo and Cyrus Sulzberger, and the more historical ones concerning Indochina and the Spanish Civil War.

This feeling of Malraux's presence in the book is achieved through the use of indirect methods which Malraux would describe as 'oblique', whereas a more direct approach would have produced a clearer, but no doubt a less accurate image. This image is not a 'posed' photograph, it is by way of being a cinematic image – it moves, it is perhaps a bit blurred, but Malraux comes to life in it.

Mindful of Malraux's own attitude towards any biography of himself[*] – which is one of professed lack of interest – we have included at the end of the book a synopsis covering the important events of his life and the dates of the publication of his works. Only in Professor Walter Langlois' chapter do we find details of his childhood and adolescence, for after his Indochinese venture Malraux's life and work are so closely intermingled that his books are the clue to his biography.

This book is constructed on horizontal rather than vertical lines: the chapters are related to each other, composing a network of intersections and cross-sections and even going off at a tangent so that what might appear to overlap or to be repetitive produces, in the final analysis, an increase of contrast such as is obtained by the simultaneous development of negatives placed one on top of the other.

This multi-sided approach, which Malraux likens to the beams of anti-aircraft searchlights tracking an aeroplane in the sky, makes a linear biography obsolete. It avoids the pitfall of reducing a character

* For further reference, see Jean Lacouture's comprehensive work, *André Malraux*, Deutsch, 1975.

to the mere objective elements of his life and seems to me particularly suited to a study of Malraux in so far as he can be defined by a twofold unity – dual and integrated; the first between his life and his work and the second within the work itself. For if it is always artificial to atomize a work, to divide it into isolated chapters (even if this technique has heuristic advantages), it would be all the more absurd to do so in Malraux's case. So this book does not presume to be exhaustive, but to be sufficiently open to provoke and welcome different approaches and other points of view.

The connection between the different chapters soon becomes apparent. It is interesting that Isaiah Berlin should attempt to analyze Malraux's Marxism and that Françoise Dorenlot, Hugh Thomas, Manès Sperber and Cyrus Sulzberger should also mention it; and that in the end these opinions which sometimes converge and sometimes diverge should show that Malraux had been interested in Marxism in so far as it seemed to him to carry with it a possible metamorphosis of the world, and that paradoxically he had become a Gaullist for similar, ethical rather than ideological, reasons: what he saw in de Gaulle was a kind of supreme artist, capable of resurrecting historical and mystical France.

It is likewise appropriate that Gaston Palewski should sketch the historical background of de Gaulle and Malraux's friendship, just as it is useful that Françoise Dorenlot, Manès Sperber and Girija Mookerjee should add their points of view. It is of course because he was an anti-communist and an antifascist that Malraux was a Gaullist, but also because his ideas on decolonization were very close to those of General de Gaulle – a problem which, as we shall see, has been at the root of Malraux's political vocation. Both believed in the power of the word, and every speech of theirs was an act.

An approach of this kind implies a certain element of risk, as does the attempt to sum up an author who is still writing, for if, as Malraux puts it, 'the range becomes increasingly accurate', it may also happen that it completely misses the target (I leave it to the reader to spot when). Whilst some chapters may lift a mask, others may add one.

For the same reasons I think it equally important that Manès Sperber in his article on 'Malraux and Politics' should speak of Malraux's ideas on aesthetics and that Jean Leymarie, in discussing his creative power, should mention his revolutionary commitments; that André Holleaux, who describes his administrative work at the Ministry of Cultural Affairs, should refer to his theories about art; that Hugh Thomas, who studies his activity during the Spanish Civil War, should end up by speaking of General de Gaulle; that Tadao Takemoto, who analyzes Malraux's relations with Japan, should touch on his relations with India, and that Father Pierre Bockel, speaking of Malraux's attitude towards religious faith, should record the life of 'Colonel Berger' (alias Malraux) in the maquis of Corrèze. It is also true that the Indochinese expedition as seen by Walter Langlois is a quite different adventure when related by John Lehmann. Equally the importance of the part Malraux is supposed to have played in the Chinese Revolution varies from one author to another. Likewise the absence of women in Malraux's work is given different interpretations, whether it be by John Lehmann, Freddie Ayer or Hugh Thomas.

But in the end all these differences are differences of outline – the centre of the image is brought into sharper focus.

This book, for all its apparent diversity, confirms the twofold unity which in my opinion is characteristic of Malraux's work. This is clearly demonstrated by the fact that Malraux wrote several chapters of *L'Espoir* in between air battles.

II

The first question that springs to mind in reading this book is whether Malraux does not have a sort of ontological repulsion for anything organized or established. As we shall see, he could not stand the over-academic teaching of the Ecole Turgot, and took over his own education; it was on his own, without the help of the Ecole d'Extrême Orient, that he undertook excavations in Indochina; he took an active part in the Spanish Civil War until it became a traditional war; nor was the Resistance all that conventional either in its methods or in the risks involved; he left politics when de Gaulle retired, foreseeing a return to the old rules of the game.

This explains, no doubt, why Malraux is loved neither by the Right nor the Left. (*Les Conquérants* was banned in the USSR and in Italy when it was published in 1928.) Basically he is disliked by *anyone who is a professional of any sort*; he is considered as a cheat and a marginal man. He is a bit like those young Spaniards called '*espontaneos*' who jump unauthorized into the bullring, but Malraux kills the matador's bull and the matador is left looking a trifle ridiculous. Maybe this also explains why none of our contemporaries understand better than Malraux what takes place in those mysterious regions where the past meets the present and the present the future.

He feels the same repulsion for any established church, and it may partly account for the fact that he broke away from Marxism. This agnostic, fascinated by religious thinking and religious concepts, has never been interested in religious dogma, be it Buddhist, Taoist or Catholic. What interests him is what religion makes of men who practise it and how it helps them to find in themselves 'enough strength to transcend their nothingness'. Here again is the same horror of what is established. He sought in other religions the answers to the questions raised by Christianity. When François Mauriac in his memoirs suggested that Malraux's temperament was deeply religious, and that if he hated the Church he did not despise it, he may have had in mind the passage of *L'Espoir* in which Guernico sadly states that the Church has forgotten Christ's message and become nothing more than an empty ritual.

Though he is a pilgrim in quest of transcendence, Malraux's curiosity concerning death is neither religious nor psychological, but purely metaphysical. He has the machinery of the mystic, but his faith is a kind of faith in nothingness.

III

This book also brings out what I, for want of a better word, shall call the *timeless aspect* of Malraux. As a writer he does not seem to have had any period of 'youth' or 'maturity': these are merely chronological points of reference. His maturity at twenty was no more astonishing than his youth at seventy; in 1923 it required not only a great spirit of adventure, but also a tremendous gift for organization – seldom found in a young man of twenty-one – to start excavating in the jungle of Cambodia; and in 1973 there were few septuagenarians who volunteered to fight in Bangladesh.

It was on the boat coming back from Indochina that he wrote most of the *Tentation de l'Occident*, which John Lehmann regards as a work of secondary importance but which I personally consider very important: first because the seeds of all Malraux's ideas on art are to be found in it: metamorphosis, timelessness, transmutation of myth and the discovery of the comparative method. He was to develop these ideas in *La Psychologie de l'Art* and *Le Musée Imaginaire* and I think they have helped to change our attitude towards art and the way we look at it. *The Tentation de l'Occident* is also historically significant because it is the first non-specialist work to state in new terms the dilemma between Europe and Asia. This all-encompassing vision of art, apparently the fruit of age and maturity, was revealed to Malraux when he was only twenty years old!

There is also a 'timelessness' in his relationship with artists and their work. Artistic creation – both past and present – fascinates Malraux, and he is equally at ease with any artist, be he alive or dead. Contemporary artists return the compliment: I have never discussed Malraux with any painter or musician without feeling that they considered him as one of themselves. He is at home on Olympus and he finds it just as natural to be on friendly terms with Michelangelo, Braque, Titian, Tolstoy, Picasso, Baudelaire, Giono and Nietzsche as with Dante, Alexander the Great, Mao Tse-tung, Stendhal, the two Lawrences, Matisse, Dostoievsky . . . and even Victor Hugo.

But this 'intimacy' with culture, history and artists is not only the fruit of his imagination – some might even say of his delirium. Malraux has been, and still is, the friend of painters. He has haunted studios and he has drained bottles of red wine with Picasso; he has spent time with Fautrier, Masson and Braque among others; he accompanied Le Corbusier to his building sites; he was the friend of André Gide and Paul Valéry and knew all the writers of *La Nouvelle Revue Française*. He stepped into publishing by way of the printing shops where fine editions are produced. After his return from Indochina he travelled widely in the Near and Middle East and again to Asia, where he went to many archeological digs and visited new museums. As far as art was concerned he was always 'on the spot'.

This 'timelessness' naturally takes on a spatial dimension. In the *Postface* he added to *Les Conquérants* in 1948, Malraux shows himself to be among the first to have understood the phenomenon of the internationalization of culture, which he opposes to the political illusion of internationalism. Through this concept of the multiplicity of cultures, he very early on acquired a planetary vision of the world which he explains as follows in the *Antimemoires*: 'the passion that Asia and the civilizations of the past kindled in me so long ago – ethnography – was due to a basic astonishment at the forms that man has been able to take, and also to the light that every foreign civilization sheds on my own, to what was singular or arbitrary in one or other of its aspects.'

'Timelessness' of his memory: it appears absolute and final. He remembers everything, and at any moment can delve into the most fabulous store of props imaginable. In spite of that he remains free, untrammelled by his immense knowledge. His thought is always fresh and continually renewed: every dawn is the dawn of a first day, nothing is ever settled or finally classified, the challenge goes on. He keeps producing another 'rabbit' from his hat. The word modern no longer means anything: the system with its feedback effects is integrated – the everlasting movement of the sea. There is no final full stop. He manipulates his writings with the same freedom, moving a passage from an old book into a new one, warning us that an apparently self-sufficient book was only the third part of something yet to come, and including in a new book a twenty-year-old text. Or else he does the opposite, as in the *Postface* to *Les Conquérants*: a trick borrowed from musicians who sometimes use the same theme in various compositions.

The timeless quality of his work itself tends to make us forget how disconcerting and new his technique as a novelist was in the Twenties. Because of this, I would have liked – but it could not be fitted in – to include a chapter on Marlaux's technique and style, to study the poetic element in his novels and in his books on art – for there are few non-political works (quite apart from his oratory, which by nature is lyrical and poetic) in which the poetic vision flashes so continuously. In fact the quotations in the present book are like so many passages of verse, hence the problems of translation throughout; so difficult indeed that as I look through the translation of some of his books I am amazed that Malraux should be read at all on the other side of the Channel or of the Atlantic.

The timelessness is revealed again in the only film he made, *Sierra de Teruel*, now shown under the title of the novel, *Espoir*, the film being based on one of its episodes. Shot in 1938, it was only released in 1945, as it had been considered dangerously revolutionary at the outbreak of the Second World War. It was very warmly praised when it was shown again in 1970 and 1975 (cf. Marion, *André Malraux*, col. Cinéma d'aujourd'hui, Seghers). The making of the film by Malraux in the middle of the Spanish Civil War, its disappearance (for the Germans had got hold of the reels), its reappearance after the war thanks to the fact that a copy had been placed (by accident or design) in a box labelled *Drôle de Drame* – all this was like a blood and thunder serial.

'Timelessness' again in his intellectual perception; Malraux seems endowed with a mental radio transmitter-receiver which is more sensitive and more sophisticated than other people's. He appears to obtain an immediate result from calculations which would take another critic a lifetime. This speed, the simultaneous workings of his mind, make him go right to the heart of things. He is like that when you meet him: although perfectly courteous, he never wastes a moment making small talk.

Every country, every village, has its own 'world's end', and every human being has his – the extreme limit of his universe. This is where Malraux seems to live permanently. But let us make no mistake, Malraux is no dreamer living on the edge of his dreams: the man of vision should not be taken for the visionary.

He lives in a kind of permanent intellectual exaltation which is not the same thing as restlessness. His attitude to practical problems is, in fact, extremely down-to-earth – what he calls 'an aptitude for action'. He is meticulous and precise, as you can see from his handwriting. André Holleaux says that, as a Minister, he was concerned about details – which were actually more than details – like the colour of the asphalt on the Place de la Concorde. His professional work as an art publisher required precision and technical know-how. And whatever his detractors might say, the Escuadrilla España was operational.

I would have liked to devote a chapter of this book to 'Malraux the Publisher', for we must remember that he came to literature through selling, discovering and publishing books. He worked at first for the bookseller Doyon, then for the art dealer and publisher Kahnweiler, where he served a kind of apprenticeship on the actual make-up of books. Then he was artistic director for Gallimard, and it was there that he first conceived his *Tableau de la Litterature Française* (of which the 'Colloquy' is possibly a very distant cousin), and that he founded the collection 'Univers des Formes' of which he is still a director. Several times in his *Journal*, between 1919 and 1923, André Gide pays tribute to Malraux's competence, then on 18 May 1929 he writes: '. . . this book owes its success to Malraux's enthusiasm and good taste', and on 2 January 1932: '. . . priceless help from Malraux, I could never have managed without him'.

These simultaneous workings of his mind, linked with his immense intellectual generosity, lead Malraux to a kind of passion for explanation: understanding so much that we do not understand, he wants to make us do so. But his sensory – above all visual – awareness is such that he also wants to make us see. It is not only the eyes of blind statues that he wishes to open. Even Nixon realized this when, according to Yves Salgues,* he confessed to a journalist: 'I thought I was consulting a disorderly mind, but I found myself in front of the most illuminating light of our time.' I have heard several politicians, bewildered by some event, remark: 'I would like to know what Malraux thinks of this.' For them he was a sort of great 'guru' of the West, and as he amusingly said to Pierre de Boisdeffre, he is not to blame if the world has suddenly started to look like his books.

Malraux is an analyst – an analyst of meaning – a sort of human computer fed by intelligence and sensibility, and unlike electronic computers he has no 'limits': indeed the machine sometimes seems to produce almost too many results. But this kind of Pythian labour is

* *Historia*: November 1975.

achieved with the greatest natural ease – even if this ease is sometimes a little complicated – and also with a great deal of humour. (Another gap in this book is that there is no mention of Malraux's sense of humour, of his smile which is quite different from Voltaire's, for Malraux is often on the brink of despair. Some of the quotations will illustrate this sense of humour and so will many parts of the *Anti-critique*.) His analysis is done in an unassuming manner: Malraux does not consider himself more extraordinary than anyone else, but certainly not less so. He would like us to see what he sees, and he has for us the same feelings that we have for the blind man we help across the street.

In this didacticism, which is a form of generosity, there is a desire to communicate his knowledge to the person who does not know, and his vision to the person who does not see, to be the intercessor and mediator between ourselves and a reality which escapes us. In all this there is no judgment but rather a kind of non-involvement, something like the non-involvement of the analyst, although psychoanalysis is strangely absent from Malraux's work, or perhaps not so much absent as unexpressed. What is absent is Freudianism (here again Malraux's distaste for anything dogmatic), whereas Jung's less rigid theories are more compatible with Malraux's view of man and the world.

But accompanying it all, as several contributors to this book have pointed out, there is an immense kindness, which is the reverse of false modesty and springs from his compassion for mankind. In his *Anti-memoirs*, Malraux admits: 'I have a tendency to think myself useful.'

It has often been said that de Gaulle loved France, but not the French. Malraux loves both mankind and men. He is interested in the essence of man: this essence which expresses itself through art and action. This is why he stands on a level with the great characters of our time, (and with those of the past), just as he does with ordinary people. Let us recall those peasants sitting on the doorstep of their farm at the end of *Les Noyers de l'Altenburg*, the strangers in the museums whose eyes, like ours, he opens (even if we sometimes become what André Gide calls 'his victimized audience'), the old woman for whom he pleaded with one of the sailors who made up the guard of honour holding back the crowd at General de Gaulle's funeral: 'Let her through, it would have pleased the General.'

IV

But alongside this kindness, there is drama, tragedy, anguish – the fundamental Pascalian anguish – the ultimate question: 'what are we doing here?' Malraux has searched for the answer everywhere and asked everyone. Surely his travels and explorations, his meetings with the great men of our time, are the sign of a secret hope that perhaps someone has the answer, or that it exists or has existed somewhere?

He went to Indochina looking for Khmer statues and came back with revolutionary ideas: in Indochina, a taste and a desire for action became part of what until then had been merely aesthetic sensitivity. Thereafter his travels were stages in his quest, food for his questions. Here I would like to quote *in toto*, as Vandegans did in his remarkable *La jeunesse Littéraire d'André Malraux*, Jean Prévost's description of Malraux at the time:

A chastised child, a soft-hearted rebel who has hitherto exchanged kisses with nothing but death: thus was Malraux on his return from Asia. Under the cover of excessive politeness, theories and whimsical daydreams, he tried to shelter himself from people and things. Pen in hand he rasped at life. The ample and tenacious recurrence of death and sadism turned his work into an act of revenge. He found fulfilment in his genius. Action, more than years, made him a man. Danger lent muscle to his heart; yet he seems capable of repose. He had reached the peak of the watershed. Which way should he turn? What should he say?*

He did not go to Spain just to see, or, according to Trotsky, as a war correspondent, and if he went to see it was not to look, but rather to get a vision more than a picture. He was not a tourist, but 'weary of our ancient world', as Apollinaire put it, he was anxious to know if other cultures would give him the answers ours denied him.

The exoticism in Malraux's novels is a convenience, not of the practical but of the poetical order; his characters are not so much Chinese, Spaniards or Germans as they are men. Denis Marion, who took part in the shooting of *Sierra de Teruel*, points out that: 'The enemy remains anonymous. Although this is propaganda, it is free from hatred and contempt.'

Malraux simply sets the scene. His love of exoticism for its own sake can perhaps be traced to his reading Pierre Loti's books when he was very young; but he broke away from it in an outburst of fantasy – his only tribute to Cubism and up to a point to Surrealism (again the same horror of establishment) – by writing *Lunes en Papier* and *Ecrit pour une Idole à Trompe*.

A further gap in this book is that there is only a passing reference to his early works. Although enlightening, they are not essential to the understanding of Malraux's work in general, and this may explain why none of the contributors has felt the need to enlarge upon them.

* *Les Caracteres*, pp. 106–7, Albin Michel.

Malraux, however, was already suggesting in *Lunes en Papier* that 'killing death' was the final solution to all our troubles . . .

What he keeps seeking is the meaning of life, and therefore of death as it appears in the various cultures and the various religions. This constant interest has even been considered obsessive; but writing about death does not imply fear of it, and as he says himself in *Lazare*: 'The importance I have attached to the metaphysical side of death has given rise to the notion that I am obsessed with it. You might just as well say that biologists concerned with the study of birth go about looking for jobs as wet-nurses.'

How could he not be particularly interested in death when it has so insistently and so strongly beset him: the violent death of his grandfather, whose skull was split open by his own axe as he was felling a tree; the suicide of his father; the death of his half-brothers (Roland, killed during the bombing of the *Cap Arcona* a ship transporting prisoners on the North Sea; and Claude, who died in Bergen-Belsen in the *Nahct und Nebel* section); the death, through a tragic accident, of Josette Clotis, mother of his two sons; the death of his two sons, Gauthier and Vincent, in a car crash in 1961; the death of Louise de Vilmorin, whom he had known in his youth and with whom he hoped to end his days; the death of General de Gaulle. Metaphysical anguish takes on a personal dimension. As Sperber told me: 'Malraux is the unhappiest man I know.'

His work is impregnated with human suffering; evil and death are omnipresent, and if this agnostic has a sense of the sacred, it is in action and in art that he sees salvation: there is no sense of sin. His universe is akin to that of Graham Greene, but as regards sin totally opposed to it. Greene's and Malraux's novels are strewn with deaths and suicides; their heroes are sick of the world, but they also have a taste for it and it excites their curiosity. In each case events, news items and their own experiences are amalgamated by a kind of metaphysical cement. But in spite of their similarities, the world of each remains foreign to the other. Malraux feels that man can found his greatness on nothingness, without the help of religion. On the other hand Greene believes that man can only be saved by following the more dubious paths of failure and humiliation.

This search for transcendence – for what is beyond man and lies at the very heart of his being – is linked to a sort of personal spiritual evolution in which the world is for Malraux no more than an immense 'projective material': the ambiguity of people and things allows him to project his own phantasms, his own doubts and hopes.

Here again we see a process of almost mystical fusion. (As I have already stressed, I do not think at all of Malraux as a mystic, but his faculty of understanding coupled with his creative power bring forth results comparable to those connected with mystical experiences.) It is unlikely that during the last twenty-five minutes they spent together General de Gaulle said everything Malraux attributes to him in *Les Chênes qu'on abat . . .*, but undoubtedly he said them during the course of their friendship, that twenty-five-year-long conversation. For me there is no finer book on de Gaulle.

Probably Picasso did not say everything reported by Malraux in *La Tête d'obsidienne*, but no one, to my knowledge has contributed so much to the understanding of this painter. Equally it is highly improbable that the volunteers who fought on the Republican side held, between skirmishes, conversations on Liberty and Death worthy of the Bloomsbury Set. Hugh Thomas, authoritative historian of the Spanish Civil War, acknowledges that *L'Espoir* has 'absolute historical credibility' and believes that this novel will stay alive in people's memory long after the textbooks have been forgotten.

This point of view coincides with that of Professor Gombrich, who does not succeed, in spite of his efforts, in overcoming a kind of fundamental rejection of Malraux's theories and cannot accept that Malraux 'reveals the presence of a mystery without providing the solution to an enigma'. Nevertheless and paradoxically, he ends his contribution to this book – in which he accuses him of not having invented anything new and of having worked almost exclusively from reproductions of works of art (whereas we know that Malraux has done more field work than anybody else) – by saying that future generations will continue to read Malraux when the works of specialists are collecting dust on library shelves.

Malraux has never ceased to seek the Minotaur, and art has been his Ariadne's thread. In this quest, action and creation are always closely intermingled: life turned into art by creative power, art which is above all an attempt 'to reveal to men the greatness within them and which they ignore', as he wrote in the preface to *Le Temps du Mépris*.

Quest and struggle. For a man who does not like war, Malraux has fought a great deal: first in Spain, then with an armoured division in 1940, and finally in the Resistance. But as he admitted to Cy Sulzberger, 'war has always been around him'. It was during these battles that he discovered that *'fraternité virile'*, which he saw as a second weapon to fight destiny, art being the first. For a man so haunted by love of mankind, finding fulfilment in battle may seem strange: after all the greatest lovers of animals are the first to shoot them.

But he has always fought these battles in the name of liberty. Hence the interesting and significant recurrence of the theme of liberty in the chapters by Walter Langlois, Pierre Bockel and Girija Mookerjee. His purpose was to fight man's enslavement by man, the denial of liberty which he first came up against in Indochina. As Minister of Cultural Affairs he strove to promote this concept of liberty. For instance when the Odéon-Comédie Française Company was on tour in London in the Sixties, Laurence Olivier told Jean-Louis Barrault that he could not believe that a State-subsidized theatre could put on a play like Jean Genêt's *Les Paravents*.

For the sake of this same liberty, in 1973, he gave evidence in favour of Jean Kay, the young man who tried to divert an aeroplane of medical supplies to Bangladesh.

V

But through all these travels and adventures, all these commitments, all these dashing deeds, a legend inevitably has developed. A powerful legend, and not a new one, for as early as the Indochinese period there was a Malraux 'myth'. To me, one of the most surprising things in Malraux's life – where subjects of astonishment are not scarce – was that when the Indochinese authorities had found him guilty of stealing statues, the greatest figures in contemporary French literature signed a petition requesting his release – after all, he was only a twenty-one-year-old youth, practically unknown, who had only published *Lunes en Papier* and extracts of *Ecrit pour une Idole à Trompe* in literary reviews and edited a few works for book-lovers.

The myth must already have existed at the time. Was it due to his spellbinding personality? We might do better to seek a less obvious explanation. Could it not have been an act of allegiance by his literary peers towards a writer they held to be one of them? François Mauriac, André Gide, André Breton, Louis Aragon and many others had signed the petition.

So the legend goes back a long way in Malraux's biography. I am well aware that he was handsome, moody, elegant and incredibly brilliant, but that does not explain everything. There again, I wish someone had mentioned Malraux's 'dandyism', apparent in some of his attitudes, as well as in the elegance of his clothes, which stands out in all the photographs taken at every stage of his life.

We can only state that the legend exists and that Malraux has never done anything to dispel it. In spite of certain indisputable facts, people will go on believing, for example, that he played a part in the first

Chinese revolution: Paul Morand says so in *Papiers d'Identité*; we also know that in the foreword to the German edition of *Les Conquérants* it was stated that he had been the Kuomintang 'Assistant Commissar for Propaganda' (cf. Manès Sperber's chapter).

It has often been said that Malraux nurtured his legend: he simply refrained from either denying or confirming anything (General de Gaulle did the same). This attitude is consistent with his indifference for 'what matters only to me'. Malraux fights shy of introspection, but he is a Romantic. This led Professor Henri Peyre to refer to him as 'Malraux, the Romantic', and François Mauriac to call one *Bloc-Note* on Malraux: '*Le Romantisme au pouvoir*'.

VI

When I was just launching into this book, I cast a fly over a few writers I had in mind to explain to them what I wanted the book to be like. I had either written or told them that one sentence at the beginning of the *Antimemoirs* summed up my intention: ['Man's] image is not to be discovered in the extent of the knowledge he acquires but in the questions he asks.' Paraphrasing him I expressed the hope that the reader would find here a picture of Malraux, not so much in the accumulation of dates, facts and anecdotes, but in the questions he has put to the world . . . and in the questions the world has put to him.

I meant this book – prone by its very nature to becoming a mere juxtaposition of unconnected essays – to be bound together by the underlying theme of the *Question*. This theme is to be found throughout Malraux's works. He wrote in his preface to Manès Sperber's novel *Qu'une larme dans l'Océan* . . .: 'Our civilization, which both in its sciences and in its thought is founded on questioning, has started to recognize one of its secret voices in the highest forms of interrogation.' It is with pleasure that I find that this general orientation, adopted at the outset, should be to some extent endorsed by Malraux in his *Anti-critique*, when he writes that contemporary Western thought 'often substitutes for answers a dialectic of questions'.

The unity imparted to the book by this theme of the *Question* should reflect the unity of Malraux's life and work through the manifold aspects of his thought, action and creative achievement. This unity arises out of the inextricable mixture of what Malraux is, what he does and what he says. It is an organic unity, as it were: 'the artist has to immolate himself in order to achieve his creation,' as Paul Claudel put it. Malraux's work springs from the insertion of himself into the historic fabric of his time. His work is both enigmatic and obvious, personal and reticent; the work of a man who has been flayed alive, but although he writes in the first person the author does not give himself away; a work soaked in reality yet detached from the present; obsessed by the dignity and the ignominy, the liberty and the servitude of mankind, it is dominated by contemporary problems, but far more by the ultimate question: 'What are we doing here?'

Faced with the complexity of his life – lived with 'avid lucidity', according to Malraux himself – we must go beyond even the very concept of unity and proceed to a more dynamic idea, which would better express 'Malraux's system', the concept of integration. For here we have an elaborate complex, open on every side, where nothing is static, where there is a permanent interchange between the man and what he has conceived in a movement within which the author, his history, and his work are integrated: what he is, what he has done and what he has said.

Creation in art has always obsessed Malraux, even in the midst of the most intense action (some pages of *Les Noyers de l'Altenburg* were written on the eve of battle, as were some chapters of *L'Espoir*); creation has been his only answer to the existential question and the answer has left him unsatisfied. François Mauriac pinpointed this essential dissatisfaction when he said: 'The authenticity of Malraux is attested by this contemplation of nothingness from which adventure does not deliver him.*

Therefore I think that, in spite of the omissions and inadequacies that I have pointed out and those that I am unaware of, this book will have been a step towards a better appraisal of Malraux's enigma, which might well be his own metamorphosis.

It is a book of questions that raise other questions – but to quote Malraux in *La Tête d'obsidienne*: 'What does it matter if you do not approve of my answers, provided you cannot ignore my questions?'

---

* François Mauriac: *Nouveaux Mémoires Interieurs*, Folio Flammarion 1965, p. 172

PART I

*

CHAPTERS OF A
SINGLE LIFE

WALTER G. LANGLOIS

*

INDOCHINA: THE INITIATION

In a recent interview, André Malraux observed that 'the monuments in a man's life do not add up in orderly accumulation. Biographies which run from the age of five to fifty are false confessions. It is his experiences that situate a man.' Certainly his two-year sojourn in Indochina as a young man was a major biographical experience for him, because it profoundly influenced the course of his whole life.

Georges-André Malraux was born into a middle-class family in Paris on 3 November 1901. His father, Fernand Malraux, was French-Flemish in origin, and his mother, Berthe Lamy, was of French-Italian background. The first four or five years of young Malraux's life were not particularly tranquil because his parents were not well-matched temperamentally. (They separated when André was about five years of age and were eventually divorced.) Doubtless the best times of this very early period were when the boy went to visit the Malraux family home in Dunkirk. His grandfather, Alphonse Emile, a man of exceptionally strong personality, believed in the virtues of hard work, and he had expanded the modest fishing business he had inherited into a small fleet of ships and the ownership of several maritime enterprises.

Unfortunately, some time before André's birth the family fortunes had suffered a drastic decline as the result of major uninsured property losses, and this disaster encouraged the old man's tendency to eccentricity. Yet young André felt great kinship with his grandfather, and he evidently had a particular admiration for his sense of justice. In the fictional portrait he later painted of him (in *La Voie royale* and *Les Noyers de L'Altenburg*), he recounted two revealing anecdotes. On a certain occasion when none of the town's leaders would rent the local Jewish community building in which to gather for worship, the old man

– a devout Catholic – protested strongly that such an action was grossly unfair, and that very evening he offered a wing of his large house, free of charge, to the Rabbi of the congregation. Similarly, when he felt that the municipality had unjustly refused space for a travelling circus to make camp, he offered part of his property for that purpose. Photographs of young Malraux during these visits to Dunkirk show an alert child, elegantly dressed in the bourgeois fashion of the day in a velvet suit with a lace collar, or in a sailor's uniform.

When Malraux's parents separated in 1905, André and his mother went to live with Adrienne Romania, his maternal grandmother, in Bondy, a small town about eight miles north of Paris. For the next decade, the boy shared the little apartment above the family-owned grocery store. During these years he was certainly influenced by the strong and independent character of his Italian grandmother. Although he himself has almost never spoken of her, his ex-wife Clara has painted a rather striking portrait of Adrienne. Tall and proud, with great intelligence and natural dignity, she was a woman very much aware of what was going on in the world around her. When she saw something amiss in society, she would urge that something be done, adding that 'in my day, people took to the streets' on behalf of social causes.

Malraux went to school in Bondy for several years, but the level of instruction presented little challenge, so in 1915 he decided to try for a scholarship to a private institution in Paris. To prepare for the competitive examination he enrolled in a special tutoring class run by the daughter of a local policeman. In a photograph of the class he stands out as poised and intelligent, perhaps somewhat of a dandy; his teacher remembers him as a tallish youth with sharp eyes and an intense manner. He already had some of the facial tics that were to afflict him for most of his adult life. He was unusually independent and self-disciplined, with certain qualities of leadership already evident.

Malraux won his scholarship, and he did very well in his studies in the Paris school. However he became increasingly restless at the slow pace and narrow scope of the traditional curriculum, and when it came time to move up to a *lycée* he decided to take charge of his own education. During the next five years – until he left for Indochina in 1923 – he explored three areas which particularly interested him, and which have remained major preoccupations throughout his life: literature, art (especially that of ancient civilizations), and what one might call the philosophy of world cultures. He had an unusually alert and retentive mind, and through reading, personal contacts, and frequent visits to

Parisian galleries, museums and libraries he rapidly acquired a very broad intellectual background.

In this period Malraux supported himself in part through the purchase and resale of books for the thriving French bibliophilic market, and this activity – together with his subsequent work as editor-publisher of several series of limited editions – brought him into the mainstream of the literary life of the capital. He soon had many writer friends, not only among his contemporaries (Pascal Pia, Marcel Arland and Jean Paulhan, for example), but also in the older generation (André Gide, Max Jacob, Jean de Gourmont). His marriage in 1922 to Clara Goldschmidt, daughter of a well-to-do Jewish banking family and herself a budding intellectual, brought him into contact with an even wider circle of people. Not surprisingly, he was soon invited to collaborate on a number of the little reviews that proliferated in the immediate post-war years. Then, in 1921, the art-dealer and luxury-edition publisher, Daniel-Henry Kahnweiler brought out Malraux's first book-length work, a fantasy prose-poem called *Lunes en papier*, illustrated with woodcuts by Fernand Léger.

During this time, Malraux also became acquainted with many of the artists who were working in Paris, and in 1922 he published his very first essay on an artistict subject. It was a preface for the catalogue of an exhibition of the work of Demetrios Galanis, a painter whom he admired and who subsequently became his life-long friend and collaborator. It was in this text, written when he was only twenty years old, that Malraux revealed one of his basic intellectual beliefs: 'We can feel only by comparison,' he wrote. 'The Greek genius will be better understood through the contrast of a Greek statue with an Egyptian or Asian statue than by the examination of hundred Greek statues.' In just the same way, he noted later, we come to know ourselves by looking at people who come from cultural backgrounds and traditions that are *different* from our own.

Malraux's concern with the differences between world civilizations was motivated by something more profound than a Romantic's interest in exoticism, for he was fully aware that such variations were based on certain fundamental philosophical or metaphysical ideals. In the troubled days of the early 1920s, when European intellectuals were insistently calling into question the underpinnings of their whole Greco-Roman and Christian heritage, such considerations came to preoccupy him more and more. Marcel Arland later alluded to this aspect of his friend Malraux's concerns when he observed that by his early twenties this metaphysically sensitive young man had 'lived more, thought more, suffered more, than most of those who are officially "elders". His admirable intelligence intensifies this torment; it has flung him toward all the possibilities that presented themselves to him, one after another; he envisions them . . . but he retains the lucidity that nurtures him until the end – an intensity that makes an artist of him, and a restlessness that pushes him forward without ceasing.' Although financial considerations may have played a certain role in Malraux's decision to go to Indochina, as his ex-wife insists, surely such restlessness, such intense intellectual and metaphysical anguish and the need to probe some of the non-Western answers to the human condition were even more profound and authentic motivations for his trip to Asia.

On 13 October 1923, André and Clara Malraux left Marseilles for Indochina on a self-financed expedition. They hoped to find some artistic remains of the Khmer civilization of Cambodia. Malraux's boyhood friend Louis Chevasson was to follow shortly afterwards. All archaeological work in France's Far East colony had long been monopolized by an institution called L'Ecole française d'Extrême Orient, headquartered in Hanoi, but young Malraux had been able to convince officials in the Colonial Office in Paris – which also had jurisdiction over the area – to grant him an official research 'mission'. Actually this amounted to little more than permission to go into the area, and the right to call upon local authorities to furnish native helpers. Malraux's project was to rediscover the ancient Royal Way of the Khmers, a pilgrim road linking the sacred capital at Angkor with other regions of the country. He was convinced that it would be marked with the remains of temples and shrines, in much the same way that churches dotted similar routes across medieval Christian Europe.

In view of Malraux's lack of professional training and the fact that he had obtained his 'mission' by bypassing the usual channels, it is not surprising that his reception at L'Ecole française d'Extrême Orient in Hanoi was not particularly warm. Officials there, jealous of their prerogatives, were not at all pleased that an outsider – and a rank, self-taught amateur at that – should have been given permission to explore in what they considered to be one of their private reserves. The acting director took a certain pleasure in pointing out to Malraux that a recent administrative decree stipulated that all archaeological materials found in the colony had to be left *in situ*, for subsequent evaluation and exploitation by the Ecole. Young Malraux was hardly prepared to turn over any discoveries he might make to someone else, and the interview ended inconclusively.

After outfitting themselves in Phnom Penh (where they were joined by the recently arrived Chevasson), André and his wife proceeded up-river to Siem Reap, in the Angkor area, where they obtained horses, several ox-carts with drivers, and a guide for the trip into the jungle. Because of various difficulties, Malraux had decided to give up his rather ambitious original plan to search for the ancient pilgrim route and to concentrate instead on relocating Banteay-Srei, a little temple some distance from Angkor. This ruin had been accidently discovered by a French surveyor a decade earlier, but the Ecole in Hanoi had never done much more than make a preliminary survey of the remains.

After two days in the jungle, a guide from a village managed to lead the Malraux party to the neglected site, lost in the bush. In spite of its dilapidated state, several walls near what had been the small central sanctuary tower were still partly standing. On one of them Malraux saw a lovely high-relief carving of a *devata* or *apsara*, a female Buddhist deity. The slightly smaller than life-size sculpture was cut into several superimposed stone blocks, one of which had fallen to the ground. By dint of considerable effort, Malraux and Chevasson were able to dislodge these stones, and they loaded them onto the ox-carts, together with several smaller figures discovered among the debris of the roof pediment. Then they returned through the jungle to Siem Reap, where they caught the steamer that was to take them down river to Saigon and the ship for France. But during a brief overnight stop at Phnom Penh, Malraux and Chevasson were rudely awakened by several colonial police, demanding to examine their hold baggage. When the Banteay-Srei carvings were discovered, the two men were informed that they would be formally charged with taking materials from an archaeological site.

According to French judicial practice, in a matter such as this a special Examining Magistrate (*juge d'instruction*) is appointed to prepare the preliminary dossier of inquiry and to recommend whether or not the accused ought to be brought to trial. The case against Malraux was evidently quite weak, for although he may have technically violated a recent administrative decree by removing materials from a ruin, he certainly had done nothing more than what archaeologists (both professional and amateur), government officials, and a number of private citizens had been doing in colonial areas of the world for years. In any case, the first Examining Magistrate was prepared to recommend that the charges against the twenty-two-year-old youth be dropped, and the sculptures simply handed over to the custody of the Ecole in Hanoi. However, for reasons that are not entirely clear (but which may be related to Malraux's involvement with 'Bohemians' in Parisian

literary and artistic circles), the local French colonial officials insisted
on pressing the matter further. A second Examining Magistrate was
appointed, but when he was equally reluctant to recommend prosecution he too was dismissed. The third judge was more cooperative,
and the case was finally tried in Phnom Penh, on 16 and 17 July 1924.
According to eye-witnesses, Malraux presented an energetic defence,
but the administration brought considerable behind-the-scenes pressure
to bear, and on 21 July he and Chevasson were convicted of having
removed stone sculpture from a classified site. The sentences they
received were very severe – three years in prison for Malraux and
eighteen months for Chevasson, without parole. However the two young
men were left at liberty pending an appeal.

Meantime Clara Malraux had returned to France to urge her
husband's friends to come to his aid. Thanks in part to their intervention – and to the fact that Malraux's lawyer was able to point out
numerous irregularities in the prosecution dossier – the October appeal
hearing in Saigon went rather favourably. The court reduced the heavy
Phnom Penh sentences to one year in prison for Malraux and eight
months for Chevasson – with the possibility of parole. Yet this was not
enough for Malraux. Through his lawyer he announced that he was
appealing the matter to the Cour de Cassation in Paris. (When the case
was finally heard there some months later, the findings of the two
colonial courts were set aside on a technicality; eventually, sometime
in the 1930s, the whole matter was simply dropped.)

Malraux had gone to Indochina on an archaeological mission which
was planned to be fairly brief, but because of his imbroglio with the
authorities he had been forced to spend long months in Phnom Penh
and then in Saigon, preparing his defence. This enforced stay gave him
an opportunity to observe the workings of the colonial administrative
bureaucracy at first hand. To someone as imbued with Republican
traditions as he was, it was not a very edifying sight. In principle the
French idea of having the native children of the colonies guided by a
benevolent authoritarian father may have been defensible, but in
practice this paternalistic system had degenerated into the grossest
kind of exploitation. In Cambodia and even more in Vietnam (Annam
and Cochinchina), Malraux saw a proud people with a long cultural
tradition treated as virtual slaves and foreigners in their own land,
while corrupt and short-sighted bureaucrats from France used their
power to build huge personal fortunes. To Malraux, the system had
come to represent middle-class or bourgeois capitalism at its very
worst.

While in Saigon, Malraux met several liberal lawyers who were actively working for social and political reform in Indochina. One of these, Paul Monin, was particularly respected as an outspoken defender of native rights and as an advocate of the kind of Asian nationalism represented by Sun Yat-sen's Chinese Kuomintang party. On finding that they had very similar political and social ideas, Malraux and Monin decided to join forces and establish an opposition newspaper. Such a publication would help to expose and document the misdeeds of administrative officials; even more important, it would propagate a new and positive ideal of Franco-Indochinese collaboration, based on something other than authoritarianism. In retrospect, the general programme of the paper – and of the Young Annam political movement with which it was associated – appears as a moderate Indochinese nationalism, closely linked to French Republican traditions. The main purpose of the crusading young editors was to bring an end to the oppressive paternalism of the colonial administration which had permitted abuses to go unchecked for so long.

Supported by funds from several native businessmen, the first issue of *L'Indochine* (as the new daily was called) came off the presses on 17 June 1925. In spite of great administrative harassment, the eight-page folio paper continued to appear regularly until 14 August, for a total of forty-nine issues. At that time the Vietnamese who was responsible for printing it, weary of the threats made against him by the bureaucrats, finally told Malraux and Monin that he would no longer accept their business. After a frantic search, which took Malraux to Hong Kong and probably China, the two young men located and purchased an old press, and then – several weeks later – some Roman type. Their paper, rechristened *L'Indochine enchaînée*, reappeared at last on 4 November 1925. Although reduced to small magazine size, it came out fairly regularly twice a week during November and December of 1925, and – after a month's interruption caused by a press breakdown – in February 1926, for a total of twenty-three issues, before ceasing publication entirely.

From the beginning, Malraux took a very active part in preparing materials for the paper. In addition to short items of various kinds, satirical pieces, and a fanciful tale ('Expédition d'Isphahan', published under a pseudonym), he contributed a number of major documentary exposés of the various corrupt and illegal practices being engaged in by those in authority in the colony. These included several gigantic land swindles, flagrant violations of rights guaranteed by law, collusion and bribery extending into all levels of the bureaucracy, and tortures and murders committed by French soldiers and police in the name of 'order'. However by far the most interesting of Malraux's texts are the various political editorials he wrote – occasionally as co-author with Monin – to elaborate the paper's position on Franco-Indochinese collaboration. They furnish an invaluable insight into his earliest political thinking, and they clearly document the direction of an ideological commitment that has often been misunderstood or misrepresented in the years since.

The masthead of *L'Indochine* proclaimed that it was a 'newspaper for Franco-Annamite reconciliation'. This positive element was the basis for the policy of collaboration which Malraux hoped would replace the outmoded 'domination' mentality and bureaucratic framework that had made so many abuses possible. The outlines of his general political programme are particularly visible in two editorials he wrote. The first of these, published on 4 July, was revealingly entitled 'Upon What Hard Facts Should An Annamite Effort Be Based?' The appearance of a French newspaper advocating a programme of collaboration between French *colons* and natives had apparently provoked a flood of mail from Indochinese intellectuals. These individuals, shaped by French culture and Republican traditions absorbed during their schooling, were increasingly angry at the unjust authoritarian system under which they were forced to live. They clamoured to know how they could help bring it to an end. In his editorial of reply, Malraux began by noting that 'in order to make Annam a free nation where two peoples live on a footing of equality . . . it is indispensable that the first part of your life be sacrificed. You can set up a real Annam, but it is your children who will enjoy it'. While admitting that the vast majority of the French colonials came to the peninsula to make money, he emphasized that there was nothing intrinsically wrong with such capitalist motivation, *provided* that these Frenchmen earned their profits by hard work, and not by graft.

As for political reforms, a majority of the Indochinese apparently felt that action through the Chamber of Deputies in Paris would be most effective, but Malraux realistically pointed out that there was another kind of pressure which would probably bring quicker and more lasting results. Yet a radical change must first take place in the thinking of the educated elements of the native population. Instead of seeking the security and prestige of minor bureaucratic posts – virtually the only jobs open to them – they must obtain specialized training which would fit them for certain important technical positions. 'Let each family realize that to be any kind of technician is much better than to be a clerk in the administration,' wrote Malraux. 'There are no [native] technicians. They must be numerous in twenty years. Make engineers of your sons, construction foremen, doctors. Make of them, above all, agronomists.' After these Indochinese youths had received a technical training (preferably in a specialized institution in France), they should then organize themselves into unions and professional societies under aggressive leaders. Malraux admitted that this method of bringing about change was slow because it required a long period of training, organization and sacrifice. However in his eyes it was by far the best way – not only because it was non-violent, but even more important because it was based *on the work* of the petitioners.

In these editorials Malraux emerges more as a conservative than a 'revolutionary'. He obviously wanted to do away with the flagrant abuses which had grown up in the colony, but he appeared quite convinced of the virtues of capitalism, private enterprise and competition. Although he wanted strong workers' unions, he did not share the Marxist view of Western society as a constant struggle between different economic classes. If he opposed what the French colonial system had become, it was above all because it went directly contrary to his deepest humanist convictions. He wanted the French and Indochinese to live together, not as masters and slaves but as equals, because as men they *were* equals. The natives had a fundamental right to the same educational and economic opportunities, to the same justice and personal freedom as Frenchmen. To deny them these things and treat them as unworthy inferiors was a betrayal of France's long political tradition.

In spite of its general reasonableness and moderation, the Malraux-Monin programme was anathema to the arch-conservatives in the colony. They correctly saw it as a major threat to their power – and to their incomes. The government-controlled Saigon press raised loud cries of 'Bolshevism' against *L'Indochine*'s proposals, suggesting that such reforms would bring chaos to the country. In rebuttal Malraux wrote his most moving political editorial, entitled 'Sélection des énergies'. In this essay of 14 August, he centred his attack on the short-sighted policy which deliberately selected only the most servile Indochinese to go to France for further education. Any native youth who showed independence and strength of character was immediately classified as 'dangerous' by the administration and prevented from leaving the colony. This policy, noted Malraux with sarcasm, had evidently been formulated in 'the most serene regions of happy stupidity', for it was obvious that it would 'bring about – in a very short time – the most dangerous assault that our colonization here could experience'. By deliberately thwarting the efforts of potential native leaders to prepare themselves for participation in the economic and political life of their country, the colonial administration was paving the way for a revolt that would one day drive France from the peninsula forever. In a particularly eloquent passage, the twenty-three-year-old Malraux spoke prophetically of the uprising that would surely result from all this frustrated nationalist energy:

Every power that feels within itself a will to expand and the controlled violence that makes certain people colonizers sets itself as a first task the seeking out of strength. Those whom Rome sent to the marches of the Empire, those whom Tai-Tsong sent into the depths of the Gobi, those whom our Kings sent to Louisiana, applied themselves above all to ferreting out, among the scattered forces that were opposing them, what elements of resistance, vigour, and energy lay hidden, in order to bind them to their cause by granting them – unmistakably and without contest – the prerogatives of masters. Never did a great king, never did a great statesman forget to seek out this characteristic of quickly provoked independence and honour by which the strong are recognizable.

Our policy in Cochinchina and in Annam at the present time is very simple: it affirms that the Annamites have no reason whatsoever for coming to France, and it immediately creates *against us* a coalition of the noblest characters and the most tenacious energies of Annam. It appears that politically motivated and financially greedy idiots are applying themselves with rare perseverance to destroying what we have been able to create, and to awakening in this old land – sown with great memories – the sleeping echoes of more than six hundred revolts.... [Let us show] that we know how to do something besides direct against ourselves – thanks to an ingenious system – one of the finest, one of the purest, one of the most perfect streams of energy that a great colonial power could turn upon itself.

Unfortunately Malraux's perceptive appraisal of the situation fell upon deaf ears. The conservatives in the colony refused to believe that the time for change had come, and they stubbornly refused to modify their authoritarian system. For a brief period, the appointment of a new Governor General from the ranks of the French Socialist party seemed to offer some hope of reform, but even this proved to be illusory. By late December of 1925, weary from illness and from the enormous energy he had expended in his struggle against the authoritarian bureaucracy, a frustrated Malraux decided to return to France. As he put it in an editorial of farewell to his Indochinese friends and supporters: 'The people – in France – will not permit the sufferings whose marks you bear to be inflicted in their name.... The great voice of the people must be raised to ask the leaders for an explanation of all this heavy affliction, of this devastating anguish that hangs oppressively over the plains of Indochina. Will we obtain Freedom? We cannot know yet. At least we shall obtain a *few* freedoms. That is why I am leaving for France.'

After his return to Paris in 1926, Malraux set to work on behalf of the Indochinese cause, but his struggle quickly expanded into something more broad than just an indictment of the abusive colonial system. He soon came to demand major reforms of the French government itself, so that it would be removed from the domination of the conservative bourgeoisie, a class which to him represented the worst elements of Western capitalism. More and more a Leftist, he wanted to put power into the hands of the people, so that far-reaching political and social changes could be effected, both in France and in her colonial empire. In this expanded struggle, the Indochinese problem tended to become submerged in broader concerns, and Malraux almost never again spoke specifically about Indochina or his plans for reform there. Yet, in retrospect, the experience was unquestionably a crucial one for him, a major 'monument' in his life.

Indeed, before going to the peninsula, the young man was not at all involved in political or social questions. Preoccupied with literary and artistic matters, his interests had been almost entirely aesthetic. But when he had come face to face with the enormous injustices that characterized every aspect of life in the colony, the grandson of Alphonse Emile Malraux and Adrienne Romania felt his social conscience awaken with a start. In a little-known comment, he alluded to the circumstances of his transformation from an intellectual dilettante into a social revolutionary: 'For me, a revolutionary is born from a resistance. Let a man become aware of certain injustices and of certain inequalities, let him become aware of an intense suffering – that will never suffice to make a revolutionary of him. . . . For this, it is necessary that at the moment when he seeks to intervene on behalf of that suffering *he meets a resistance*.' It was precisely the stubborn conservative colonials' blind resistance to any change in the status quo, to any attempt to correct the abuses that crushed the natives at every level, which made Malraux an increasingly militant social reformer. It was his social concerns which soon led him to the literary and philosophical heights represented by *La Condition humaine* and *L'Espoir*.

ISAIAH BERLIN

*

MALRAUX, THE RUSSIANS OF THE THIRTIES AND MANY OTHER THINGS, *OR* IS THE PARTHIAN LANGUAGE REALLY LOST?

A conversation between
Isaiah Berlin and Martine de Courcel

When, in 1967, André Malraux went to Oxford to receive his doctorate Honoris causa, *he gave a lecture in the Sheldonian Theatre and opened the new Maison Française. While at Oxford he stayed with the Berlins.*

    I.B.   Malraux was, of course, very tired when he came to this house after his lecture. I felt that he thought he had an amplifier in front of him at the Sheldonian Theatre, whereas it was in fact a tape-recorder. And so he talked in a low voice, in French – in Oxford not many (including myself) understand rapidly spoken French – and he suddenly realized that the whole thing was not going well, and became depressed, and stopped – it seemed to us all – half-way. I cannot remember what he said, only that it seemed original and interesting, and referred to classical attitudes to beauty, history and death; but he seemed to become bored with his own remarks, and came to a sudden end. After the lecture he was driven to my house and he was very tired, and then he had a drink . . .

    M. de C. . . . And then it was *l'amour fou*. When we had lunch in London you told me that Russia was the link between you and Malraux. What did you mean by that?

    I.B.   I don't know about *l'amour fou*, but he then began talking about all kinds of subjects, and I asked him what his journeys to Russia in the Thirties were like, whom he had met, and what did he feel – and he came to life in the most remarkable fashion. It was quite clear that he had been absolutely fascinated by his experiences in the Soviet Union in the Thirties, when he came across many writers who had not yet been crushed by Stalin – at least, not yet crushed completely – and he talked in the most vivid and fascinating fashion about his experiences, and about the works of these various people, particularly Pasternak and Olesha, both of whom he met and liked, and a celebrated journalist who had reported the Spanish Civil War and was later liquidated. It was clear that he felt that he had entered into a new world in Russia, of people who were in some way fresh and original and not encumbered by the conventional kind of literary talk of the West. He found in Russia what I found when I went there many years later, although of course the number of people even a non-Communist foreigner could talk to then was perhaps greater. These Russian authors didn't talk (at least not on the occasions when I met them) about the weather or literary earnings or publishers or periodicals or rival groups; there was no small talk, no obstacle between them and the object they wished to talk about – Hafiz or Chekhov or Wilde or why Dr Cronin but not E. M. Forster had been translated into Russian – and there was something very direct and fresh and spontaneous. This moved Malraux greatly, and he returned to it with obvious pleasure and fascination.

I had a feeling about him then that he was in search of some kind of experience which would take away the patina of the conventional world and make things look new and fresh. I wondered whether he obtained some experience of this kind in Indochina, when he went there in the Twenties. He was fascinated by these Soviet writers and their directness of vision and non-commercialism. He realized that they were living under very difficult conditions. There was rigid censorship and mounting persecution even then, sometimes very violent; but he talked about Russia with a degree of eloquence and passion which made me feel that he had got on to a subject which had laid its spell on him; that we were not simply having a polite conversation between host and guest on an official occasion, but that I had turned out to know something about a world which he knew too, that we were fascinated by the same kind of people and by the same kind of values among these people. And this created an immediate bond of sympathy – at least, I felt it: I don't know if he did . . .

M. de C. You were, as he wrote to you on the fly leaf of the *Antimémoires*, 'son complice'.

I.B. Well, that is perfectly true; after that there was no looking back, after that it all went marvellously well. I can't remember in detail what he said about Russia, or particular descriptions that he gave, but he was literally fascinating.

M. de C. During that lunch you told me also that Malraux needed '*piqûres*', that he first had *la piqûre chinoise*, then *la piqûre espagnole* and that de Gaulle was *l'ultime piqûre*.

I.B. I think that was a terribly vulgar thing to say, if that is what I said. I hope I didn't; but if you remember it, I probably did. If so, I regret it and withdraw it. It isn't that at all, no, it seems to me there are many ways in which people become Marxists: sometimes out of social idealism, because they react acutely to injustice or poverty or exploitation or misery, because they want social equality, or want to end the oppression of one human being by another, bullying, slavery, sycophancy, domination. I didn't think he belonged to that category.

M. de C. Which one did he belong to?

I.B. Difficult to say. There are people who become Communists because they think it is scientific, and they think it is important to be rational and to organize the world in a rational way instead of letting things – circumstances, uncontrolled events – dominate one. That wasn't it either, though he may, of course, think in these terms. I doubt it. I think that there are people who become Communists because they are oppressed and disgusted by the corruption and squalor of the world in which they live. Some want to escape from it, others to purify it, and they want to remove, scrape off the horrible mildew, remove this suffocating feeling of living in the midst of this awful, grey world. In fact, funnily enough, when I talked to Pasternak in Russia he accused me of looking at Russia with charmed eyes. 'Here we are,' he said, 'living in a dreadful, sordid, stifling society, this ghastly pigsty, and you – you look at everything with completely fascinated eyes. How can you? You idealize, you romanticize everything here, when life is only there – art, "personalism", Herbert Read – only there, in the West.' Well, I think that although, of course, we are very different, I am sure – and Malraux is in any case a man of genius and I am very far from that – I think that he too, to some extent, was interested and fascinated by the same spectacle, because all his life, I suspect, he must have looked for some renovation of things, what the Renaissance, when it went back to Greece and Rome, called *renovatio, restauratio* – a return to brighter, simpler, grander values than their own world appeared to generate. It may be a craving for the future, but if so, it is disguised as a craving for the past.

Malraux talked about visions of splendour. There were three phenomena he most admired: one was Alexander the Great – because he was very handsome and died young, and died of his vices, all of which seemed to him (as they did to John Kennedy) to be heroic vices – the second was T. E. Lawrence, with whom he seemed to me to identify himself to some degree – a romantic, bold, dissatisfied, unashamed, exhibitionist adventurer, who took pride in his fantasies, who also looked for renovation in exotic and remote societies, among primitive peoples – the third was the Parthians, *les Parthes*, because they alone had not been defeated by the Romans. The three things amounted to some kind of Romantic search for heroic values: hence, perhaps, his decision to support the hero de Gaulle, whom he felt to be simpler and larger than life, free from doubts, ruthless, all of a piece. I don't know. Malraux asked to be shown the room in All Souls College which T. E. Lawrence had lived in when he was a Fellow in the Twenties, just as Gide had wanted to see Oscar Wilde's rooms in Magdalen. In the end, with the help of Professor Ernest Jacob, we identified it: he looked at it – it is a perfectly ordinary little college room, of course, like anyone else's – with absolutely fascinated eyes; exactly what Pasternak thought was so absurd about me in Russia. I thought that I understood Malraux's feelings. In fact, I think he is a hero-worshipper, although none of his heroes, except perhaps de Gaulle, and maybe Mao, belong to the twentieth century. Lenin, Trotsky, were not figures in his *panthéon imaginaire*.

I think he wants to live at the height of experience, and seeks fulness of life. There are people who loathe *le juste milieu* more than anything else in the world, who want to be at some extreme – it doesn't matter whether it is the extreme Right or the extreme Left who want to be on the very edges of being, who are bored by 'everyday life'. If I talked about *piqûres*, that was a particularly vulgar and inadequate way of saying that what he wanted was to be lifted by some unique sensation to an enlarged and heightened sensibility of some sort, which some find in religious, some in artistic experience. In the case of Malraux, his acute visual sensibility plays a central part in this, but above all, I think, contemplation of heroic people, acts, individuals – splendour: some unimaginable ideal of splendour, which he, of course, perfectly well knew, and knows, cannot literally be realized. If this is Romanticism, it is so in a classical framework. I think that the painter David had something of this – perhaps David's attitude towards Napoleon was not altogether unlike Malraux's attitude to de Gaulle. Napoleon said to David after he looked at his magnificent *Sacre*: 'C'est très bien fait, Monsieur David, c'est très bien fait.' I am sure that if de Gaulle ever said anything like this to Malraux, he must have experienced similar sensations – which I understand, and sympathize with.

M. de C.   You said that Malraux's problems seemed personal, always remained personal?

I.B.   Oh, I don't know what I could have meant by that, perhaps that it was nothing to do with theories. I think that he rather romanticizes himself, which is to me another sympathetic characteristic. I don't mean that he permanently lives in a world of fantasy or illusion, far from it, though I think that sometimes he may have fantasies, and is glad to do so. But I think that he does resemble the Romantic tradition of the nineteenth century. I suppose that the most characteristic representative of it is Baudelaire – the *poète maudit*, the *âme damnée* – whose vision has in it something wild and contemptuous and tragic, intoxication with black wickedness, the Satanism Mario Praz writes about, which is not bogus, not counterfeit, which really does respond to something genuine in such people's natures. I think that Malraux has a touch of that, yes; it is not decadent and not sentimental; there is something very dry and realistic and penetrating about him. What interested me, what made his conversation delightful to me, was not merely his charm, which is considerable, nor his eloquence, which is remarkable, but an extreme sense which I got from him of acute discrimination between the genuine and the counterfeit; he really does know what he wants, he knows what he is looking for, what gives him these sharp sensations which make him live, make him feel that he is alive. I think that Byron somewhere speaks of the desire for sensation – to be conscious of oneself as existing even though it be in pain – and I think that there is that Byronic element about Malraux, wedded to a curious, sharp, ironical kind of realism, which was there in Byron too. He didn't talk about Byron: but that's what he liked about Alexander and T. E. Lawrence, and the wild, unconquered Parthians. This had a very Byronic ring to me. And there was also the defying of men and nature, *contra mundum*, a traditional Romantic image of the lonely thinker. Malraux doesn't seem to be a man who believes much in working with a team, or leading a party, or altering his principles or his convictions to adapt himself to some mass movement in order to feel that he is leading the masses, or at least marching with them towards some goal. He does not, I think, mind detaching himself, if need be, and pursuing his own path: there is surely some desire for solitude in his feelings. And some self-dramatization and self-romanticization also – much scorned in our day but to me, I admit, rather refreshing; the whole thing the exact opposite of Sartre, for example.

M. de C. When I first thought about the subject I wanted you to write on in this book, it came to my mind that it could be, 'Malraux and Marxism'. I then went on to think that 'Malraux and the Marxist Adventure' would convey better Malraux's relationship with Marxism, and that in fact 'Malraux and the Marxist Temptation' would even be more accurate. I now feel that we are not really going to talk about

Malraux and Marxism at all, because he was never actually a Marxist in the proper sense of the word.

I.B. I have no idea to what degree, if any, he was a theoretical Marxist; of course he must have been one in some sense. I don't know whether he would describe himself as a Marxist at any period, but I can't talk about Malraux *and* anything, because I don't know him and one cannot judge people by their books. One would get a very odd conception of what Tolstoy's own personal character was like if one only had *War and Peace* and *Anna Karenina* to judge by. You may say, you may well say, that it is more important to understand *Anna Karenina* and *War and Peace* than it is to understand the individual personality of Tolstoy. That may be so. But if one wants to understand Tolstoy himself, one has to have lived with him, to hear the voice, the intonations, see the gestures, have a direct vision of the individual himself, for a sufficient length of time. Deducing people or trying to reconstruct them from brief meetings, still more from their works is, I think, never much good.

M. de C. You must admit that in the case of Malraux, Marxism was not mere intellectual play, nor a way to enjoy intellectual comfort, it was in fact a commitment: he was involved in the Chinese revolution, and he was even more involved in the Spanish Civil War, to the extent that he actually organized and led the Escuadrilla España. It was indeed not an abstract approach, but a physical involvement.

I.B. Oh, I am sure that action is very important to him, because I think there is a craving for some sort of heroic life in him. But I think he's rather like – I don't know, I may be quite wrong and what I am going to say may be terrible nonsense – I think there's something about him which probably existed in the early years of Christianity, when people who were not particularly interested in the Christian theology, nor even in the view of Man and of God which Christianity unfolded, but who were oppressed by the exhausted – or what they felt to be the exhausted – stifling edifice of the pagan world, people whom Christianity liberated, for whom it was a transformation and a revolution, a vision of infinity which made all things new, a new heaven and a new earth, restored an earlier, younger world. Perhaps it sprang from a neo-primitivism, as if history were cyclical, and this was the beginning of a new cycle. That, I think, is what Malraux may be like, what may have attracted him originally to left-wing movements whether in Asia or in Europe, or in Russia. He is certainly fascinated by Asia. When he went to the Ashmolean Museum in Oxford what he most wanted to look at were Chinese, Persian, Afghan things. We all knew, of course, of his

fascination with China and with Indochina. It may be that he wanted
to experience some sort of contrast, conflict, almost between the old
Western civilization and something which would excite it into a new
vitality by producing a spark, by bringing two cultures together and
creating a collision.

I think the idea of a sort of collision of conflicting values, and the
emergence from this of something new and fresh, and not simply a
gradual evolution of something which had in embryo been there all the
time – that, I think, may be what in some way moved him. That is why
he talked about Russia very much as I tend to think of it, as a world
which for various political and historical reasons had to a large degree
been insulated from what was going on in the West, and which therefore
for Westerners preserved a kind of strangeness, a Jansenist, *au-delà*,
quality, in which some things, some writers, some values, some forms of
experience were brighter and larger than life, more authentic; where
human beings behaved more like human beings; where what they said
sounded more genuine, in some ways more childlike but also more
sincere. That, it seems to me, is what attracted him – a certain poetical,
uncontaminated quality in the lives of people he met.

This, of course, often happens to people who live under tyranny:
because they are isolated, forcibly isolated, from the outer world, and
are reduced to bare essentials, and to leading a kind of controlled,
aborted, and therefore childlike life, they sometimes are purified by this,
kept from growing up, and so free from the defects of freer, more easy-
going, more open and more blasé societies. This is one of the by-
products of being forced into private life, when public life is dangerous
or forbidden. This, I think, he did encounter in the Russians, particularly the Russian writers and artists whom he met. We, or rather, he,
talked about their charm and imagination in a vein of happy nostalgic
reminiscence.

What he likes to talk about, I think, is exceptional people. While he
was at Oxford he had various tasks to perform: to receive an Honorary
Degree, and to open the new Maison Française, and so on. In the course
of this he had to meet a certain number of official representatives of the
University and was himself accompanied by official academic persons
from France; and although he was quite pleased to be doing this, I
think, he really seemed to want to resume talk about the interesting
persons outside the Western world whom he had met or had thought
about; he found it rather difficult to do this with most of the perfectly
polite but slightly bewildered Oxford dons, some of whom, perhaps, if
he had known them better, he might well have found interesting, but

whom there was no opportunity to meet at length if one was engaged upon a purely official visit of this kind.

When we were alone in our house, he would, with evident pleasure, resume his very vivid and fascinating descriptions of Bukharin, for example, and other old Bolsheviks who, in his opinion, knew that they were doomed, and knew that they would end badly, but who at the same time marched towards their fate in a manner which he found irresistibly interesting. He liked talking about 'fatal' men and women, obsessed lives, lonely Byronic souls: for example, I remember a long conversation about Lou Andreas Salomé, about whom a book had just been published, who lived in Russia, then in Germany where Nietzsche had become infatuated by her, and then became the mistress of Rilke, and ended by captivating Freud and becoming a psychoanalyst herself. The life of this peculiar, gifted and fascinating woman absolutely gripped him. And he talked of other people who led self-absorbed lives. He didn't want to talk about Victor Hugo, who struck him as a terrible, noisy bore, although he thought he was immensely gifted. But he talked about Delacroix, whom he liked because he was proud, bitter and grim, and above all, on his own, a man by himself, *solitaire*: Hemingway, he thought, was a phoney *solitaire*, unconvincing, no good; he knocked him out. He liked uniqueness, if possible with a *maudit* strain; hostile, doomed figures who despised accommodation of any kind. Defiance is what he seemed to like best; in spite of his official position, in spite of being a member of the government, in spite of apparently seeming to be a wholly dedicated, conformist Gaullist by this time, the idea of defiance, preferably with an element of dandyism and swagger – refusal to transact, the insistence on self-expression at the expense of everything – clearly attracted him. I expect I am painting the wrong picture, because I seem to be simply painting a picture of a characteristic nineteenth-century Romantic – he's not that at all – I'm afraid I'm not very good at psychological vignettes – I really must stop.

M. de C. I remember that conversation about Delacroix, and how you tried to reconstruct his life, with Malraux handing on a piece and you supplying the next, and so on. But I also remember that you talked about music.

I.B. Yes, we talked about music a little, and he obviously didn't really like music much. He offended Stravinsky greatly, you remember, by describing music as an 'art mineur'. He was, however, very proud of discovering a funeral march by the Belgian composer Gossec (at the time of the French Revolution, or perhaps a little after, but at a time of revolutionary change). He ordered this to be played at the public funeral – no not a funeral, I think it was a commemoration – of the great Resistance leader Jean Moulin; he was clearly pleased about finding the piece by Gossec, with that particular pleasure which amateurs always have when they discover something which professionals haven't told them about – I know the feeling all too well.

M. de C.   When 'the God failed', people like Koestler and Stephen Spender were left in the dark, but for Malraux there was the possibility of salvation through art.

I.B.   No, he didn't strike me as being saved. Stephen Spender was a very short-lived Communist, for not more, I should say, than three or four months in all; he was a great friend of mine, and still is. I am very devoted to him. Communism was an irrelevant episode in his life. After all, everybody who had any heart at all was attracted to something of the kind in the terrible Thirties. I was only saved from temptation to work for or with the Party by the accident of witnessing, the Russian Revolution in some of its less attractive aspects as a child, and later, from a distance, watching some of its gloomier consequences. I don't think salvation is what Malraux is looking for, or obtains; no, I think art means a great deal to him, simply because he has a passionate attitude towards creativity as such, and he conceives it in a Romantic spirit. I think creation for him is individual self-expression, and not simply the creation of an object: it is human communication by these exceptional beings who are larger than life, see more, suffer more, see through more, despise more, understand more, despair all the more – that's his conception, I think, of what great men, major actors, are like.

One of the things I enjoyed – and perhaps he did too – was our last conversation, on the way to the airport, of a kind that undergraduates have with each other. We began talking about whom (if we could go into the past) we would have liked to meet, to ask to dinner and so on. I was sitting next to the chauffeur. I turned round asking him, 'Now, if you had to ask Plato or Socrates for lunch, which one would you choose?' He answered without hesitation; 'Certainly Plato, it would not be very easy, but one would eventually get him to come – he is such a snob.' We went on to consider whether Plato would have snubbed Dante, and there was more of this kind of thing. He always came back to Alexander the Great whom he wanted to meet very much indeed, and I didn't want to meet at all, I thought he would have been too savage, arbitrary, but that was exactly what he liked. He wanted to go to Ctesiphon to meet some Parthians, but he wouldn't, he agreed, have understood a word they said because their Greek must have been appalling – the Parthian language is completely lost – but he didn't mind that; what he wanted was to gaze upon them. Our conversation became one of mounting gaiety, in which all kinds of fantasies were built up. It may seem an extraordinary thing to say about a man of such talents, who has lived so eventful a life – that there is something ungrown-up about him, which is peculiarly attractive, something very young, very unexhausted. If the right subjects are touched upon, and the right atmosphere conveyed, a great fountain of intellectual gaiety springs forth, of rare quality, and to me very delightful. There is nothing pompous about him, nothing stuffy or solemn, in spite of a clear sense of his own importance. Provided the subject stimulates him at all, he goes off at fantastic tangents, which carry one with them. All I can say is that it was to me an extremely exhilarating and delightful visit, and I had that particular sensation, which one has with certain types of men touched by genius; namely an enormous heightening of vitality, and increasing flatness and regret after they are gone, though a sense of excitement lingers on for some time after.

He is an eloquent genius, with no philistine fear of brilliant flights of rhetoric. After the unsuccessful lecture in the Sheldonian Theatre, on the following day he opened the new Maison Française; he sat on the platform with a somewhat Napoleonic expression, and seemed only half to listen to the speeches of everyone else. Then he rose, and for, I suppose, about four minutes spoke with the most magnificent eloquence about the obligations of those who wore the gowns of university teachers, the obligations of intellectuals in the terrible world of sex and blood and banality in which we were living. Most people there, I think, were rather embarrassed by this old-fashioned kind of rhetoric, and thought it unsuitable to our time and circumstances – the English don't take very well to the grand style of this type: but I thought it was absolutely splendid, and think so still. This kind of eloquence is what W. B. Yeats used to defend against those who believed in wringing the neck of rhetoric, the deflation of words to the shape of the flatness of experience in an exact and excessively austere fashion. Malraux believes in poetical afflatus, and this is a thing which is exceptionally unfashionable today.

HUGH THOMAS

*

THE LYRICAL ILLUSION: SPAIN 1936

The Spanish Civil War broke out in July 1936 at what seemed an ideal moment for the anti-Fascist cause in Europe as a whole. At last, an English student, Philip Toynbee, could say at Oxford, the gloves were off in the struggle against Fascism. Blum's Popular Front government had taken office in France in June, and the anti-Fascist demonstrations in Paris were the largest hitherto known. The outbreak of war in Spain seemed to offer a chance of undoing the weakness which the democracies had shown over the German occupation of the Rhineland in February.

Most sympathizers with the Spanish Popular Front government (and the revolutionary and other parties that supported it, once the fighting had begun) believed that the 'generals' rising' in Spain had been a co-ordinated part of the Fascist European offensive: the day before yesterday, Italy; yesterday, Germany; today, Spain; tomorrow, France, Austria, Czechoslovakia; even aloof England in the end would fall. People noticed, as did Scali in Malraux's *L'Espoir*, that clear proof of this prior coordination had been given by the discovery of flight instructions to Italian airmen before 18 July, the date of the rising in Spain: 'Two columns: *From* ... *to* ... and dates. 16 July (so *before* Franco's rising): La Spezia; then Melilla; 18, 19, 20; then Seville, Salamanca. ...'[1] So the long-awaited war against Fascism could begin. '*Oggi in Spagna, domani in Italia*' was the slogan of Carlo Rosselli's social democrats of *Giustizia e libertà*; '*Der Heimat ist heute vor Madrid*', sang the Germans of the Thaelmann battalion in the international brigades; even for Jaime, one of the Spanish socialists in *L'Espoir*, 'the Popular Front was that fraternity in life and death ... under that huge sun and the Phalangist's bullets ... he fought with a full heart'.[2] André Malraux, who had in May visited Spain, during the '*primavera tragica*', as co-President of the Comité Mondial des Intellectuels Contre la Guerre et le Fascisme, returned to Madrid in July, observing what was happening both for the immediate benefit of readers of *L'Humanité* and for his friends in Blum's goverment, and for the long-term benefit of his novel and film, *L'Espoir*; he immediately flung himself, with the total concentration upon the matter in hand for which he was famous, into the struggle, as *voyeur* turned actor, by helping to organize the shipment of French aircraft for the Republican defence. It was then that he organized the famous air squadron of volunteers and mercenaries to help the Republic, the Escuadrilla España (which will be discussed later in some detail).[3]

Though Malraux was certainly regarded by the Communists and the anti-Fascist movement generally as the brightest ornament in their following, he was not a member of the Communist party, and indeed was never really a Communist in outlook. His language was never tarred with the brush of Marxism. Also, as David Caute put it: 'He never really cared about plans, about social security benefits, about production statistics and easy-to-come-by abortions. The heirs of the Enlightenment did. . . . Whereas they cared about the destination, he cared more about the journey itself, the struggle, the heroic camaraderie.'[4] The war in Spain offered precisely this opportunity in an incomparable manner; on the doorstep of France the Russian revolution was re-enacted – as tragedy, it is true, not as farce, but with the symbols the same: Trotsky's armoured train drove again at Talavera. Malraux went to Spain as *l'homme engagé* par excellence; in his novel, based directly on his experiences and what he saw (though rearranged, so that it is in some senses an anti-history, as well as anti-novel), the Communists are certainly in the centre of this resolute group of men marching towards death, with their brains never dull; but everyone else gets their chance on the dais (or pulpit), as one would expect from one who, though a fellow-traveller of the first class at the time, nevertheless defended Trotsky in 1937 and contributed to the cost of his bodyguard. Malraux's denunciation of the Russian attitude to the freedom of the artist at the Moscow Writers' Congress in 1935 was probably the last public speech of opposition in Russia. Furthermore, the excessive preoccupation among Spaniards with death coincided with Malraux's own: 'Each of them knew that, for those waiting for him, his own death would be nothing but the smoke of cigarettes nervously lit, where hope struggled like someone choking.'[5] Malraux was then speaking of the men in his air squadron but that is how he saw the prospect himself.

Malraux's time of action in Spain was between July 1936 and March

1937, the first eight months of a civil war which would last until March 1939. His part as commander of the Escuadrilla España began in August. He collected together in France, by public subscription, a number of Potez 54 bombers, some Blochs and later a few Dewoitine fighters, together with Haile Selassie's private light aircraft which had come on the market, and hired some pilots, some of whom came to him through idealism, some through interest in the very high salaries that were paid by the Republic at the beginning. This interesting team – with never more than six aeroplanes in the air at the same time, never more than nine ready to fly, never more than twenty in all – saw action fairly continuously from August to February, in the Tagus valley, at Toledo, in Aragon, around Madrid, and at Màlaga. Malraux's own role was to orgnaize, galvanize, inspire and observe, for he had no pilot's licence and knew nothing of aeroplanes before this – only having, like Magnin in *L'Espoir*, a passion for them.[6] He took part in many missions, but was never wounded. The squadron was first established at Barcelona, then at Barajas, the airport of Madrid, then moved in November to Alcantarilla, not far from Albacete, and then to La Señara, near Valencia.

Of the effectiveness of this squadron much has been said. It was a time when the Republican conduct of their air force left much to be desired on every side and scapegoats were sought, then and since. It certainly can be argued that, if the Republic's aircraft had been used with the dash and energy with which the German, Italian and rebel 'fliers' conducted themselves, they would have been in a strong position. Instead, their aviation was spread out, pointless bombing attacks were carried out against non-military targets such as Our Lady del Pilar of Saragossa, and such combat flying as happened was marked by bravery ('courage, too, was a homeland'[7] but once again it was not enough) and incompetence. After a while things improved: by September some excellent Russian pilots were flying, and by the end of October, the war was transformed by major Russian intervention.

On this period, and of the performance of Malraux's Escuadrilla España generally, some have been harsh: for example, General Hidalgo de Cisneros, head of the Republican air force, was particularly critical of Malraux in his memoirs.[8] Nevertheless Hidalgo became a Communist and his judgments were probably affected by Malraux's defection from close alignment with the Communist cause. (Much too can be said that is critical of Hidalgo's conduct of the Republican air force.) Nevertheless. other critics should perhaps be heard: Colonel García Lacalle, subsequently head of the Republican fighter force, wrote that:

of the extremely numerous group of people who arrived with Señor Malraux few, very few were or had been professional airmen. The majority were assistants, that is writers, artists, photographers, women, children and I don't know what, everything but aviators. In consequence, we had to complete the crews of the Potezes with Spaniards. If I remember properly, I believe that it was only once that we successfully filled a Potez with its whole crew French. . . . One day I found myself in the Hotel Florida in Madrid in one of the huge dining-rooms, entirely full of people, the most extraordinary people you could imagine. I asked who they were and they replied that they were the crew and the families of the Malraux squadron. . . . I, therefore, knowing that there was only one Potez in service at that time, went immediately to Lieutenant-Colonel Cisneros and I asked him to turn them out, which he did.[9]

A similar picture of life at the Hotel Florida, though with different value judgments of the efficacy of the group, was given by Pietro Nenni in his diary: 'Malraux has organized an "aviation de fortune" which has rendered inestimable services. Thin, almost sickly, his handsome face moulded by intelligence, Malraux spends himself with all his heart, as a true combatant. He lives the passion of Spain before writing of it [a good prophecy]. Around him two categories of aviators and combatants: the mercenaries and the volunteers. The one have only one angle, that of the contract; the others, that of faith.'[10] Koltzov, the correspondent of *Pravda* in Spain and 'friend' at that time, it was said, of Stalin himself, also introduced a picture of life at the Florida with his dispatches for *Pravda* and then into his Spanish diary: noting, in the tradition of his friend in Moscow, that 'there are ten men there who are undoubted spies and a dozen loafers who intrigue scandalously against André and Guides [Abel Guides, a prominent socialist flier, an "idealist", in the squadron] at the bar'.[11] The bomber chiefly used by the Malraux squadron was the Potez 54, a plane which, since it was so slow and heavy and required so many people to man it, was nicknamed the collective flying coffin. It was 90 kilometres per hour slower for instance than the Junkers 52 (160 kilometres per hour compared with 250 kilometres per hour). Some fighters were later attached to the squadron.

By late 1936, the Spanish Civil War had ceased to be an affair for amateurs, however gifted. The Russian aid force had really taken over the Republican command and General Smuskievich (known as General Douglas) imposed upon Malraux and his team, such as were left of it, the heavy hand of Soviet centralized bureaucracy. Earlier on it had seemed, according to his commissar thirty years later, that Malraux had felt that with a few men, a few aircraft, he could play a decisive role.[12] Now such illusions of revolutionary elitism were over. Malraux then withdrew into propaganda, literature and, later, the manufacture of the brilliant film based upon two sections of *L'Espoir*. He was to be seen, as many remembered, at the International Congress of Writers at Valencia and Madrid in 1937 and he was still in Catalonia in 1939, the film unfinished. (The last scenes were shot in France. Shown to a selected audience in Paris in July 1939, its general release was banned as revolutionary film by the government after the outbreak of war. That it survived at all was quite fortuitous.)[13]

Malraux the propagandist of the Spanish War should not be forgotten. His meetings at the Mutualité in Paris on the platform with Marcel Cachin or other Communist leaders or with Gide or Benda, remained in the memory of many for years, not so much for the style of his speech but for his appearance, his unmistakable grandeur of effect: for Mauriac, one observer at the Mutualité in 1937, Malraux, a Saint-Just on arrival, 'seemed laborious when he opened his mouth'.[14] But he remained unmistakably the hero, the man of action turned writer, to the French audiences to whom he spoke in those years. To his American audiences, on a lecture tour to raise funds in 1937, he was sometimes incomprehensible – to big audiences he spoke with almost untranslatable rapidity and eloquence, reported *Time*.[15] To others, he was unforgettable. Alfred Kazin recalled for years afterwards Malraux's description of the procession carrying the wounded aviator through Aragon which appeard later in *L'Espoir*, and is the conclusion of the film of it: 'When I raised my eyes the file of peasants extended now from the heights of the mountain to its base; it was the grandest image of fraternity that I have ever encountered.' Kazin thought that Malraux's 'rhythms were so compelling that audiences swayed to them'.[16] Malraux's aim in the US was to urge writers to active politics. In Hollywood, he was asked how he could write with the war going on. He replied: 'It gets dark at night.' The ivory tower, he said, was no place for writers who had a cause to fight for. If they lived, their writing would be the better for the experience of battle. If they died, their deaths would make them living monuments. This message must have seemed a little chilling for the US in 1938, but there is no doubt that it had a tremendous effect – perhaps in the end as great an effect as Malraux's actual fighting with the Escuadrilla España.

The testimony of Malraux's action in Spain is, of course, *L'Espoir*, an extremely ambitious novel which seeks to report, in prose which often seems to be the best writing Malraux ever produced, not only what happened but what people thought was happening: at least as important. No doubt few conversations in Spain in 1936 were on quite such a high level as those reported in *L'Espoir* – as Azaña, himself a philosopher-statesman, remarked, 'it takes a Frenchman to make a philosopher out of an officer of the Civil Guard'.[17] Still the dialogue, the comments, and the action, within the chosen framework, have absolute historic validity. For example, the originals for the characters who in *L'Espoir* are responsible for the siege of the Alcázar in Toledo obviously spoke in a less consistently stylized manner. But Malraux was not Zola: he desired to express less what reality was in the simple sense of what was going on, than its significance. I find it hard to believe that the real chief of operations in the Air Ministry in Madrid in 1936 would have said, as Malraux makes his 'Vargas' say:

> My dear Mr Magnin, we are both sustained and poisoned by two or three rather dangerous myths. First, the French: the People, with a capital P, who brought about the French Revolution. Right, I grant you that. That one hundred pikes can win over some rotten muskets does not mean that one hundred hunting rifles may win over one good plane. The Russian Revolution complicated things further. Politically it is the first twentieth-century revolution, but you must also remember that from a military point of view it is the last nineteenth-century revolution. There were neither aviation nor tanks for the Tsarists, only barricades for the revolutionaries. How did the barricades come about? In order to fight royal cavalries anywhere, since the people never had any themselves. Spain today is covered with barricades, against Franco's aviation.[18]

But this was nevertheless a brilliant statement of the view of intelligent men on the Republican side, if expressed a little too well.

By giving ideas pride of place, incidentally, Malraux solved a problem which comes to all novelists if they write about foreign countries. Novelists can almost never establish their characters in depth if they are of a different nationality. Before philosophical problems, however, frontiers vanish. (How different is Malraux from, say, the gifted English writer Gerald Brenan, who not only wrote well but lived in Spain for nearly twenty years yet decided, after spending five years on a huge historical novel about Spain in the twentieth century, to give it up and burn it: 'I did not know nearly enough about Spain and Spaniards'.[19])

Malraux selects as his main characters persons whose dilemmas were the difficult ones: for example, Colonel Ximenes, the colonel of the Civil Guard in Barcelona, who keeps his men loyal to the government during the rising there. Azaña might object to his philosophizing but the position of men like Ximenes was one of the most difficult in the

Civil War. They were not men of the Right, they were conventional officers and had not even been approached by the military plotters. Therefore they instinctively fought to defeat the rebels, to find themselves the midwives of revolution. They fought on in the Republican army, and played a large part in its organization, often disillusioned by Communism, sometimes like General Miaja becoming 'fairweather Communists', and faced often, in the end, either by the repression of France – which meant either death or years of imprisonment – or by exile and poverty. For them, the illusion was seldom lyrical. Manuel asked Colonel Ximenes why he called his men 'children': 'Should I call them "comrades"? I can't. I am sixty years old. It simply doesn't work, I feel as if I'm acting. So I call them "chaps", or else "children".'[20] (Actually, the man who was certainly the original of Ximenes, Colonel Antonio Escobar, was shot by Franco's authorities in 1939.)

Another well-selected character is Manuel, Communist sound engineer in the cinema, who moves quickly from being the commander of a small group of volunteers to brigade commander (ultimately army commander). His Communism is sophisticated, *montparnassien* like his dress, driven by anticlericalism despite the impossibility of forgetting the church. His life has been dominated by the fact that he was once seriously in love:

It was as if I were dumb. I could have been that woman's lover, but it would have changed nothing. Between her and me, there was a wall: there was the Spanish Church. I loved her, and when I think about it now, I feel that it was as if I had loved a madwoman, a tender and childish madwoman. Look here, Colonel, look at this country! What has the Church achieved other than the establishment of a kind of horrible childishness. What has it done to our women? And to our people? It has taught them two things: to obey, and to sleep. . . .[21]

Women, incidentally, play no part whatever in *L'Espoir* save as victims. Once, only, we catch a picture of La Pasionaria, the Communist leader, leading a demonstration. She is, however, seen by the American reporter 'Shade' whom we take to be Herbert Matthews, representative of so many other Anglo-Saxons – Vincent Sheean, Sefton Delmer, Henry Buckley, Hemingway and Dos Passos, who interpreted events in Spain for the benefit of the public in their countries with almost as great commitment as Malraux himself.

Manuel is a Communist of the *type militaire* rather than *type abbé*, in the interpretation of 'Colonel Magnin'; a middle-class Communist, of course, able to appreciate the beauty not only of nature but also of dangerous situations – even of the lights placed by secret Fascists for the benefit of enemy aeroplanes – 'In the transparent peace which had descended over the Sierra, the rising darkness was filled only by the silent language of betrayal.'[22] Manuel has often been taken to be Gustavo Duran despite the latter's subsequent denial that he was ever a Communist (see also p. 52); but there were many young Spaniards such as he, drawn into the Communist movement in 1936 by its members' propaganda, courage in battle and ultimately access to Russian weapons; educating themselves in politics through the extraordinary circumstances.

Nearly all the characters are eminently representative – some, it is true, more than others. For example, le Négus, the Anarchist, successfully described in action, is mentioned as being always fighting against something rather than in favour of it: 'His were always negative passions. Yet it no longer works. He hears his people on the radio, calling for discipline, and he envies the young Communists.'[23] It is not a very probable thought by an Anarchist transport worker, though the sympathetic treatment of both le Négus and Puig, another Anarchist, show how far Malraux was even in 1937 from being a conventional Communist. Similarly Guernico, the Catholic writer who seems modelled on José Antonio Bergamín, a friend of Malraux, seems less successfully drawn. But these minor qualifications should not alter the fact that these characters stand up firmly, authentically and even inspiringly, today, as they did in 1937. The courage of Hernández before his execution, after the march as a prisoner through the streets of Toledo, remains a convincing picture of what happened to thousands of doubtless articulate officers: 'Toledo shimmers in the luminous air which trembles at the foot of the mountains by the Tagus: Hernández is learning what history is made of. Once more, in this country of women clad in black, is rising the ancient race of widows.'[24]

Events which subsequently assumed an almost mythical significance, too, convincingly crowd the pages of *L'Espoir*. For example there are the critical problems: why does Ramos become a Communist not an Anarchist? The white Russians who desire to fight their way back through Spain to their homeland: 'Many Russians, who were once white, who served in Spain, did so to prove their loyalty, hoping later to be able to go back to their country.'[25] (There were also white Russians on the other side: Koltzov, the *Pravda* correspondent, found the notebooks of the white Russian General Fok, who had commanded the artillery at Perekop in 1920, outside Saragossa in 1937.)[26]

There are also excellent illustrations of the received ideas character-

istic of the time: the English volunteer for the air squadron with his
Plato,[27] 'the people, without leaders and almost without weapons. . . .'[28]
– a false view but one widely held ('they have leaders, they have
weapons'[29]); ' "The people is magnificent, Magnin, magnificent!"
said Vargas. "But it is helpless".'[30] There are also the paraphernalia
of the Spanish War: the significance of aeroplanes – indeed the Spanish
War was the first conflict in which aviation played a decisive part; and
the telephone, unsung protagonist of the conflict, as the first pages of
the war make obvious, and other pages (the battles around the
Telefonica in Madrid, presaging less glorious ones around the Telefonica
in Barcelona in 1937). Finally, there are the legends more or less
surviving of the hostages of the Alcázar of Toledo,[31] and also the cadets
of the same fortress;[32] the massacre of Badajoz;[33] the Moors (*les
Maures*);[34] 'the Russian planes are coming';[35] also the American
volunteers;[36] and Unamuno's last lecture gets a brief hearing;[37] the
legend of the Italian Savoia aircraft – 'by far superior to anything the
Republicans had'.[38] Finally there is the description of the battle of
Guadalajara, which resulted in a Republican victory over, specifically,
the Italian volunteers sent to Spain by Mussolini: a victory which
could be represented as the moment of greatest hope for the Republic.
L'Espoir, it was almost the same, surely, as *L'Espagne*, from now on, for
anti-Fascists?

Of course, this turned out not to be the case in the sense that, by the
time *L'Espoir* was published, hope had evaporated. All northern Spain
with its mines and industry was lost, and from November 1937 onwards
the only hope could be that the Spanish War could be subsumed in a
general war; an apocalyptic vision which only the strongest – such as
Juan Negrín – could stomach.

When one considers these and other ideas in the context of what is
now known more clearly, some become to some extent revalued. Take,
for example, the comment made that the Italian airman was found to
have papers saying that he set off from Italy before Franco rose. This
idea has had a long life. It derived from papers, dated 15 July, alleged
to have been found on the body of an Italian airman who, flying from
Italy to Franco-held Morocco on 30 July, crashed in Algeria and was
found by the French. All the evidence from diplomatic and other
papers now available is that Mussolini was approached for help by
Franco after 19 July, that Mussolini was at first circumspect, and
finally changed his mind when he heard the French government were
sending some aircraft to their friends of the Spanish Popular Front.
Historians have then pondered over the mysterious '15 July', Could it

be that the pilot concerned began his turn of duty on 15 July, and then had it changed about 26 July? The simplest explanation is the most difficult to accept: that there were no such papers. The French Ministry of Air in 1936, strongly pro-Republican, merely said that such papers had been discovered; but they never existed. If they did, they were forged. The Left as well as the Right were ready in the 1930s with lies as well as ideas.

A minor point, no doubt, but there are very many minor matters where the lyrical beliefs of the epic days were plainly wrong. Take the frequently repeated assertion that the people were 'without leaders and almost without weapons'. This is not really true; nor was it true to say 'against the Government, three quarters of the army, as usual'.[39] People certainly thought those things in Madrid in 1936. The truth is that the army was divided almost in half by the rising of the zealot Right. Malraux is right in terms of the numbers concerned to speak of the enemy so often as 'Phalangists', or 'Fascists', for they were often such, being volunteers for the Fascist 'crusade', not regular soldiers. The zealots included, it is true, most of the *africanistas*, those officers who had such brutal experience of combat in Morocco in the 1920s; but they did not leave the Republic unarmed. The Republic was never short of rifles in 1936 – or should not have been. The trouble was that the rifle was regarded as a symbol of liberty, or revolutionary prowess, by the members of the working-class organizations, so innumerable weapons were kept hidden at home or exhibited in the streets. In addition, the initial superiority of the Republic in artillery disappeared because, in the confusion of the first days in the Sierra, a mass of material was abandoned in the battle. It was wrong for Magnin to imply that the Republic had fewer aircraft than the rebels at the time of the rising. If the Germans and Italians sent extremely useful Junkers and Savoias in July, August and September, the French let the Republic have something over fifty aircraft – Potez and Marcel Bloch bombers, Dewoitine fighters and Loire fighters too. The cry 'Comrades, the Russians planes have arrived' was one which led to the transformation of the war, giving the Republic air superiority from then until the summer of 1937, but, even so, the timing of the remark is wrong: it should appear not at the end of Chapter xiv of ii (*Sang de gauche*) of Part ii (*Les Manzanares*) but closer to Chapter iv of Part i.

So much for pedantry. There are, too, some omissions which the author of *L'Espoir* must perhaps regret today. We hear much for example in the novel of the nights of Madrid in summer – 'Mosquitoes buzz around them. They talk. Night settles over the field, solemn as on any great space; a warm night, like all summer nights.'[40] The phrase will now always remind the historian of another memory of Madrid in that August, written (only a little later), like Malraux's paragraph, some time in 1937, by another voyeur-cum-actor, the President of the Republic between 1936 and 1939, Manuel Azaña, recalling the tragedy of the murders in the Model Prison: 'Personal recollection: Evening of a Madrid August: I watch the square through a window: little whisps of smoke: signs of unease: news of the fire in the prison: nightfall: that all is finished and that there is calm: at 11.30 telephone conversation with Bernardo Giner, Minister of Communications: first news of the events: slaughter: *la noche triste*: problem, in search of my duty: desolation ... mourning for the republic ... uncontrollable sadness. In the evening, tears of the President of the Council....'[41]

Not only does the reader of *L'Espoir* derive no idea of the tragic and pointless murders of so many people on the Republican side far from the battle-line, but the position of such men as Azaña is not reflected. Unlike Malraux's characters, he was not in search of his destiny; only of his duty.

Of course, there are many other such matters where good debating points can now be made against the partial historical picture which the book conveys. It is important to appreciate that the action of *L'Espoir* takes place entirely between July 1936 and March 1937, before, for instance, the Communists' pogrom against the POUM or the Anarchist collectives in Aragon, before the setting up of the sinister police force, the SIM, and before disillusion with Communist methods was widespread – among Anarchists on the political ground that the Communists seemed to be destroying the revolution, among 'liberals' on the ground that Communist methods were unacceptable even if their aims were sensible. In the end, therefore, it is the phrases in *L'Espoir* which, regardless of history, stay in the memory like lines in great poems: 'In the dusk of an equestrian portrait, amid the scent of pine and herbs growing among rubble, the Sierra unfolds its decorative hills down to the plain of Madrid over which night descends as over the sea. An incongruous sight, the armoured train, huddled in its tunnel, seems forgotten by a war which has departed with the hot sun.'[42] This passage has an energy and fascination which defies any analysis of what it is purporting to describe. The vitality of the prose will survive the work of pedants (such as myself) who may prove that such and such an interpretation of the author is historically misleading; and will therefore also remain as a true expression after all of the quality of those *fuerzas vivas* (live forces), whose clash led to the Civil War in the first place.

A. J. AYER

*

ANDRÉ MALRAUX:
THE EARLY NOVELS

My knowledge of the works of André Malraux goes back to the early 1930s, when I first read *La Condition humaine*. It made such a strong impression on me that for many years afterwards its principal characters and even the details of the story remained fixed in my memory. I did not at that time know anything about the author, and it was only some years later that I had the curiosity to read his earlier novels *Les Conquérants*, *La Voie royale* and *L'Espoir*. I learned from *L'Espoir* that Malraux had fought on the Republican side in Spain and when, in the character of an intelligence officer, I made my way to Toulouse in the autumn of 1944, I discovered that he had been one of the leaders of the local Resistance and had played an outstanding part in the liberation of the city. This increased my admiration for him, so that when a few months later I was asked to meet him at a dinner in Paris, I eagerly accepted the invitation. Unfortunately, something in his manner combined with my shyness to make me almost tongue-tied and I gained nothing from the meeting, or from another more relaxed encounter at a party a few days later, beyond the impression that he saw himself primarily as a man of action. I remember that he criticized a certain well-known author for not being one, and seemed to imply that this detracted from the value of his work. It struck me as an odd choice of literary criterion, but one that I could understand his adopting. It was clearly also one that very few writers were going to be allowed to satisfy.

I think that I have read the greater part of what he has subsequently written, gaining most pleasure from the *Antimémoires*, and least from the works on art, but never quite so much pleasure as from those four early novels. Having re-read them recently, after an interval of many years, I still think most highly of *La Condition humaine*, t ho some ways I was more moved by *L'Espoir*. This was perhaps due less to its literary merits than to its theme, which revived my strong feelings about the Spanish Civil War. The book ends on a note of guarded optimism, which is made more poignant in retrospect by our knowledge that the heroism which it celebrates went for nothing. Even the legend is not unsullied. We can still admire the spirit which led men to volunteer for the International Brigade, but we have learned too much about the party which controlled them.

The Communists come best out of Malraux's book, because of their recognition of the need for discipline if there is to be any chance for the war to be won. They are contrasted favourably with the Anarchists, who fight as individuals and tend to desert their posts if the odds against them appear too great. In general, Malraux presents his characters fully-fledged. He is interested in their actions, and the qualities which they display in them are kept constant. The one character in *L'Espoir* who develops throughout the book is the young factory-worker Manuel, by profession a sound-engineer in a film-studio and something of an intellectual, who is shown gradually acquiring the sense of responsibility and the hardness which fit him for military command. One of the stages in this process is his refusal to do anything for two of his men who have been condemned to be shot for cowardice. He understands and pities them but sees that in the pursuit of victory pity cannot be afforded.

Manuel is thought to have been modelled on Lister [see also Hugh Thomas, p. 47 in the present book], who became one of the leading Communist generals, and it is fair to assume that most of the main characters in the book are taken from life. That it is in this sense a work of reportage does not detract from its value, which consists in its evocation of the mood of the Spanish people, the vividness of its set-pieces, such as the description of the air raids on Madrid, and the authenticity of its battle scenes. The exploits of the small international air force, a mixture of volunteers and mercenaries, fighting with obsolete machines against the superior numbers and equipment of the German and Italian flyers, before the arrival of Russian aid, are particularly well rendered. This was the force in which Malraux himself served and one that he did much to organize.

At the date at which *L'Espoir* was written the cause of the Spanish Republic was, as I have said, not yet obviously lost. Franco's troops and their Italian allies had been driven back from Madrid. *Les Conquérants* also celebrates a temporary victory for the Left. Appearing in 1928, it displays Canton in 1925 under the control of the Kuomintang in uneasy alliance with the Communists, attempting an economic blockade of Hong Kong, with Chiang Kai-shek's army preparing to advance north towards the capture of Shanghai and Peking. The villains of the piece, the British imperialists and the Chinese war-lords, are mostly off-stage, and the main concern of the book is with the interplay of forces and the conflict of personalities within the revolutionary movement.

Unlike *L'Espoir*, *Les Conquérants* has a single hero, Pierre Garine, a man in his early thirties, of Swiss and Russian parentage, who has become director of propaganda for the Cantonese government. He is shown as working with the Communists, notably with the Russian Borodin who figures in the novel in his own person, but not as being one of them. He is portrayed rather as a romantic revolutionary, a modern conquistador, and it is from the description of such men as conquerors that the book derives its title. There is a slight suggestion that men of this sort have had their day, and that the future belongs to the disciplined party worker, but the doubt is raised whether the outlook of the Communist party, with its distrust of individualism, is suited to China. This may have been written in the hindsight of the failure of Russian policy to prevent the Kuomintang from turning on the Communists; another historical episode which furnishes the setting for *La Condition humaine*.

Garine is not seen in depth. We are told something about his background – a conviction in Paris for helping to procure abortions, from wholly disinterested motives, his joining and deserting from the French Foreign Legion. We watch him in action – there is a scene in which he summarily shoots one of a pair of captured enemy agents in order to terrify the other into talking – but we do not get much insight into his motives, beyond his desire to do his job efficiently. There is just the suggestion that he suffers from an inner void for which he needs to compensate by the exercise of power. He speaks of himself as being fundamentally a gambler and as one who has learned that 'a life is worth nothing but that nothing is worth a life'. He stays at his post though the climate has destroyed his health, and when he is at last persuaded to leave Canton it is implied that he has not long to live.

It was perhaps gratuitous for Malraux to make Garine a dying man. The imminence of death has no marked effect on his behaviour, and the story did not demand a tragic ending. But once more the value of the book lies not in the handling of its characters but in its dramatization of historical events, its portrayal of a city in ferment. Already, in this youthful work – 'ce livre d'adolescent', as he subsequently called it –

Malraux displays his power to engage the reader in the actions which he is describing. In this sense his writing is cinematic.

The remaining two novels are both records of defeat: in the one case personal and in the other political. The defeat is personal in *La Voie royale*, which is remotely modelled on a youthful enterprise of Malraux's own – his abortive attempt to smuggle works of art out of Indochina, then still a French possession. The novel tells the story of two men who organize an expedition to explore the ancient Royal road which leads through the Cambodian jungle to Siam, with the real intention of discovering ruined temples which they plan to pillage of their sculptures, and thereby make their fortunes. One of them, the young Frenchman Claude, may be to some extent a self-portrait, though we do not learn much about his character. The hero of the book is his accomplice, Perken, again a conquistador, a much older man, a Dane who, more or less in the service of the Siamese government, has established a personal ascendancy over some of the native tribes. The story reaches its climax in a scene in which Perken advances alone and unarmed to bargain with the chief of a hostile tribe for the release of a white man whom the tribe has blinded and enslaved. He is successful in this but falls on a dart which wounds him in the knee. Infection sets in and there is no hope of saving him. The Siamese send out a punitive expedition and Perken, a dying man, goes forward to protect his people. Claude decides to go with him, abandoning the sculptures which he has found. The book ends with Perken's death.

This is the only one of these early novels in which the reader is made conscious of an attempt at fine writing. It is as if the lushness of the scenery had broken in upon Malraux's style. If the work succeeds, it is again through the creation of atmosphere and the sense of adventure which it communicates.

La Condition humaine is a more ambitious work than either *La Voie royale* or *Les Conquérants*, and of much higher quality. It retains the urgency which characterized the earlier novels, the power to create atmosphere, and the cinematic skill, but it achieves a depth which they lacked. For the first time Malraux succeeds in creating characters who exist apart from the events in which he involves them. The scene is set in Shanghai in the spring of 1927, with a popular rising organized by the Communists, and the Kuomintang army advancing on the city. The local Communist leaders know that Chiang Kai-shek will have no further use for them once he has secured Shanghai, but the party line forbids them to organize resistance to him. They receive orders first to surrender and then to bury their arms. They connive at an attempt by a Chinese terrorist to assassinate Chiang, but it fails; the terrorist throws himself with a bomb under one of Chiang's cars, but Chiang is not travelling in it. Chiang has the Communist leaders arrested and executed, as they actually were, by being burnt alive in the furnace of a railway-engine. Only one of them, a Belgian and a minor figure, escapes and makes his way to Russia.

If the novel has a romantic hero, it is the Russian Katow who gives his cyanide pills to two of his Chinese comrades and goes resolutely to his martyrdom. He does not, however, dominate the book, playing indeed a lesser part in the story than his associate Kyo, half French and half Japanese, or the Chinese terrorist Tchen. There are other characters who are more vividly drawn, such as Kyo's father Gisors, a professor of politics who has taken refuge in opium, the industrialist Ferral who cares only for power, the ruined art-dealer Clappique, a fascinating mythomaniac living by his wits.

The book contains brilliant set-pieces: the opening in which Tchen assassinates a sleeping stranger, in order to procure a warrant which will give the Communists arms; Tchen's first abortive attempt to assassinate Chiang, when he goes into a shop to wait for Chiang's car and cannot detach himself from the merchant in time; the scene in which Ferral, who has been humiliated by his mistress, buys the whole stock of a seller of birds of paradise, and sets these birds loose in her hotel room; Clappique's setting out to warn Kyo of the trap which has been set for the Communists, himself needing to escape from Shanghai and expecting to receive from Kyo the money which will make this possible, but visiting a gambling-house on the way, succumbing to the gambler's need to lose all his money, and missing his appointment; Ferral's vain attempt, back in France, to persuade the establishment to finance the restoration of his ruined industrial empire. There is no over-writing. The style is subordinated to the action; and the action maintains an almost continuous level of intensity.

Here too the Communists come out well, but they come out well as individuals and as men of action; we do not learn much about their political beliefs. Since their main motive is that of respect for human dignity, they might as convincingly have been portrayed as Anarchists, except for their reluctance to go against the party line. In later years, Malraux was to become very hostile to the Communists, or at least to their adherents in France. In a postscript to *Les Conquérants*, consisting in the text of a lecture which he delivered as a Gaullist in the spring of 1948, he attacks them for their lying propaganda, and for their acceptance of the principle that the end justifies the means. This is not so sharp a change of front as it might appear at first sight. To the extent that Malraux was drawn to the Communists in the decade before the Second World War, it seems to have been a romantic rather than an intellectual attachment. He saw them as champions of the oppressed, and in Spain he respected their efficiency. There is, however, no evidence in these novels that he accepted the body of Marxist theory. What they do show is that it was not yet altogether clear to him that the end does not justify the means.

Politically, there is some affinity between the Malraux of the 1930s and another writer who went to fight in Spain, George Orwell. Both were individualists, and each of them combined left-wing sympathies with the conservative values of patriotism, self-reliance and discipline in action. I suppose that Orwell was the more puritanical, though in personal relations neither priggish nor arrogant, perhaps also the more romantic and the more keenly aware that power corrupts. Malraux seems to have been more of an adventurer. It is to their credit that Marx would have seen them both as sentimental socialists.

In Malraux's case, the socialism comes out most strongly in *L'Espoir*. Of the three historical novels, it is the most straightforwardly political. In the other two cases, the cause matters less than the personalities and experiences of those who are fighting for it. If we sympathize with them, it is because we are drawn into the action. This could apply even to a reader whose political sympathies were on the other side. Thus, it is one of the merits of *La Condition humaine* that when the industrialist Ferral is at the centre of the stage, we see things from his point of view. He is not a sympathetic character, but one comes to respect his lucidity, his lack of hypocrisy and his driving force. He makes a stronger impression as a person than the Communist leaders, who are a little too much idealized. So in their different ways do Gisors and Clappique.

A remarkable feature of all these early novels is that their world is almost wholly masculine. There is a brief scene in *Les Conquérants* where a wife mourns her husband who has been tortured and murdered by the terrorists, and one in *La Voie royale*, where Perken savagely enjoys a prostitute, but this is intended only to throw light upon Perken – the woman remains anonymous. In *L'Espoir*, women do not figure at all, except as extras who very occasionally are given small speaking parts. There are two female characters who achieve some prominence in *La Condition humaine*. One of them is Ferral's mistress Valérie, a dress-designer valuing her independence, who resists Ferral's attempt to dominate her. When she rejects him Ferral takes his revenge on the sex by treating a higher-grade Chinese courtesan as if she were an ordinary prostitute. Again one feels that these women were put in only to enlarge our knowledge of Ferral. The other is Kyo's wife May, a German doctor working in a hospital and sharing his political activity. There is a scene in which she confesses to a passing infidelity, and Kyo is hurt and resentful, even while acknowledging her freedom to do what she pleases. Here too the interest is focused on Kyo's attitude rather than on May's. She figures also in the last scene in the book when, having escaped arrest and on her way to Russia, in the hope of being trained as an agitator (or if that is not possible, working as a doctor in Siberia), she visits Gisors, who has taken refuge in Japan. She expects him to come with her but he refuses. The Marxism which he has taught is no longer a living thing to him, now that his son is dead. His resignation is contrasted with her need for some form of action, which will allow her to feel that she is avenging Kyo. But, apart from being allowed the last word, saying with bitter pride that she hardly cries any longer, she is made to serve mainly as a foil to Gisors.

It need not be taken as a defect in the novels that women play so small a part in them. The same is true of most of the best stories of adventure. They play no significant part in *Kim* or in *Treasure Island* or in Saint-Exupéry's *Vol de nuit*. It could be objected that *La Condition humaine* at least is designed to be something more than a story of adventure. It would belie its title if it did not have general implications about the ways in which men live. It does have some such implications. There is a general view, which is found also in *L'Espoir* and *Les Conquérants*. It is the view of men in the Hegelian relation of master and slave. For all its success in characterization, *La Condition humaine* is primarily just an illustration of this theme.

Even so, the philosopher of whom Malraux reminds us is less Hegel than Schopenhauer. His novels are studies in the exercise of the will. He is concerned with the attempt of the slaves, the common people of Spain or China, or wherever it may be, to liberate themselves from their masters, and he sees that this can be done only through collective action. But there have to be leaders to take the necessary decisions and impose the necessary discipline; leaders who realize themselves in action, even if they fall short of having an appetite for power. Like Rousseau's legislator, such men incarnate the general will, even if their decisions sometimes run counter to the individual wills of those for whose benefit they are being taken. It is by assuming this responsibility that adventurers become conquerors. To a reader of these early novels, it should not be at all surprising that Malraux became a passionate adherent of General de Gaulle.

PIERRE BOCKEL

*

MALRAUX AND THE
CHALLENGE OF FAITH

Translated by Robert Speaight

I knew André Malraux personally before I became acquainted with his works, and anything I say about him will be the evidence of one who saw, heard, lived, and felt with him, and who sometimes read his thoughts. I shall not be speaking as a philosopher, a theologian, or a literary critic, whose business it is to dissect and classify. But what I can witness to is none the less important because it does not pretend to be exhaustive.

I am a priest and Malraux describes himself as an agnostic. It was the war and the French Resistance which threw us together in the same adventure, and established between us, no doubt for as long as we shall live, a relationship in which the quest for transcendence and the faith in a living God are questions which never cease to arise—sometimes explicitly, often silently, but always with a view to the salvation of mankind.

How did it all begin?

It was in July 1944. The Allied troops had just disembarked in Provence, and the army of General de Lattre was moving up the Rhône valley. The scattered elements of the ss Division Das Reich were turning round in circles, caught at every crossroads by the *maquisards* who had come out of hiding. The towns of the South-West, from Toulouse to Périgueux, had fallen prey to a Resistance split up into political groups after effective demobilization. Because our own provinces had not yet been liberated, the Alsace–Lorraine maquis were able to escape the degeneration of a noble adventure into the mire of insurrection, theft, rape, and ignoble revenge. The task of regrouping, disengagement from the muddy towns, which we had nevertheless helped to liberate, and of rejoining the army advancing in the direction of the Vosges, called for a commander of exceptional quality. André Malraux, just freed from prison, came forward to put himself at the head of what was soon to become the Brigade Alsace–Lorraine.

I was at first reluctant to accept his offer to serve under him. His halo as a member of the International Brigade during the Spanish Civil War and his reputation as a militant of the extreme Left were at that time calculated to frighten me. I was nervous of entering Christian Alsace under a chief with such strong political attachments. So my relationship with André Malraux got off to a rather bad start. Certain of my comrades needed all their powers of persuasion to convince me of the chance that was being offered us. My friends had met him before I had, and when I met him myself I knew that they were right.

Our first meeting was short and rather brusque. We were at Ussel, during the early days of our advance towards the east, when I was summoned with the command: 'Colonel Berger wishes to see you.' So there he was, this strange Colonel with the elegance of a cavalry officer, and the legendary little beret which distinguished him from the regular army. But it was his face that revealed the most striking contrast between the ranking officer and the adventurer in a just cause. Below the high forehead and the famous lock of hair which fell across it, one could read the look of piercing intelligence on features that were still young, ravaged by tics, and extremely mobile. This was the impression that Malraux made upon me. The interview was brief and almost chilly, and I was still on my guard when the Colonel's car drove off. Gide had certainly been right when he had said that 'in front of Malraux one doesn't feel very intelligent'.

Most fortunately, our second meeting – and this was the one that mattered – corrected the somewhat severe impression of the first. It took place at Besançon, and this was one of the great moments of my life. Recalling it in a book recently published (*L'Enfant du rire*), I wrote as follows:

I realized then, and almost instantaneously, that – at least on my side – our meeting was providential; that it was one of those things which have to happen in order that so many other things may be disentangled and bear fruit. Perhaps because I was at the same time a priest and his accomplice in that adventure, we were soon talking on a level where no confidences are required to produce agreement. Through the quivering excitement of a brotherhood in arms, I could see, albeit confusedly, the birth of a mutual communion which had no need of direct communication.

From that moment I could sense in my interlocutor, who was soon to be my companion, the same kind of understanding which was my own vocation and destiny. I did not stand on his level of intelligence and culture, but I could feel intuitively what he could see immediately with his mind, and what he was able to communicate by the sheer vibration of the links that bound us together.

And so it has come about, all through the adventure that we shared, and later through our friendship, that Malraux the unbeliever has always been for me – and perhaps without realizing it himself – like a reflection of my own faith. Curiously enough, by the way he acts as well as by the way he thinks, he has reminded me of certain of its aspects that I had forgotten, and revealed to me certain of its dimensions that I had not suspected. His vision of transcendence, as he catches it on the face of a saint, or perceives it in every human heart, or finds it in a work of art, has deeply affected the way that I look at men and women. At the same time he would question me about my own faith, for he hopes that the civilization of tomorrow will be visibly stamped with religious belief, and he already sees the promise of this. Without it, he maintains, no civilization is viable or lasting.

There are at least four kinds of question with which Malraux confronts the conscience of a believer.

André Malraux, mirror of the Christian faith. Of course he is not a believer, at any rate not in the strict sense of the word. Although atheism horrifies him, he counts himself among the agnostics. I tempted him, not long ago, with the argument that Pascal put into the mouth of God, hoping to learn something more about his own search for faith: 'You would not be looking for me, if you had not already found me.' But instead of giving me the personal answer I was waiting for, he eluded my question with a long discussion on Pascal, disguising his own feelings under a strange cloak of modesty. One can only enter into a religious discussion with him if one refrains from attacking him like a stupid and disrespectful missionary who will annex for the Church any suggestion of the sacred or any manifestation of charity. Malraux is not a Christian without knowing it; he is an unbeliever so ardently in search of the transcendent that the world of Christianity has become his own universe. To be sure, he has all the appearance of a man to whom Christ is no stranger; the Christ who gave life to St John, who inspired St Bernard, and who made of Francis of Assisi the founder of a new world through an expression of the faith rediscovered at its source. But the grace which took hold of Max Jacob or Claudel does not seem to have touched him, and we owe it to ourselves to respect a secret which does not belong to us.

Nevertheless, Malraux believes in transcendence. But what sort of transcendence? In the way he looks at mankind, at the men he had enlisted to work with him, I have always seemed to discover a profound respect; and this he would willingly identify with the contemplation of that 'eternal part' which he defined, in a letter he wrote to me on 28 April 1948, as 'man's desire to subordinate himself to that which, in himself, is yet greater than himself'. Transcendence, thus understood, comes to appear like immanence, a deep presence within. Although I knew this already through Scripture and theology, I had never seen it so clearly in the eyes of a man. Biblical terms like 'the ark of the covenant' and 'the temple of the Holy Ghost' now corresponded with reality, and gave a new meaning to my life.

Malraux's deep and diffident definition of transcendence goes hand in hand with a radical commitment to the service of mankind, and to human brotherhood. I was often a witness to this. He wrote to me in the same letter that he thought it essential we 'should put the emphasis on our defence of what is eternal in man, whether or not we regard this as bound up with the Revelation'. This letter brought me very close to him. No doubt our mutual convictions did not spring necessarily from the same source, but I thought of the passage in St Paul: 'Ever since God created the world His everlasting power and deity – however invisible – have been there for the mind to see in the things he has made.' (Romans 1:20). So in what way was I committed at his side in the name of transcendence? And what are the Christian values that he helped me to recognize?

Malraux's adventures sometimes have a symbolic power in the way that they reproduce an epic of times past; sometimes they have a limited and precise objective; but they always envisage the liberation of man himself, as well as a particular territory. To set free, at much risk and peril, a people fettered and humiliated, and to do this in the name of justice and brotherhood, is to acquire for oneself the dignity of a free man.

To enlist the people of Alsace and Lorraine in the recovery of their own land is at the same stroke to create free men capable of putting a population on its feet. What do I mean by a free man? I mean precisely the man who can submit himself to what, in himself, is greater than himself, to that transcendence which is all a part of him. This was how Malraux taught me the true meaning of liberty, and at the same time the true meaning of sacrifice. 'There is no greater love (and no greater freedom) than to give one's life for those one loves.' I had never realized so keenly the connection between liberty and death. I read the passion of Christ; and I could read it also in the frightened look – the look of a startled hind – in the eyes of those who were shedding their blood and would presently have no eyes to see with, because they had one day answered 'yes' to the free man they had rediscovered beneath the ruins of the man humiliated. Our clerical technique of organized apostolate makes me smile when I stand in the presence of a man – of a witness – whose slightest gesture revived the spark of liberty in the meanest of our volunteers; who very often reminded him that he had been confirmed by the Holy Spirit, and that a gospel of love had been preached to him as a child. For at the heart of our great campaign of liberation, in which we fought as one man – with arms, alas! but without hate – we realized at every moment the close connection between love and liberty and death; for death was seen as the loving offering of life. The Mass celebrated in the woods took on an astonishing significance: 'This is my body which was given . . . this is my blood which was shed' – while the bullets crackled and the shells whistled overhead. 'I salute those of us who died yesterday and those of us who will fall tomorrow' – as Colonel Berger, alias Malraux, said to us between two bloody engagements.

Malraux taught us the meaning of liberty, and at the same time – perhaps without knowing it? – he revived the faith of the believer. By his intelligence and wide culture, his sensitivity to the religious nature of man on every continent, from India to the Western world, and at every stage of history, he opened our horizons and planted in us the seeds of that ecumenical obsession which now dominates my life and thinking.

The Catholic and Protestant chaplains who were at Malraux's side in the same adventure felt this with a particular intensity. Pastor Weiss and Pastor Franz represented the Reformed and Lutheran churches; there were Father Bonnal, the Jesuit, and the Abbé Maurel; and we made up a truly pastoral community at the heart of a single parish. Very often, as the fortunes of war gave us the opportunity, we relieved each other in going to the help of a comrade struck by a bullet and lying on the ground. I can still hear Pastor Franz telling me how he had just heard the confession of a Catholic soldier on the point of death.

In spite of his severe expression, and a grandiloquence which he likes to charge with a suggestive and persuasive symbolism, in spite of his taste for the heroic canvas, and a certain reserve where his private feelings and those of others are concerned, Malraux has a natural tenderness which is easily moved to charity. So many of his actions, attitudes and words recall the Beatitudes – and here, too, I can speak from experience, past and present. I am grateful to him, finally, for reminding me, with the most delicate tact, of what is essentially demanded of a priesthood which he values so highly. Nor is he unaware of this power of revelation; it has put Christians greatly in his debt; but he did not allow it to influence him.

Malraux looks at transcendence in its highest human manifestations. That is to say, in the face of sanctity and in the artistic expression of the faith. He invites the world to look in the same direction as himself, and to surrender, as he does, to the seduction of supreme beauty.

Lives of the saints that come to us from pious biographers are generally boring; our allergy to the past sets them at one remove, and we are not easily touched by them. But when Malraux speaks of St Bernard or St Francis of Assisi they come to life again. He brings them before us so vividly, and his face so lights up as he does so, that they seem to be alive in the depths of his consciousness. One wonders whether the tragic note that always strikes one in his conversation is not inspired by the regret at not being able to feel himself completely at one with them. In his panegyric at Rouen on 31 May 1964, during the commemoration of Joan of Arc, he exclaimed:

How should we understand this girl of seventeen, if we did not catch beneath her marvellous simplicity, the incorruptible accent of the Prophets who stretched out their hands in menace or in consolation towards the Kings of the Orient, and in pity towards the Kingdom of Israel?

Or again:

When they questioned her about her submission to the Church militant she replied, troubled but without hesitation: 'Yes, but God must be served first.' Nothing she said depicts her more clearly. In face of the Dauphin and the prelates and the men-at-arms, she put secondary considerations aside and went straight to the point.

And Malraux added, troubled also maybe, but unhesitating: 'Ever since the world has been what it is, this is the genius of action.' Finally, as he described her sufferings: 'The first flame shot up, and with it the appalling cry which, in every Christian heart, was to echo the outcry of the Virgin as she saw the cross of Christ erected against the livid sky.'

I might compare these phrases, where hope seems to pierce the mist, with certain surprising observations that I heard from the lips of Malraux himself. 'You know very well that nobody can escape from God'; or again: 'I would willingly go with you to Benares or to Mecca, but Jerusalem would be a different matter; I should have to speak the words of Christ at Gethsemane.' And yet his admiration for his friend Jean Grosjean, a champion of Faith, knows no limits; neither does his veneration for Bernanos, whose spiritual heir he considers himself to be. It is only with a certain modesty that I venture to quote from a letter he wrote me on 4 October 1971; it was in reply to a note I had sent him after he had made known his intention to go to the help of the people of Bangladesh:

> Realize that everything I do, in face of what one must call the destiny of the world, I feel to be all the more justified. I sense that you are with me. How much time is left to us? It doesn't matter. I can't tell you why, but if you are in the Sahara, and I am in Bangladesh, we shall still die together – and I should like you to know that you will help me to die nobly.

So even in the mystery of the communion of saints, he enlisted me at his side. His allusion to the Sahara refers to our common sympathy for the missionary order of the Little Sisters and Little Brothers of Père de Foucauld; perhaps it was only circumstances and a failure of courage which prevented me from joining them.

I cannot resist the temptation of reproducing from *L'Enfant du rire* Malraux's account, on his return from the Sahara, of a scene he had witnessed there and which had deeply moved him.

> In the middle of the vast Saharan desert we saw three little dots on the horizon. As we drove along, the dots became three advancing silhouettes, and then, as they reached us, three smiling faces. And what a smile it was! The desert came to life because three little Sisters were slowly walking in the glittering vibration of infinite space. They seemed to be inspired by a mysterious presence which gave them strength and sweetness and joy. We stopped and invited them to get into the car. They thanked us very politely, and apologized for declining our hospitality. 'We haven't very far to go,' they said. In fact it was a good fifty kilometres to Hoggar; we could see the strange mountains beyond the mirror of the sands. So we went on, and through the exhaust of the engine we saw the little Sisters lay down their packs on the edge of the trail and then, immediately, resume their march. No doubt they were thinking of some poor Tuaregs who would be passing that way. Where were they going? After all, their destination didn't matter very much, since their destiny was to walk with the Christ whom they carried in their hearts.

André loved to talk to me about our mutual friend Edmond Michelet, the comrade and partisan who served impartially both the people and the State by living the Beatitudes of Jesus Christ. It was a totally Christian affection which united the two men. Michelet carried in his soul the living Word of God, just as Péguy had it enshrined in his heart, and with it he carried the cathedral of Chartres and the apocalyptic inferno of Dachau; and between the spirit of Michelet and the spirit of Christianity, which may have inspired the Resistance, and certainly inspired Péguy at Chartres, there is a connection of which Malraux cannot be unaware. In the one and the other, in the faces of the saints and the heroes, and in the artistic heritage of the Christian centuries, he can recognize one of the highest manifestations of that transcendence which makes a man greater than himself.

Malraux questions me about my own faith. It always seemed to me that I was the only one to profit from the exchange of views on religious matters which marked my relationhsip with Malraux. I was convinced that God was speaking to me through the voice of an agnostic, and I thought this was quite possible; no doubt because I felt a very poor creature in the presence of an intellectual giant whose humanity equals his intelligence. So the letter from which I have quoted moved me not only by its testimony of friendship, but even more by the feeling it gave me that, within this friendship, God played a bigger part than either of us.

Looking back, I remember certain remarks from which it is easy to tell the sort of questions about the faith that Malraux puts to an interlocutor who is also a believer. Owing to the modesty in which he likes to wrap his own relation to transcendence these questions are generally 'oblique' – a term he is particularly fond of. More often than not they touch upon the themes of grace and death. With the former he is preoccupied even to the point of obsession, as if he saw in it the ultimate revelation or experience enabling one to cross a gap which is at once narrow and infinite. One day, after I had not heard from him for several years, I went to see him at the Ministry for Cultural Affairs. He was extremely puzzled. In fact he had spent some hours in vainly trying to get in touch with me on an urgent and personal matter – and there I was in front of him for no other reason than because I wanted to see him again. As if the coincidence was a reality which must be the cloak for some deeper reality, he asked me straight out: 'Is that what you call Grace?' I didn't know what to reply. But more than once since then he has asked me: 'What is it that you call Grace?' My book *L'Enfant du rire*, for which he has written a generous preface, gives a partial reply to the question. Here he writes: 'We cannot discover the cause of a vocation, and the author suggests that it has no other cause but the groping of grace. He is less concerned with the "why" than the "how". His "how" is more convincing than the "how" of Renan, because it is based on a less rational psychology.' The 'how' takes one back to one's own experience; and Malraux concludes his preface by asking a number of questions.

A book like this one teaches us what a Christian expects from a revival of the faith, confirmed by a return to its sources, and discovering its formula, no doubt, in the belief that true religion is communion with God. It may be that a believer sees, first of all, in transcendence the most powerful means of this communion. It is certain that for an unbeliever the most important question of our time is this; can there be communion without transcendence and, if not, on what can man base his supreme values? Upon what transcendence, apart from revelation, can he base his communion? Once again I hear the whisper that I heard not long ago: what is the point of going to the moon, if you commit suicide when you get there?

You can imagine that we often spoke about death; but only once, I think, did he question me about the life to come. The circumstances were particularly tragic. We were about to bury his two sons, Gauthier and Vincent, both killed in a car crash. The two coffins lay in a tent erected in the little Parisian cemetery of Charonne. We stood beside them; a crowd filed past, deeply moved; and already the light was failing. André then took me by the arm, and passing in front of the open tomb where his sons' dead mother, Josette Clotis, was awaiting her children, he led me into an alley of the cemetery. Overcoming his modesty, he asked me shyly: 'Would you agree to celebrate a Mass? You know how it used to be when we buried the men fallen at our side?' And then he tried to justify his request by the life of the children who had been crushed to death; they were not atheists; they had even been baptized, etc. It was as if he were saying to me: 'They were my children anyway, so ...?' I agreed. He had understood that I should not have ventured to take advantage of my priesthood to impose, even by way of suggestion, an initiative which only he could take. So he was almost happy to anounce that the funeral would be postponed until the next morning. The same crowd of officials and good folk met the following day in the little church of Charonne, where the remains of Gauthier and Vincent were carried in procession. The Mass was celebrated in a devout silence through which you could hear the secret prayer: '*Requiem aeternam . . .*' After this all we had to do was to lay the children beside their mother, for she too was intensely with us at a moment which seemed abstracted from time.

Hope. As a 'prophet of our time', André Malraux looks forward to tomorrow. Is it with the same eyes that he studies the depths and horizons of history? I cannot say. If there were a close connection between his perception of transcendence and his vision of the future, the latter would have taken on an eschatological dimension, and his earthly hopes would have been transformed into the expectations of faith. Many Christians discover in supernatural hope the supreme compensation for despair or scepticism about the immediate future of a world or a civilization irretrievably corrupt. But Malraux brings to these covert expectations the accent of a natural hope. He believes, and proclaims, that the world of tomorrow will be religious, and that if it is not religious it will not survive. This conviction, based on his profound knowledge of man and of history, forces the believer to look closely at the world he inherits, dark as it may appear, and discover the first signs of that metaphysical thirst and renewal which are to mark the civilization of the future.

Will the natural hopes of Malraux reinforce and illuminate the hope which draws its strength from the faith? Will he finally discover in the hopes of believers the supreme justification for the hope which he places in man?

GASTON PALEWSKI

*

A SURPRISING FRIENDSHIP:
MALRAUX AND DE GAULLE

Translated by Robert Speaight

For both André Malraux and myself, twenty-five years of our lives were spent in devoted observation and passionate service of General de Gaulle, and in constant dialogue with him. For my own part, I had followed him since 1934, and this background of a common effort and hope, sustained over so many years, may well have been responsible for the special warmth that existed between the General and myself. But from June 1940 our close and constant relationship gave way to a different *rapport*. Irrefutable logic and sentiment led de Gaulle to put himself in the place of France. His voice, alone, was raised in defiance of the chorus of voices that came to us from France, discordant or unanimous as the case might be. From the moment he appeared to personify the nation by what he did, and to give it a kind of mystical reality, we served him with a quasi-religious devotion, although we were sometimes surprised by the direction in which he was leading us. But we knew that what he did was in some way connected with what we could dimly discern beneath the silence which had fallen on a country defeated, occupied, and muzzled.

Where others brought incidental or political support to the General, André Malraux came to us with a different experience and authority. His ascendancy over the young reminded one of Barrès, but a non-conforming Barrès. His practical experience of Communism had enabled him to live 'a novel of energy' – and this 'energy' was not *national* but *international*. What he had looked for – although he was quickly disillusioned – was an excuse for that heroic brotherhood without which he cannot act. His nobility of mind: the universal breadth of his culture; his formidable dialectic; the power to connect and compare one thing with another, and the quick transitions of his thought, which are the gift of his encyclopedic memory; his feeling for the tragic, as he meets it from day to day; his sense of sacrifice; his Tolstoyan humanism; the pathos of his incantation and the leap of his spirit towards the sublime which echo in his speeches as well as in his fiction – all this gave him a prestige which has only increased with time.

He has never been afraid to put himself under another person of outstanding quality, for he knows that here he has nothing to lose. The greater the man, the less he is diminished by the sacrifice of himself. Nothing could have robbed Malraux of his place among the great voices of our country. He entered into the epic of de Gaulle, as we all did, like a man entering a religious order – but what he brought to him was so much more.

One day I shall write the story, which has never been accurately told, of how we came back to Paris. I shall try to show how strange the situation actually was. People credited General de Gaulle with all the responsibility of omnipotence, but in fact we found ourselves shut in the Hôtel de Brienne – the residence of the Minister of War in the rue Saint-Dominique – as if we were under siege. The place was surrounded on every side by a mob of organizations, movements, parties and journalists. These were manipulated and infiltrated by the Communist Party with incomparable skill. The intellectuals were certainly not exempt from this stranglehold whether they believed themselves to be Communists, like Picasso and Eluard, or whether they were Communists without proclaiming themselves as such.

The Communists were ready to take their revenge. Everything was ready for their coup d'état. The scene had been set, if slightly put out of gear by the quick arrival of General de Gaulle in Paris from Rambouillet at the very moment when von Choltitz surrendered. Once we were established in the rue Saint-Dominique, the agents we had sent to France, themselves indoctrinated and subdued, came begging us to go immediately to the Hôtel de Ville and proclaim the Republic. This was to be followed by the 'spontaneous' appointment of a provisional government chosen from a cleverly composed Committee of Public Safety. With his superior good sense, General de Gaulle had no difficulty in scenting the manoeuvre. 'Proclaim the Republic! What is the point of that? It has never ceased to exist.' The motto *Liberté, Egalité, Fraternité* always accompanied the broadcasts of the Free French, and our Official Journal confirmed that we meant what we said.

General de Gaulle was a thousand times right. From the moment a French organization, however weak and fragile, took the place of a feeble government to honour its alliances and work for the liberation of the native soil from the invader, that organization became the legitimate government of France. It was founded to speak and to act in the name of the country, whose near-unanimous acclaim supported and ratified what we had done.

As we have seen, the plot was foiled. The Communists held their ground only in certain strongholds where the illness of the Paris Préfet de Police enabled them to take over the Préfecture, order the arrest of their potential opponents, and make a show of discharging their weapons – which merely served as a pretext for arming the so-called patriotic militia. But although the Communist Party had failed in its bid for power, it continued its work of infiltration. The instinctive hostility of writers to public authority gave it an audience in the daily and the weekly Press. The situation was all the more absurd in that the majority of great intellectuals outside of France had supported us. From the very beginning, the active support of a Bernanos, a Focillon, a Maritain, had a considerable effect. In the delicate circumstances which produced a division of power in Algiers, and even before the arrival of representatives from the Resistance had allowed the authority of General de Gaulle in face of General Giraud to be firmly established, the intellectuals in Algiers discovered in General de Gaulle their natural spokesman. The painter André Marquet, who had taken refuge in a pretty house overlooking the ravine of La Femme Sauvage, had wished to present the General with one of his pictures showing a warship flying the tricolour on a Bastille day. The presentation of this picture was a festive little occasion at which Marquet was surrounded by everyone who mattered among the intelligentsia of Algiers, with André Gide at their head, just arrived from Tunisia. They realized then that the General who told them: 'Art has its honour in the same way that France has hers' was an intellectual like themselves, and that his actions had a Cartesian perfection.

This adhesion by the intellectuals of Algiers was all the more important since the rebirth of the political parties faced us with a problem which had to be solved. Already, before the war, they were no longer compatible with the national unity which the situation demanded. I had previously suggested to Paul Reynaud the publication of a text declaring the need for national unanimity at a time when the dictatorships were threatening the democracies; when any split between the forces of the nation, and their fragmentation among the parties, constituted, if not an act of treason, at least a sign of weakness incompatible with so great a peril. But these parties, which the courageous and unfortunate Pierre Brossolette had excommunicated, begging his socialist comrades to merge into a large movement of resistance, showed considerable signs of life. Under their various labels they demonstrated the will to be born again. It was an ambiguous rebirth. The MURF, led by Edouard Herriot, gave concrete shape to a peculiar collusion between the Communist and the Radical Parties. The Independents were indistinguishable from the old Right. And the MRP made it possible for the Christian Democrats to come to life again, and exist side by side with those resistant forces of the Right who were preparing their renaissance as a party to the right of Centre.

In face of the parties and their rebirth, was it possible to discover among the Resistance movements those elements capable of bringing new vigour and health to the political life of the country? The Communists realized very well how risky this would have been for their own activities. They wanted to turn their Front National, which had annexed François Mauriac and Louis Marin, into a sort of basic nucleus for all the movements of resistance resolved upon political action.

It was at this moment, in January 1945, that the initial congress of the MLN for the first time brought the Communist tactics to a dramatic halt. It included the united movements of Resistance (Libération, Combat, Franc-Tireur, Défense de la France, Libération-Nord, and the OCM – Organisation civile et militaire) which had infiltrated the public administration during the war. To be sure, André Malraux was not their only spokesman. André Philip and others brought forward their arguments and showed their determination. But it was the great speech of André Malraux which ensured their triumph. What did he say – he whose name was a synonym for revolutionary action?

The government of General de Gaulle is not only the government of France, but the government of the Liberation and the Resistance. So it is not for us to question it. It is right that the government should say: 'War and revolution are contradictory terms.' When it is faced with all the problems of foreign policy, when France is obliged to feed the allied armies or put trains at their disposal, it is inevitable and necessary that all its energies should first be devoted to securing the military triumph, and that the revolutionary problem should be tackled later. The Communist Party is not a collection of people with the means of persuasion; it is a collection of people with the means of action. . . . If we want to mobilize our energies, as they have recently been mobilized, we must employ a technique similar to that of the Communists; that is to say, we must maintain within our movement a discipline equal to the discipline of the Communist Party, with the same heroism, however burdensome and difficult are the demands which that discipline makes upon us.

If, as I think, the great majority of us are opposed to the idea of fusion, I am equally convinced that this same majority wishes to find the point at which the groups of the Resistance can act in unity. And I say to all of you who were capable of unity when you had nothing, that you will be capable of restoring that unity, now that you have everything in your hands. It is a question of yes or no – and I say yes.

This speech came at exactly the right moment to support us, when the old parties, under new labels, were preparing to resume the reins of power. I recall my astonishment, tinged as it was with a sceptical enthusiasm, as I learnt of Malraux's stand, which gave us the support we needed. I asked Corniglion-Molinier to arrange a meeting between Malraux and myself. He had won his spurs in developing the Free French air force; both his gift for command and his legendary bravura had marked him out; and I knew that he had been at Malraux's side in trying to discover the capital of the Queen of Sheba, and also in the Spanish Civil War. The meeting took place in Malraux's apartment in the avenue Gabriel, which harboured me for several weeks after the resignation of General de Gaulle.

André Malraux has recalled this first conversation in his *Antimémoires*. Each of us was carefully feeling his way with the other. But there was a human contact which had no need of words. The rather disquieting legend which people had tried to create around this great personality dissolved of its own accord after one had seen him for a few minutes. He revealed himself as the man he was, crammed full of knowledge, experience and vision, living with the masterpieces of every age. They were arranged in his mind, composing one beside another a kind of pictorial background against which his personal adventure stood out. This was personal but not selfish, for although he was eager for action the only action capable of nourishing his dream was cemented by social generosity and carried on within the context of a kind of heroic fraternity. Paradoxically, he had looked for it in the ranks of the Communist Party engaged in the fight against National Socialism, but Spain had opened his eyes, just when Picasso was caught in the maze from which he could only escape through exile on a Mediterranean shore.

André Malraux had discovered this fraternity in armed resistance. The Brigade Alsace-Lorraine had given him an epic stature. I felt at once that he was indispensable to us. Focillon was a great mind, but he was known only to specialists – and he was dead. Brossolette and Cavaillès, alas, were also dead. Bernanos and Maritain had given us valuable support, and their thinking counted for a great deal with everyone who mattered, but they did not represent occupied France whose liberation had been our *raison d'être*. It was so difficult to find anyone amongst ourselves who could give an authentic expression of this, and who was not involved either with the mistakes of the past or the cowardly temptations of the present. When I got back to the rue Saint-Dominique, I told the General about our meeting, and said to him: 'Here at last is the man for us.' 'He will never agree,' replied the General. But the battle was won: André Malraux turned up the next day at the rue Saint-Dominique.

General de Gaulle had chosen an office which charmed him with its somewhat sad austerity. It adjoined the former office of Clemenceau, and the balcony on which 'Le Tigre' was leaning when the crowd invaded the courtyard of the building to applaud him on the day of victory. I remember that very office very well, for I spent many hours there under the portrait of the Comte de Saint-Germain and his watchful eye, and the candid gaze of Carnot – 'organisateur de la victoire'. His sober dress and burning eyes contrasted with the sceptical expression on the features of the marshals of the ancien régime whose portraits also hung there. Between the two windows stood Frederick the Great's clock, which Napoleon had brought back from Potsdam. The stools made by the cabinet-maker Jacob, with their crossed swords struck a note of the consular epic. This décor – the expression of a man so terribly alone in what he thought and what he did – should have been preserved; but some minister of the Fourth Republic, to whom such memories came as a living reproach, thought fit to efface with a hammer the Cross of Lorraine which had been sculpted on the façade, and turn an office where a great page of French history had been written into something like the drawing-room of a *pension de famille* in the 16th arrondissement.

Perhaps I should say a word about how our two characters looked at the moment of their meeting. De Gaulle had always been remote by reason of his height, which made people call him 'the Constable', and remote also through the sort of walking dream in which he had moved from 18 June 1940 to 25 August 1944, while his task still remained un-accomplished. He worked, struggled, and gave his commands from a sort of glass cell. At certain, very rare, moments, the partition was lowered – when a decisive advantage had been won; when he felt that the work to which he had set his hand was progressing and that one day he would see the end of it. But after his return to Paris a subtle change became noticeable. He was no longer at odds with the force of circumstance; he had only to face the snares or the devotion of men. The game had become more complex, and slowly, little by little, he adapted himself to it. Later, after the long days of reflection at Colombey, during his crossing of the desert, he broke with certain habits and certain ideas that he had taken for granted, particularly when they concerned the practice of government and the men who ought to be entrusted with it. He came out of his monklike seclusion, and took up a fresh attitude towards a country which hesitated to follow him once the danger had been averted, and to a world where the relative importance of France was sustained only by the superiority of the one statesman of genius to have survived, when death had taken the other great leaders of the day.

Before him, André Malraux was no longer the apparition in beret and khaki, at once youthful and disillusioned, changed by personal sorrow, who had commanded the Brigade Alsace–Lorraine. He soon acquired the manner of a minister. But there was always the same sensibility, ardent and profound, hidden behind a wall of erudition, knowledge and brilliant reflection on men and their works. These two sensibilities, each developed to an abnormal degree, this same need for a climate of grandeur and altruism, came together, and the current was set up between two exceptional human beings.

So there we have them face to face. Entrenched behind his desk, the General only too often gave one the impression of having to counteract an insidious or impertinent ambush. But no one plumbed the secrets of human nature more accurately than he, who was supposed to despise it. He saw at once that Malraux belonged to the same family as himself; that here was an intellectual who would find his fulfilment not only in books, but in the thought that gives birth to action. These two men, destined to walk side by side for so long, appeared at the same time strangely alike and strangely different. Certainty marked the one; questioning marked the other. De Gaulle went into action like a professional, Malraux like an adventurer. But for Malraux adventure is the dimension without which creation is impossible.

With the simplicity of great men, Malraux agreed to work with me for the man who had cast his spell on him, for he realized how far the opportunities that lay ahead for France were incarnate in de Gaulle. He enlisted in our service from that moment, happily, unconditionally, and without the least reservation. He brought the extraordinary pledge of his presence to our effort which was fiercely debated on every side. During the few weeks when I had the joy of working with him, before he entered the government as Minister of Information, Malraux helped us very considerably not to stray from the path we had marked out – which required that we should give our support not to any one class or category, but to the whole of France. This created a lasting friendship between us. When we met at Colombey-les-Deux-Eglises on the day of the General's funeral, we could say that we had tried to serve him to the limit of our strength, and that he knew it.

On the General's first departure from power, those who stayed with him were divided from the rest. This separation grew wider, and presently a gulf opened between the two parties. What was already latent in the subconscious of each became clear in the crude light of circumstance. One man who had been doggedly loyal in the London days now showed that he had seen in disaster nothing more than the springboard for his own career; another who had not reached ministerial rank sheltered in the semi-obscurity of public service, ready to jump on the winning side.

We began by thinking in terms of a strategic retreat. This would not last for long, and it would allow us to come back and foil the ambush of the parties. We had not reckoned with intervention from outside. It is a certain fact that, but for the Marshall Plan, the Fourth Republic would have died of a financial crisis shortly after the departure of General de Gaulle. Should one regret that matters did not turn out like that? Was the country ready for decolonization? Were we ready for it ourselves? And then we did not have behind us the bulwark of national support which managed to build itself up over the years, in defiance of the winds and tides.

The Rassemblement du Peuple Français, as the General conceived it, was to include the adherents of very different parties, and the movement counted for its success on a mood of general support. When we first tried to outline its character at Colombey-les-Deux-Eglises, it could have developed in this way. But in order to do so it should have remained in the background during its initial phase. Some were frightened off by the precedent of the Union Gaulliste. Willy-nilly, on 7 April 1947 the General emerged at Strasbourg at the head of a formation which was a wonderful sounding board, but whose dynamism aroused so many fears that all negotiation became impossible.

André Malraux was in charge of propaganda. I remember his ceaseless activity in the handful of rooms rented from Swissair in the place de l'Opéra; the marvellous taste with which he transformed our posters – particularly the sketch of Rude's statue of the Marseillaise, that really got in the guts of the passers-by; the public meetings where thousands of Frenchmen and Frenchwomen crushed against each other in the Vélodrome d'Hiver. These always finished with Malraux's grandiose incantation, crediting his listeners with his own nobility, setting out the necessity of action to assist the country, reviving the memory of its former sufferings and evoking its present misery.

It is a little sad to think that so much struggle and effort had to end in a tangle of parliamentary manoeuvres, and that only a pretorian revolt obliged the Fourth Republic to beg the man who had restored democracy to intercede for it once again.

By a strange trick of destiny, both Malraux and I were far from Paris during those fateful days. On my behalf, General de Gaulle had broken his rule of having no dealings with public authority: he summoned the Secretary General of Foreign Affairs, and indicated that he wished him to give me an ambassadorial post. This was how I came to be appointed to Rome. It was only through the newspapers that I could gauge the fever that was mounting little by little until it swept away the regime. I had come to Venice, as French ambassador to Italy, to attend the lecture which André Malraux was to give at the Cini Foundation. He was still dreaming of art, and the dream had helped to relieve his despondency. It helped him to forget the derisory aspect of contemporary affairs by bringing to life the civilizations and empires of the past, and by evoking the great periods of artistic creation. We listened to him, Vittorio Cini and myself, astounded by the way he brought before us the great Venetian works of art; the Republic of Lepanto and Tintoretto which was to become the Republic of the Carnival and Tiepolo. And his becoming Minister for Cultural Affairs did not cause the dream to fade.

I soon joined him in the government. He sat on the right of the General; I was on the left of Georges Pompidou. Facing each other as we were, our friendship added a warmer note to the austere mood of the discussions, and the General, who was very sensitive to the wavelengths between human beings, liked to have Malraux close to him, for he was glad to look at faces that were friendly to him. Shortly afterwards my appointment as President of the Constitutional Council was to give me the office opposite to Malraux's. Only the terrace of the Palais-Royal lay between us, and there we used sometimes to meet – unless I called on him to discuss the difficulties of the situation, or he knocked on my french window, with Balthus, to go out to lunch and talk things over together.

André Malraux's contribution to the work of General de Gaulle, whether in the government or as a militant of the Rassemblement du

Peuple Français, went beyond ardent loyalty or intellectual cooperation. To be sure, these were not negligible. But just as he had been a remarkable head of propaganda, so he proved to be an excellent minister. He was exceptionally precise in what he planned and in what he carried out – innovating with the Maisons de la Culture, giving a new look to Paris with the cleaning of its façades. What he brought to us was something more than a 'guarantee from the Left'. He had devoted too much of his life to working for the people, he was too preoccupied with social justice and brotherly equality not to radiate these concerns around him. For de Gaulle he acted as a kind of living reminder, not of a necessity of which de Gaulle was already convinced, but of the urgency to give this necessity the force of law. We had to go far and deep. Here the pursuit of what is covered by the word *participation* – so hard to define and to describe, so uneasily translatable into legal texts and even into a clear plan – owes much to the dialogue between Malraux and de Gaulle.

Talking to Malraux in *Les Chênes qu'on abat* ..., de Gaulle laid his hand on the MS of the Memoirs he was writing, and said: 'Between you and me, Malraux, is it worth it?' In fact the General often asked these apparently anxious questions to which his secret judgment had already given the reply. When he pretended, in some moment of disgust, that he wished to resign his authority and go – whether he happened to be the head of the Resistance or the head of the State – I used to say to him: 'But, General, what about France?' 'France,' he would reply superbly, 'will see us both to our graves.'

True enough. And now he lies in the 'good and holy earth of France' at Colombey-les-Deux-Eglises. But alongside his tomb there rises that immense Cross of Lorraine, a project for which André Malraux was responsible. It may be that Malraux, as he leaned on my shoulder during the long, sad ceremony at Colombey, said to himself that this memorial would no doubt be useful in the future, but that it was superfluous if one wanted to make France aware of its mission, and to give it confidence in its destiny. That, whatever uncertainty the future may have in store, is what de Gaulle has bequeathed to us.

And André Malraux? The three or four great books which have given him authority over the conscience of our generation will certainly remain. But also the memory of that long companionship and that unique friendship – it has no parallel since Voltaire and Frederick the Great, but that finished badly; since Diderot and Catherine II, but that was based on false appearances – between a head of state and one of the great writers of his time. They met upon the heights, and it was there that they became united. For twenty-five years they pursued the long dialogue, and each was strengthened by it. This is how posterity will see them, side by side, captivating the imagination and each enhancing the image of the other.

ANDRÉ HOLLEAUX

*

THE ADMINISTRATION OF CULTURE

Translated by Robert Speaight

In the spring of 1962 Edmond Michelet, who had just left the Ministry of Justice, sent me to see Malraux, who was looking for a Chef de Cabinet. It was, at first, a giddy prospect: I was nervous at the thought of serving a genius, and I didn't exactly see myself in the job. More precisely, I was afraid of being at the beck and call of a man who was nervy, difficult, irritable, and exhausting for those who worked for him. I found him to be nothing of the kind. Were it not for the fear of softening his character, I would say that he is a very kind man. Our working relations were extremely pleasant; during the four years that he was my chief he never subjected me to the slightest outburst, the slightest temper.

Malraux realized that any lasting achievement requires time for its development, and that the imponderable factors – the accidental, the absurd, the quixotic – are the fabric of life, more particularly at the Ministry of Cultural Affairs. He had founded it but it remained for him a machine which he was not able to manipulate as he liked. He had described it to me beforehand as having its farcical side, and often said to me afterwards: 'I told you that you wouldn't be bored.'

We met at a restaurant, as one nearly always did with Malraux; not at Lasserre's, where he likes to go today, but for once at Laurent's. Every week he invited me to a different restaurant, and we were generally alone. He catalogued them in his mind, as a bibliophile catalogues his books. The conversation would generally begin with a preface in comparative gastronomy. In these matters Malraux has the judgment of a fine artist. He is serious in his choice of food and wine, and depressed when they don't go well together. Towards the end of the meal the conversation would – always and irresistibly, as it were – turn upon de Gaulle, for de Gaulle was the beginning and the end of all

he did. If I ever happened to venture a reservation on some point or
other, I was duly put in my place.

On that first day we did not begin by talking about the succulent
steak, but about Chancellor d'Aguessau. The Ministry of Justice, where
I came from, is established in the street that bears his name, and I
realized that the highly successful novelist who was my host still had
some roots in the countryside. He spoke of Corrèze, Roussillon, and the
Romanesque churches of the Charente with an incomparable eloquence.

So I had been well and truly caught, and the next morning we met
in his office, where some familiar work of art always had its niche. He
tried to inaugurate our working relationship by presenting his Ministry
as a circus-master presents his show. He began by explaining to me how
the place was organized, and I had the impression not so much that he
was bored by this, but that he felt he was the wrong person to talk
about technical matters to a specialist in administration like myself.
'You are a Conseiller d'Etat, and all that will become clear to you as
time goes on' – which was as much as to add 'from your rather narrow
and legalistic point of view'.

After this rapid survey, which lasted no more than five minutes, he
led me out of doors, saying: 'Now we're going to see something far more
important.' We went along to the Louvre and spent three quarters of
an hour in the Cour Carrée. He told me the whole story of the Louvre,
not as Sacha Guitry would have told it, but as an historian and a
cinematographer of art. It was a broad canvas that he painted for me,
and after this baptism of stone and architecture he felt that I had been
thoroughly initiated into the life of the Ministry.

His chauffeur was the third member of the party. Malraux is always
extremely friendly with ordinary people or those modestly employed.
When he visits an exhibition, he will spend an unusually long time
with some stranger if he feels that he is puzzled, yet at the same time
capable of emotional response. The chauffeur told me that his job with
Malraux was a good one; so that was how it all began.

People think of Malraux as endlessly talkative; always playing on
the grand organ; as a mind pure and simple, without method or
timetable; an inspired poet, vague and bizarre. In fact, he is just the
contrary. At work he sometimes reminds you of an archivist, and sometimes of an airport controller.

His timetable was strict and sensible. He would arrive at the Palais-
Royal – where the Ministry has its headquarters – at 9 am, or even
9.30, for he was then living at the Pavillon de la Lanterne, which is part
of the Domaine de Versailles. Having left the previous evening at 7 or

7.30 with his papers, he would come back with the dossiers all sifted and annotated, some of them set aside for further study, and held together with paper-clips instead of the pins which I myself preferred. He was not averse to copious reports, for he liked the written word as such. He weighed the texts, distinguishing the 'serious' notes from those which he dismissed as 'cocottes', 'absurd', 'it may amuse you', or 'if you feel like having a go at it'. He has an exceptional gift for underlining the operative phrase, the essential argument.

Malraux is meticulous. A Conseiller d'Etat is commonly regarded as a hair-splitter, and yet he could get the better of me in pursuing the logic of a question with a microscope and dissecting it down to the last molecule. He knew exactly what to do with uncertain figures, doubtful tactics and specious formulas. As an example of this, he spoke to me several times about the blue in the French national flag, which he had noticed was not always of the same shade. So we researched into the blue of the revolutionary and imperial flags in order to establish its 'legitimacy' – a word he is particularly fond of.

I was his Directeur de Cabinet and chief assistant, and he saw me every day, without exception, between noon and 1.15. His private secretary, Mlle Caglione, would notify me at 11.55 that 'the Minister was expecting me'. He would begin by mentioning the topics he wished to discuss during the interview, then ask me if I had anything of my own to bring up, with an amused, furtive glance at the notes in my hand. We walked up and down in his office, four yards one way and four the other, and our talk was interrupted only when the interministerial telephone rang.

So the conversation would begin, or rather Malraux would begin to talk. I kept pretty quiet, first of all because I was only his Directeur de Cabinet, and then because dialogue is not easy with him, although he can tell quite naturally from an exchange of looks or a word dropped here and there if his interlocutor is interested and gets the point of what he is saying – or the reverse. It is not worth while interjecting phrases to reassure him. From time to time, if he wanted to give some matter deeper thought, or simply to pause before going on to something else, he would inhale the scent from one of the three or four roses on his desk. He only sat down to scribble a note on a piece of paper. Malraux knows or guesses what his interlocutor is thinking from the moment the other opens his mouth. Some people say that he has a sixth sense. I can testify to the way he reconstructed people's thoughts and fantasies simply by the expression in their eyes, their gestures, or what they said under their breath.

During the hour we worked together every day, we began by attacking the subject on the agenda, but we moved away from it very quickly, for it was not long before everything took on a timeless and universal dimension. We might be comparing our views about a budgetary credit or a governmental decree, and then Savonarola or Einstein, a painting by Manet or a flight of fancy about *musique concrète*, Sully, Las Cases, or Jacques Prévert, would interrupt the discussion. Past or present mattered very little; what had happened once, or was happening now, mattered a great deal.

Malraux is never pedantic, and he never shows off. He is always perfectly natural, with no desire to dazzle. He talks to you in such a way that you already think you know what he has in mind. He will begin by saying: 'You know as well as I do', and this is all part of his delicate courtesy. What he says, however remote apparently from the subject in hand, in fact illuminates it and forces the administrative assistant to think about it again from another angle, and in a different light. Between the technical problem and the arguments Malraux develops from it, there is a close and fine connection, although this may not at first be clear to his audience. I remember that when we were visiting the great Temples in Mexico he never said what one expected him to say, and one was almost disappointed. He brought up some minor fact, with very little relation to what we were looking at, but this immediately transformed what we had under our eyes into 'something else'.

He introduced complexities, contradictions and layers of significance into everything; appearances and illusions he pushed aside. Malraux, as Minister, was a man of imagination, a man who set the sights. He took you out of your groove, made you look at things from a new level and a fresh angle. This was the secret of his persuasive power in a technical conversation. It has been said that de Gaulle was the man of the day before yesterday, and the man of the day after tomorrow. The same is true of Malraux. With him the empire of Alexander the Great rubs shoulders with the television of 1990, Napoleon with Galbraith, Sun Yat-sen with structuralism.

When he came back to his office after lunching with a personal friend, an ambassador, a deputy, a writer, a colleague in the government, or one of his assistants, he made out a list in his own neat handwriting on little pads, red, green or yellow, according to their destination. Each carried a printed notice 'object' or 'reply on the back'. In the afternoon he followed the usual ministerial routine: receiving officials, ambassadors and men of letters. If he had a problem for his

Directeur de Cabinet, he would see him again, and leave his office at a reasonable hour for those who worked for him – between 7 and 7.30.

If his extempore performances were grandiose and poetic, a kind of private fireworks, the green pad was a masterpiece of condensation and precision. Malraux realized very well that the morning's conversation was not enough; that if it opened doors and cleared perspectives, practical action demands more traditional indications – résumés, reports, programmes, memos and timetables. The green pads were concerned with ministerial communications. They might have come to him from another minister, or from the head of some organization. I received between three and ten of these every day, for each of the subjects we had discussed in the morning if Malraux thought them worth transcribing, or for what I needed to know about an important meeting which had taken place during the day. For example, 'I have seen G.P. [Georges Pompidou, who was then Prime Minister] – he wishes X to telephone Y.'

I cannot give a list here, even approximately, of the subjects we dealt with. There was something of everything; many of the notes were of this kind: 'Who does what, and when?'; 'Put a bit of order in this bundle.'; 'I must talk to you about this.'; 'Finished, as far as I am concerned.'; and 'Amen.' Malraux was aware of the sleepy, apathetic, stupidly reassuring, and even theatrical side of administration. He felt that here were men playing a part, and that one had to get to the bottom of things, release or neutralize the springs of action.

The wars in which he had fought were not like other wars. He had twice campaigned at the side of the regular army, and he was so close to de Gaulle that he rather liked to introduce a military note into his own Cabinet, and with his own assistants. He regarded his Directeur de Cabinet as his Chief-of-Staff, in liaison with the other ministries, and even with the state as a whole.

Two or three people had been at his side for several years. They were Beuret, his friend from the publishing house of Gallimard; Brandin, a friend from his childhood; and Chevasson, who had been with him in Indochina. They had long been in the habit of exchanging views and Malraux entrusted them with missions where this was necessary. Their tasks were personal and psychological; they constituted his 'Privy Council'.

His Directeur de Cabinet was his chief interlocutor. I have never known a ministry where so much responsibility was concentrated on the shoulders of this one official, for Malraux hardly saw his other assistants at all. Heads of departments were received only exceptionally, and this

caused much bitterness. They were either administrators by profession,
or personalities from the world of art and letters – like André Chamson
and Gaëtan Picon – for whom Malraux had long held a deep affection.
They resented the distance he kept, for they regarded any contact
with him as a privilege. He appealed to them for what he called his
'coups'; shock operations that he had planned himself, and which he
kept under his personal control, such as important exhibitions or
donations, or architectural or literary projects.

One of Malraux's particular qualities was an awareness of his
limitations. With his exceptionally fertile mind, he knew that he was
neither a jurist, nor an administrator, nor a financier – at least not in
the sense in which these specializations are commonly understood. He
could transcend a problem so much that he was unable to connect with
it on the technical plane. But where other ministers I have known
claimed to be authorities in everything, and more particularly where
they were least qualified, Malraux left to his 'colonels' and his 'captains',
when they were 'really competent' – as he used to say – the job of
explaining in administrative language the ideas or inspirations which
he described in his own way.

But it would be a mistake to see in Malraux nothing more than an
ideas factory. He is also a writer who goes back over what he has
written, and scratches it out a hundred times over. The same quest for
perfection, for work well done, inspired his daily activity. He wanted to
know about certain procedures or tactics in detail; you had to explain
to him the how and the why; he came up with unexpected suggestions,
showing you some new approach, but stopping short when an assistant
made it plain to him that the technical solution he had proposed was
radically impossible.

'Could we make this into a report?' he would ask; and 'No, we can't'
I would reply. He would not insist, but two days later he would gently
return to the attack with: 'Perhaps we might tackle the problem from
another angle?' It pained me to be obliged to say no to him a second
time, and at the end of the week he would come up with a fresh and
disconcerting suggestion. At last we would find a compromise. 'But,'
he would say, lowering his eyes, 'it's a question of money' – and I
realized it only too well. There was something sadly pathetic about the
great man when he called to mind the guardians of the Temple. His
silences, and his way of gesticulating like a fencer told one very plainly
how he felt.

But in fact he was perfectly calm, and if he didn't get the funds he
agreed that there was nothing to be done about it. He had the sense of

cohesion which must exist between those responsible for affairs of State, and he was not the type of minister who tries to obtain the material help which has been refused him at any price and in any way – even by underhand means.

There was a Manichean side to Malraux. His admirations, and particularly his dislikes, were intense. He believed that every man was permanently disposed either to good or to evil. Both inside and outside the ministry there were certain devils against whom I had always to be on my guard.

When he met someone, he trusted him completely and gave him a free hand, but woe to the man whom he suspected of double dealing! Once he had given you his confidence, he would forgive any mistake or negligence, any weakness or fatigue.

He did not enjoy official inaugurations, for one must not forget that Malraux was uneasy at the idea that he was a minister like the others. It was not a question of pride; rather that he regarded his functions as extraordinary. I mean by this that he was delegated to his post by General de Gaulle, representing him at that particular level in the State. It was for that reason, and for that reason *alone*, that he was a minister. This explains why he never dreamt for a single moment of remaining at his post after the General had gone.

I am not presuming to explore in this paper the exceptional relationship that existed between them. I knew of it only indirectly, but it would be absurd to describe it as 'unconditional'. I should say that here was an intimate communion between two men bound together by the same destiny, and aware of what they had in common and of what was particular to each. If it had been technically possible, Malraux would have associated de Gaulle with everything he did, and for everything that was not of minor importance. I don't mean that he deified de Gaulle – that would be the wrong word – but there was de Gaulle and 'the rest'. Of this there can be no doubt whatever.

He was certainly thinking of de Gaulle when he excavated the foundations of the Louvre in front of the Colonnade in 1965 and 1966. He reflected that every period had brought something to the Louvre, from François I to the Third Republic, and he would add, not without a trace of bitterness: 'The General has not built anything.' A meeting with de Gaulle was a very special occasion, a treat, and Malraux prepared for it as if it were a sacred rite. Now and again I was disappointed when my prosaic suggestions found no place on the agenda of the interview.

Malraux deserves the title of statesman, for he was an artist in everything to do with the complexities and interconnections of power. Few ministers have his sense of governmental solidarity, or his respect for the responsibility of a colleague. He never tried to wear a cap that didn't fit him. 'This is the business of the Ministry for Foreign Affairs,' he would often say, 'and of no one else. So give it to Couve [de Murville].' He would have liked to have television under his control, and among his prerogatives, for he knew that today everything is done through television. It was surely very paradoxical to deprive the Ministry of Cultural Affairs of the principal instrument of 'culture'.

Interviews with the Prime Minister, Georges Pompidou, were decisive for any question within his competence, and even outside it. It was Pompidou who gave him the red or the green light. Malraux saw him regularly over several matters, which he would have rehearsed with me beforehand. Malraux was incapable of shiftiness or subtle manoeuvring; he never went back upon his word, and he put all his cards on the table. He only tried to be clever when 'Georges', as he put it, was himself aware of the game he was playing. He exaggerated – a little too freely, I thought – the secret links, shady associations, cloak-and-dagger plots. He would often explain that a man had behaved in a certain way because – as he suspected – he was a freemason, and then the anti-Fascist intellectual of 1936 would reappear in an unqualified condemnation.

The 'governmental' side of Malraux set him apart from the usual type of politician. The idea of standing for election – though he was urged to do so – never entered his head, and had the choice been forced upon him I think he would rather have been the Municipal Councillor of a village than a deputy in the National Assembly.

During the time I was really in his confidence, from 1962 to 1965, I never knew him to yield to a dishonourable request, and the same was true for as long as he remained a minister. Only if he were in doubt, would he accept the personal recommendation of a deputy. He had no contempt for members of Parliament, which deserved respect as part of the machinery of State, but while Parliament worked on one level, he worked on another, and he was not obliged to take part in its games. His views on the State were similar to those of Michel Debré: nothing great could be achieved without it. He looked at the 'man' rather than the deputy, and his judgment was more dependent, in the long run, on what he saw than on the man's political affiliation. He had very definite views, as we know, about the Communist Party, but he could respect a Communist deputy in so far as he represented France.

He would get me to read such letters from members of Parliament as he thought important, treating them as documents rather than as correspondence to be dealt with in the ordinary way. Obviously the recommendations in favour of 'dancers' who used to spice up the lives of former ministers of the Beaux Arts had no place in our files.

Each November Malraux presented the budget of his ministry to the National Assembly and afterwards to the Senate. He went up into the tribune, conscientiously clutching the notes which had been carefully prepared by his assistants. Obedient to the prescribed ritual, he read from them in a bored tone of voice; their administrative style jarred so sharply with his own that, unlike the usual orator, he did not even attempt to give the illusion that he had written them himself. When he felt that he had discharged his obligation, he became Malraux once again. The large number of deputies who were waiting for this moment in his speech furtively regained their places in the semi-circle. A total silence then reigned in the National Assembly and the Senate, those old palaces which house the French Parliament, and they echoed not to a 'speech', but to a sequence of exalted fireworks, where the Maisons de la Culture were juxtaposed to the Ecoles Primaires of 1890, Sumerian statuary to the destiny of France, and where Blood and Sex were in partnership with Death – and all this without the least desire to excite applause.

However transcendent Malraux had managed to appear during this lyrical half-hour, he did not fail to answer all the more or less electorally motivated questions of the rank and file among the deputies. He was careful to leave no one out, and if he thought his replies had been too brief, he would follow them up with supplementary letters during the following days. And after the sitting, conforming once again to the customs of the place, he would go round the corridors, pressing some deputy he met by chance into admiring the frescoes of Delacroix. Then he would make for the refreshment bar and, with any deputies that happened to be there, drink a toast to *la Fraternité*.

In a quiet tête-à-tête, without raising his voice, he would start by discussing the difficulties of an Ecole de Musique in the main town of a department, or of a Romanesque church that was threatening to collapse. And he would say something like: 'Of course we'll see to this together.'

Just as de Gaulle did not open chrysanthemum shows, Malraux did not lay foundation stones. I frequently urged him to go more often into the provinces and see what our men were doing there. But my requests rarely met with success. He feared the waste of time on programmes arranged by the Préfets, the distribution of honours before an audience of notables, the speeches after the banquets, and the cocktails of municipal councillors in their Sunday best. Still I begged him to make these journeys, for it was an article of faith at the Ministry that we worked for the provinces as much as for Paris. But his schedule shows that, despite this basic conviction, he was far more Parisian than provincial.

He was only roused to enthusiasm by certain grand celebrations: Joan of Arc at Orléans or Rouen; the Maisons de la Culture at Bourges, Amiens, Grenoble and Reims. His speeches or funeral orations were very carefully prepared; so were the Homage to Braque, and the inauguration of Son et Lumière on the Acropolis at Athens. They represented an immense effort of revision and correction, and for six days he would refuse to see anyone.

I can never pass the Place du Panthéon without hearing the echoes of that extraordinary Ode to the Dead – the speech he made when the ashes of the Resistance leader Jean Moulin were brought into the mausoleum of France's great men. It was an icy day, and before a gallery of freezing officials, in front of whom towered General de Gaulle, he called up an unforgettable evocation of what the Resistance had been.

Neither on public occasions, nor in the privacy of his office, did Malraux ever allude to his literary works, his adventures, or the fighting in which he had engaged. Never once in four years did he talk to me about his past, and it is well known that he has not even read the majority of books that have been written about him.

He is allergic to the idiom of conventional conversation. He has his own way of saying 'Good morning' or of asking about your health. He detests formal etiquette and ceremonious greetings. The receptions at the Elysée exasperated him by their suggestion of the 'last days of the Habsburgs'. Nevertheless he has a keen sense of protocol priorities, and an even keener sense of ritual, not for its own sake, but because it befits the symbolism of power and of the State. He was attached to his title of Minister of the first rank, and this was the only concession to convention that he allowed himself. In the same way he studied with the greatest care the names that he put forward every year for the Légion d'Honneur, and the rank appropriate for each of them. He was eager that the great artists, of whatever kind, should be honoured.

In spite of his prejudice against official commitments in the provinces, once there, he became himself again. Without troubling himself about titles or rank, for he settled these in his own mind and in his own way, he could spend a long time with a stranger in whose eyes he could see some interest, and he managed to stimulate the minds of those provincials who approached him as if he were a seer.

Finding it impossible, within the limits of this essay, to give a complete picture of Malraux's work at the Ministry for Cultural Affairs, I must confine myself to those aspects which had an 'epic' quality. Malraux brought himself to public attention with the cleaning of Paris in 1960. The decision to do this was taken against the advice of the experts and the architects, who warned him of the danger to stone when it has lost the patina protecting it. It was a stroke of genius. From then onwards Malraux was like a man weaving a magic spell. At every dinner table, whether in high society or in a council house, between the cheese and the dessert, people sang the praises of the new life he had given the monuments of Paris. Visitors and tourists were tireless in their admiration; préfets and mayors imitated the Minister for Cultural Affairs, and set about cleaning their own buildings.

Malraux worked with images and visions as a potter works with clay. He talked about the cleaning of Paris like a herald, but he read and annotated the most laborious reports with meticulous care. One must not forget that he had, in the highest degree, the feeling for a 'masterpiece'. But on saying this, one must be careful to emphasize that he did not wish to be taken for a Minister of the Beaux Arts. He was absolutely determined to make a break between the days when there was a Ministry of Beaux Arts and the present time when there was a Ministry for Cultural Affairs. The Beaux Arts were concerned with the great works of art, the Museums, and the historic buildings, whereas Malraux declared from his first days at the Ministry that he was working for the mass of the people, and that he wanted the people of France, regardless of any social or economic classification, to benefit from culture – just as the children of France had benefited from the educational reforms of Jules Ferry, whose spiritual heir he considered himself in some sense to be. This care for the culture of the masses was combined with a deep horror of vulgarity, and by vulgarity he was not thinking of pornography, or crudities of speech. What he meant was mediocrity.

From 1960 to 1969 Malraux was at once a bard and a pioneer. He realized that one governs with ideas, which must be carried out to the point of no return where they are taken for granted like a myth, and become essential and exemplary. He achieved this with the Press, with public opinion, with the administration, and notably with the Ministry of Finance, which was slow to respond to his initiatives, but eventually accepted his figures, with good or bad grace, after he had penetrated the defences of Valéry Giscard d'Estaing – and Giscard d'Estaing certainly enjoyed his contacts with Malraux.

It was the same with the archaeological excavations in France, too easily forgotten at a time when French scholars were working all over Egypt and Mesopotamia. Malraux set these going when the bulldozers were ploughing up the soil for important public works; and in this way neolithic flints, Gallo–Roman pottery, or – as at Marseilles – Greek remains, came to light.

Similarly, he conceived an ambitious plan for the famous 'Inventory of Monuments'. This was a very long-term project, suggested several times since the beginning of the eighteenth century; its intention was to reveal to the French their many-sided patrimony, scattered as it was in so many villages and odd places. With Julian Cain and André Chastel, Malraux excited much enthusiasm. For the past ten years bands of dedicated people, under the guidance of university professors, have been working like beavers, going from one department to another with notebooks and cameras in their hands.

He was equally concerned for the statuary of the Public Gardens, and began by putting Maillol's *Nudes* in the Tuileries. His idea was to remove the frock-coated pastiches of the nineteenth century into cold storage, but he proceeded with infinite tact, shrinking at any thought of touching the statue of Jules Ferry raised by the pennies given by schoolchildren. On the other hand he tried to convince the widow of Marshal Leclerc and the veterans of the Second Armoured Division not to celebrate their hero with a statue. This had been done for Clemenceau and Foch, and Malraux had an obsessive dislike for convention and routine.

For Malraux, de Gaulle was France incarnate, and Malraux, in his turn, was a passionate upholder of the national 'patrimony' in the sense in which the Revolutionary forbears had understood it. Time and again he spoke to me of Danton and Saint-Just. His phenomenal memory was stocked with the contents of every museum in the world – and he knew every item in their catalogues. He literally fulfilled himself when he was able to enrich the French museums with some masterpiece. This was why he paid such attention to the American or Japanese patrons of the arts who were interested in Versailles, and day after day, with Van der Kempf and Saltet, he followed the restoration of the château and the return of the original furnishings. In the same way he established a personal relationship with the great painters – Rouault, Dufy, Fernand Léger, Delaunay – or their descendants or heirs. I have in mind the conversations he had with Chagall for his Musée Biblique, or with Madame Jean Walter about her priceless donation to the Louvre of her collection of paintings. We now know, through *La Tête d'obsidienne*, of those he has recently held with Jacqueline Picasso. 'It is the Minister of Cultural Affairs,' he would say jokingly to the Minister of Finance, 'who brings the largest sum of money to France. In exchange for my countless millions, give me a few more of your paper francs.'

This concern for the national patrimony could fire him with such passion that he lost his self-control, and these were the only occasions when I have seen him really scandalized. He was indignant when he thought of his crass predecessors around 1900 who turned up their noses at the Cézannes that were offered to them, or of the merchants and heirs who gave up some notable work of art to foreign countries. In these cases he fought as he had fought with the Brigade Alsace–Lorraine, and he gave no quarter. This is how the major Proust MSS remained in France. Police, legal action – he stopped at nothing. The same passion led him to restore outstanding monuments on a grand scale; Versailles, Fontainebleau, the Invalides, the Louvre, Vincennes, Chambord, Reims cathedral, and so on. He would arrive incognito where the work was going on, giving his opinion, in criticism or approval, and worried about delays. He would see less of the directors of his own ministry than of the architects of historic monuments or the curators of museums, who came to him with reports of what they were doing, very much as a bailiff brings his report to a landowner.

Malraux was sensitive to the importance of what he called the 'approaches' to an architectural ensemble or an ancient quarter. He inspired the law of 4 August 1962 which bears his name, and which allows the creation of 'protected sectors' in any town of historic importance or architectural beauty. Avignon with its quartier de la Balance was the subject of his first struggle, and he waged it fiercely. How often in Paris we went to the Marais district, which he also saved. He knew every great private house and lent all his weight to the owners who were trying to preserve them. By 1974 fifty towns in France already had a protected quarter.

The policy of Malraux's cultural activity can be summed up in three words: quality, people, creation. For quality he was always intractable; he shared Montherlant's aversion to the mediocre and the undistinguished. In contrast to the ministers of the Beaux Arts of the Belle Epoque, who would conform to academic taste, Malraux had no prejudice either for or against any one school or talent. It never entered his head to patronize a particular style or genre, and for this reason he detested what he felt to be obstructive and conservative in the Académie des Beaux Arts. He judged the real quality of a work by its power to provoke, disturb and exalt the spectator, forcing him to come out of himself. A naive painting, even a lunatic's drawing, a canvas by Dubuffet or Fautrier, a sculpture by Giacometti, all the great artists of our time in whatever field – music, literature, architecture, and the plastic arts – were placed on the same level as the classics, no matter to what period they belonged.

The Minister was obsessed by the need to reveal the masterpieces of human workmanship 'to the greatest number', not only because they were beautiful, but because he believed that it was through great works of art that man achieved immortality. This nobility should not be the perquisite of an élite, of those privileged by fortune and education; it should be made accessible and familar to the workers and the peasants, and to the young and old of whatever social condition. He appealed to the great artists, especially ageing ones, for he was afraid they would die before making their contribution to the Patrimony. Le Corbusier, who had worked so much abroad and to whom the French had paid so little attention, was still designing, when he died, the flexible masses of the new Museum of Modern Art in the quartier de la Défense. It was the same story with Braque, who died just as he was starting to embellish the tower of the new Science Faculty; and finally with Cocteau, who was at work, before his death, on the windows for a cathedral.

Malraux, had hoped that France would be the great inheritor of Picasso, and certain passages of *La Tête d'obsidienne* leave us free to hope that the wish will be granted. They reveal the close relationship which existed, both on the personal and aesthetic plane, between Malraux and the man he described as 'the greatest maker and destroyer of forms that has ever lived.' 'If opinion is divided about Chagall's ceiling for the Opéra,' he said, 'it is not a small thing that the master has given it to France.' Masson was equally generous in designing the ceiling for the Odéon theatre; Messiaen was given some important musical commissions; Abel Gance undertook a new version of his remarkable film on Napoleon.

Malraux followed very closely, with Gaëtan Picon, the work of the Caisse Nationale des Lettres. This comes to the help of writers and poets who are not lucky enough to attract large sales. He also founded 'Art in Schools', a policy which lays down that one per cent of time and money should be devoted to the practice and appreciation of art, and he would have liked to extend this measure to the budgets of all public buildings, such as Postal and Financial establishments, for example.

His passion for new architecture was such that here one might have accused him of insensitivity, or at least of imprudence, in allowing the tall apartment and office towers to be put up in Paris. But the conjunction of different styles in art never frightened him. His syncretism made him ready to give his blessing to every variety of marriage between art and time. On the other hand he abominated the pastiche and the imitation – what he called 'absurd constructions' – and a certain commonplace Americanism which was disfiguring cities all the world over. He would have liked General de Gaulle to give his name to a modern building where France could have seen her own image, and he was sad that everything 'was lost in the sands'. This explains his attachment to Faugeron's plan for a new Ministry of National Education; the design was in his office, and he would often study it, and discuss it with his visitors. But he was quick to realize that the mental effervescence of the artists, combined with the demands and the dilatory action of the bureaucrats – what he called 'the war machinery of the civil servants' – created an impenetrable morass around these ambitious projects.

There is no doubt that he was more at home with writers and musicians, and particularly painters – for these are relatively free agents – than with film directors (for 'the cinema is also an industry') and architects (for to build is also to administer and promote). 'What in God's name is the position with Corbu?' he asked me one day on one of those famous green pads.

Malraux launched his Maisons de la Culture in a fit of lyrical enthusiasm. They had the top priority in the hierarchy of his plans. He wanted them to do for culture what the Ecoles of the Third Republic had done for education. Throughout 1961 and 1962 he felt that he was the standard-bearer of a great policy, and the visit of General de Gaulle to the Maison de la Culture at Bourges in 1965 endorsed it like a rocket in the sky. For Malraux a Maison de la Culture was designed to put the Comédie Française, the treasures of the Louvre, the great conductors, the important exhibitions, the richest treasures and highest achievements of mankind within the reach of executives' and workers' children in towns of 100,000 inhabitants and their suburbs. He gave to them the best that he had to give, and devoted one memorandum after another to the subject. But let no one think of him as an authoritarian boss. Once the impulse had been given and the result achieved, he appointed the responsible pilots after consultation with the mayors, and they were left to sink or swim. He never interfered with their artistic programme.

Neither Maurice Escande at the Comédie Française, nor Georges

Auric at the Opéra, nor Jean-Louis Barrault at the Odéon (until the break with him in May 1968), nor Georges Wilson at the TNP (with the exception of a single play by Gatty forbidden at the request of the Spaniards in 1966), nor George Planchon, nor any film director however fantastic or avant-garde, was ever lectured about his own job. If Malraux were disappointed, his face set and he dropped a remark to show his feelings; if he were satisfied, he felt that he was secretly responsible, and deeper notes would come back into his voice. He never wanted to exercise a censorship over the cinema, for he was the reverse of a dictator; he had nothing in common with a Sun King, planning, prescribing, and finding fault. He was not even anxious to convince, but merely to sow the seeds on soil which he felt was ready to receive them. 'It's for you to play,' he would often say, or again: 'Push whichever button you need.'

It hurt him when certain mayors, after the great panic of May 1968, wanted to 'normalize' the programmes of their Maisons de la Culture and bring back stock entertainment. May 1968 was certainly a break for Malraux – not as much the event itself, whose dimensions he had lucidly calculated ('We are faced here not with a need for reforms, but rather with one of the most crucial crises that civilization has ever known.'), but the divorce resulting from it between the youth and General de Gaulle – and this led Malraux to restrict his cultural activities. I was no longer working directly for him at that time, but I was close enough to feel, with him, how far the mechanisms had broken down. Disappointment had robbed his enthusiasm of its force.

One can carp at the Maisons de la Culture today, but if they were not there Amiens would be nothing more than the seat of a Préfet in Picardy, Grenoble simply the principal town of Isère, and Reims merely the most beautiful cathedral in France. They explain why Parisians now want to live in these cities, and why foreigners no longer think that France and Paris are one and the same.

As I write these lines, so many memories come back to me that I should like to speak longer about Malraux's achievements and all that he took in hand. So many important ideas were launched, so much was started, and so many credits were obtained, particularly in the field of music. One must not forget that he created the Orchestre de Paris and handed it over to Charles Munch. These enterprises were brought to fruition under Malraux's successors, for the changes we have seen in cultural activities since 1969 have affected their presentation and the ethic intention behind it, but their structure and foundations stand firm.

NICOLE ALPHAND

*

ESCORTING THE MONA LISA

Translated by Robert Speaight

Shortly after his inauguration, John Kennedy asked my husband, Hervé Alphand, to come and see him. He was the first ambassador to be received in this way at the White House. The President of the United States expressed the wish to maintain the closest relations with France in every field. After a survey of the immediate problems, he said to him: 'I think that my first visit outside the American continent should be to France, and I very much want to see General de Gaulle, whom I don't know. I have read all his books, and his opinions will be extremely useful to me as I begin my term of office.'

During the following days my husband set about arranging a visit, which was eventually set for 31 May to 2 June 1961. As soon as this was agreed in principle, each side worked on the preparations for the journey.

For Mrs Jacqueline Kennedy, in particular, it was a great event and she was anxious to give it all her attention. She had a long talk with me, from which it was clear that, after General de Gaulle, the person she particularly wished to meet in Paris was André Malraux. She had been deeply impressed by *Les Conquérants* and *La Condition humaine.* She knew every corner of the *Musée imaginaire.* Her dearest wish was to hear the comments of the French writer she most admired on the masterpieces with which she was already acquainted, for she had spent part of her girlhood as a student in Paris. We saw to it that her wishes were made known to Malraux, who at once signified his agreement.

A few weeks later the President of the United States and his wife landed at Orly – a young couple full of dynamism and radiant with beauty, placed as they were at the head of the most powerful nation on earth, 'with every heart at their command'. Paris could do nothing else but give them an affectionate and triumphal welcome.

But would Jackie Kennedy's wish to meet Malraux be realized? Only eight days previously, André Malraux had lost his two beloved sons in a tragic motor accident. When she heard the news of his loss, Mrs Kennedy said to us at once: 'M. Malraux must not feel himself bound by his promise. How could he take me round the museums after the tragedy he has just been through?'

On the first evening of their visit, at the Elysée, we were standing behind the President of the Republic, who was receiving his guests with the President of the United States. André Malraux had not appeared, and I wondered whether he would really be able to master his suffering. At the moment when the line of guests was on the point of breaking, there appeared two black, shadowy figures. We were deeply moved when we saw André Malraux and his wife pass by quickly and discreetly, and then mingle with the crowd. Malraux had shown astonishing courage in overcoming his grief to fulfil his duty as Minister of Culture.

So he did act as a guide to Jackie Kennedy. At the Musée du Jeu de Paume, he discussed Manet, Renoir and Cézanne. Below Manet's *Olympia* he had had placed Bouguereau's *Venus*, brought from Compiègne. This was a kindred subject which had received the Salon prize in the year when *Olympia* was refused, and the two pictures had never been shown side by side. At Malmaison he turned historian. Mrs Kennedy paused before a portrait of Josephine, and said to him in her gentle, subdued voice: 'What a cruel fate! She must have been an extraordinary woman.' 'A real bitch,' replied the Minister, as he recalled the stormy relations between Josephine and Napoleon. Bonds of close sympathy grew up between the great French writer and the former student who was now First Lady of the United States.

Before long the warm impulse which drew Malraux and the Kennedys together found a new expression. Anxious to give heightened brilliance to the reign of the 'New Frontier', the President had decided to give a dinner at the White House for everyone who mattered in American culture – writers, novelists, musicians and men of the theatre. He asked us whether André Malraux would agree to lend his presence to this event, and it was at once arranged for the month of May 1962. We had long discussions about it with Mrs Kennedy during a weekend spent with her in Florida at the beginning of the year. 'We mustn't allow André Malraux to be bored,' she said, 'and since he speaks English badly, we should first of all invite people who speak French.' We replied that what principally mattered was to gather round her table the greatest artists in America, French speaking or not.

My husband was in Paris during April, and he discussed with Malraux the details of the journey. The Minister found it a fascinating prospect. Not only would he speak about culture, he would also talk to President Kennedy about politics in general, for this was at a time when our points of view were at variance in many ways. The General was not prepared, in the immediate future, to return the visit which Kennedy had paid him in the previous year, 'but', added Malraux, 'he is quite glad to send on his tanks – in other words myself – and to have them set on fire to light his path.'

In fact this visit of May 1962 was a success both for the Kennedys, who wanted to introduce art at its most brilliant, into the White House, and for André Malraux, who was able to explain the French position to the President as this had emerged from his discussions with General de Gaulle. They touched on a wide range of subjects: Europe and the West, the Soviet Union, India and China. At the end of the dinner, replying to John Kennedy's warm toast, André Malraux exclaimed: 'I raise my glass to the only country, in the whole course of history, which has come to occupy the first place without having wanted to.'

Before he left, the Press invited the French Minister to answer a great number of questions, all of them political except one – and this was the last: 'And if we expressed the wish to see the *Mona Lisa* in the United States, what would you say?' 'Yes, without hesitation,' replied André Malraux. Either it would be technically impossible, he thought, and this would be easy to prove, or it would be possible, and everyone would be thrilled. In any case the General would certainly relish the idea.

So the rendezvous was fixed, and the promise was kept.

André Malraux personally devoted extraordinary care to organizing the journey of the most famous painting in the world. It is a fact that the *Mona Lisa* travelled like a sovereign. Experts were dispatched before her arrival to examine with John Walker, the curator of the Washington National Gallery, the conditions of her transport and custody. A special case was designed and built in order continually to maintain the temperature and humidity to which she had been accustomed in the Louvre. Escorted by M. Jaujard, Secretary-General of the Ministry for Cultural Affairs, and Madame Hours, one of the most eminent specialists of the Louvre, the *Mona Lisa* was favoured with a special cabin on the *France*. Never for a moment did her guardians lose sight of the thermometer and hygrometer. I observed to the charming Madame Hours, who had the chief responsibility for nursing this precious patient, that the Italian mason who had kidnapped her at the beginning of the century, and hidden her for several months under his bed in a house in the north of Italy, had not taken so many precautions – and still she had survived. But such were the instructions of the Ministry; nothing must be left to chance.

At New York harbour, lorries and another group of doctors were waiting for the celebrated traveller. She arrived in Washington under escort, a fortnight before the Exhibition was due to open, and recovered her composure in the solitary state of a locked and bolted case in the National Gallery, surrounded by armed policemen.

At last, on 9 January, the day of the private view, André Malraux, in his turn, disembarked with his wife. The dinner at the Embassy was brilliant. To honour this Italian lady lent by Frenchmen, the President of the United States himself accepted our invitation – something a President never does except for the reception of a Head of State. The Vice-President and Mrs Johnson, the Secretary of State and Mrs Rusk, the principal members of the Cabinet and the Congress were present with André Malraux for this exceptional occasion.

A series of absurd incidents followed, which can only be attributed to the mischievous influence of the *Mona Lisa*, displeased no doubt at being transported from her home, and without her consent. Three thousand guests invited too early were impatiently stamping their feet at the National Gallery; the lift which should have taken the President to the second floor broke down, and he was obliged to climb the staircase – a painful process on account of his war wound; the audience standing in the large hall found it impossible to hear a word of the speeches delivered successively by Dean Rusk, André Malraux and John Kennedy, since the microphones had suddenly stopped working. The *Mona Lisa* continued to smile, enigmatic and imperturbable.

Nevertheless more than a million visitors filed past and André Malraux's daring decision to let her cross the Atlantic was fully rewarded.

Next day, the Minister had important and difficult discussions with the President. It was on the eve of the notorious Press conference in which General de Gaulle refused the American offer to allow France to participate in the nuclear agreements reached at Nassau between England and the United States. It was also just before the General took his very firm stand on the subject of Great Britain's entry into the Common Market. Without himself announcing the decisions that Paris was about to make public, the Minister for Cultural Affairs was able to prepare the ground and convey to the President of the United States that Franco-American relations would be seriously troubled.

Yet the photograph taken after the interview at the White House shows two men, both of them laughing. The President, as he went towards the porch, had said to Malraux: 'Well, Mrs Kennedy's grace will settle all that this evening, and we will not talk about Lafayette!' Malraux, clutching at his shreds of English, replied: 'Who is this guy?' The photograph taken at that moment shows the two men laughing. Malraux's comment on it was 'Laurel and Hardy'.

The last evening of the Minister's stay also ended on a pleasant note. We were invited to Virginia, about twenty minutes from Washington, to the country house of the Robert Kennedys. A horde of children and dogs were there to welcome us. Everything was simple and uncomplicated, as if they were receiving neighbours or relatives. Ethel Kennedy said grace before the meal, as she always did, but, out of respect for her guest, she said it in French. André Malraux was enchanted by this '*bon enfant*' atmosphere.

It was in this way, and on these different occasions, that André Malraux was able to become acquainted with the United States, both officially and informally, although, of course, he had already toured America as a propagandist during the Spanish Civil War. I believe that he loved the country and that, preceded by the fame to which his genius entitled him, he was received at the White House, and by the various groups that welcomed him, as a very special envoy of French culture, and as the closest confidant of the Head of State. Kennedy, in particular, realized that he could not find a better interpreter of Asiatic problems; and Nixon, in his turn, remembered him when, on the eve of his first visit to China, he asked the opinion of only one foreign adviser – André Malraux.

PART II
*

THE TEMPTATION OF
THE EAST

CHANG MEI YUAN

*

MALRAUX AND CHINESE THINKING

1925: 'A new China is coming to birth, as yet elusive to ourselves [the Chinese]. Will it be shaken by one of those great collective emotions, which have so often convulsed it in the past? More powerful than the chant of the prophets, the whispering voice of destruction echoes to the farthest limits of Asia'.[1]

Malraux has been interested in China since he was a young man. Like many other young Frenchmen between the two wars, he did not escape the new *mal du siècle*. He tried to free himself of it by throwing himself into action, and China seemed to give him not only the opportunity for revolutionary activity, but also the possibility of a 'break with the European past', and a chance to cure the disease of his own civilization. Malraux's orientalism is essentially based on the reading of Chinese philosophical works, translated by the Reverend Léon Wieger, on his contacts with the Paris School of Oriental Languages, and on his private researches at the Musée Guimet. In addition, he has deepened his literary knowledge by personal contacts with the Chinese people. What he thinks about China is expressed in terms of a confrontation between East and West. His work has inspired many critical studies, but no one until now has examined the influence of Chinese thought traceable in certain of his early writings.

One certainly cannot blame Malraux for a failure to assimilate all the schools of Chinese philosophy, for these are fairly numerous. He has been chiefly influenced by Confucianism and Taoism, the two currents of thought which are best known in the West. Confucianism used to be regarded, even in China, sometimes as a philosophy and sometimes as a religion. In conformity with Western opinion at that time, Malraux seems inclined to the former point of view. He dissociates Confucianism

from religion in making Ling observe, in *La Tentation de l'Occident*, that
it 'developed neither in dependence on religion, nor in following it'.[2]
In separating the two, Malraux does not take into account the religious
nature of the Chinese. Confucianism – though apparently secular and
positivist – very often refers to Heaven, and to Providence, a kind of
deity, who reigns there. Confucius considers that the highest degree of
intelligence that he has acquired at the age of seventy is no longer to
transgress the laws which this Providence has laid down.[3]

If Malraux says nothing about the religious aspect of Confucianism,
he has shown the basically human and social role of this philosophy.
He demonstrates how far Confucianism has determined the individual's
rule of conduct towards himself and his neighbour. Thanks to its maxims,
the Chinese is impregnated with a kind of tranquillity 'which excludes
the possibility of conflict'.[4] This corresponds, up to a certain point,
with the attitude of the 'great man' mentioned by Confucius in his
Analects: 'The great man is exempt from sorrow and fear.'[5] In *La
Tentation de l'Occident*, the Westerner A.D. learns from the Chinese Ling
that 'the irresponsible Oriental struggles to raise himself above a
conflict where he has nothing at stake.'[6] Where the Chinese mainly
feels himself free of responsibility is over the questions of life and death,
but he is always responsible for his behaviour while he is on earth.
We find the same idea behind the attitude of many of Malraux's
protagonists when they are called upon to act.

Throughout his life, the Chinese strives after perfection. This
perfection is so important that it seems to be the principal aim of
Confucius' great study. According to Ling, it springs from 'the intensity
of emotion which a feeling excites in us'.[7] It follows that the master or
the 'great man' is neither the painter nor the writer, but the man who
knows how to carry this emotional intensity to its highest pitch.[8] Since
perfection is identical with Confucianism, the old mandarin Wang-Loh
deplored that with the disappearance of Confucianism 'the possibilities
of perfection which it enshrined'[9] would be lost.

On the one hand the teaching of Confucius makes the individual
aware of himself by demanding perfection of everyone, on the other
hand it disposes a man to a 'watchful neglect of his own culture'.[10]
Any individual particularity is held to be a stain on a woman, and
undesirable for a man. Personality itself is inconceivable in China.[11] In
contrast to Westerners, the Chinese have no wish to be aware of
themselves as individuals, but they set out 'to be neither seduced nor
arrested by this illusion [of themselves]'.[12] Such a conception is so
embedded in Chinese thought that Mao Tse-tung once said to Malraux:

'Western individualism has no roots among the Chinese masses'.[13] The absence of the idea of individualism has greatly impressed the Westerners, and proved to have much attraction for them, for young European intellectuals – including Malraux – saw in it an eventual antidote to the excessive individualism of their own civilization. Malraux's commitment to revolutionary action is perhaps bound up with this hope.

In the place of individualism, Confucianism exalts the altruism which shows itself in human relationships. Malraux was quick to understand that Confucianism was 'the greatest of *human* systems'[14] (the italics are the author's). He also understood that filial duty was among the powerful elements of this sytem. In his article on 'Young China', he thus emphasized its importance: 'I thought I was getting close to China when I saw that no act could be separated from filial duty.'[15]

Thanks to the doctrine of filial duty, the bond between parents and children has always been very close. For example, the parents intervened directly in their children's marriage; they could betroth them at a very early age to someone they would see for the first time on the day of their wedding. Obviously such a marriage takes little account of love between a man and a woman. In this respect, Ling is influenced by Western culture, and ventures to express his doubts about the system that used to prevail. Malraux is well aware that for the Chinese, deeply rooted in their traditional culture, the primary end of marriage is procreation: in the character of Tcheng-Dai he gives us the sad example of a man without children, obsessed by his solitude in a life which is a living death.[16] Confucianism teaches every Chinese that for a married couple to have no children is the greatest sin against filial piety.[17] In relegating love between husband and wife to the secondary plane, Confucianism does not exclude it from marriage, as certain passages in *La Tentation de l'Occident* seem to suggest. Malraux makes no mention of Mencius, the best known Confucian after Confucius himself, and it is he who refers most frequently to married love in his writings. Has it ever struck Malraux that if love precedes marriage in the West, in the China of tradition it follows it?

The filial piety of Confucianism extends also to the relationship of a man to his masters and to those older than himself. Malraux illustrates this in the case of the two terrorists, Hong and Tchen. Hong's feeling for Rebecci, the 'feudal bond' between Hong and Garine, Tchen's respect for old Gisors, his reluctant affection for Pastor Smithson, all spring ⸂rom the same filial piety.

The Confucian doctrine of man's relation to his fellow men is also based on altruism. Malraux gives it a very ironic application. In the course of an argument between Hong and Borodin, the former defends his role of terrorist and asks 'Don't you think that it disgusts me? It's because I find it so painful that I don't always make others do it, you see?'[18] It is extremely doubtful whether Borodin really understands that Hong's justification is founded on the doctrine of Confucius which instructs us 'not to do to others what we should be unwilling for them to do to us'.[19]

Malraux has been greatly interested in Confucianism, but I think that he discovers more defects than merits in the system. In fact, he praises the thought of Confucius in only two places. In a poetic style, and through the mouth of Wang-Loh, he describes the influence of Confucianism on the Chinese: 'It has formed their sensibility, their thought, and their will. It has given them the feeling for their race. It has created their picture of happiness.'[20] The author goes on to emphasize how this philosophy has radiated over the whole of China: 'If Confucianism falls to pieces, the entire country will be destroyed.'[21] This does not prevent Malraux from regarding the social ethics of Confucianism as the basis of both the qualities and the shortcomings of the Chinese people.[22]

In his critique of Confucianism, Malraux has essentially in mind the social context of this philosophy, the tendency of the Chinese 'to be more aware of their social condition than of their individuality'.[23] If he does not make this point explicitly in *La Tentation de l'Occident*, he does so in his article on Young China. Here he shows how paternal love could be sacrificed in the name of tradition. Because of his excessive consideration for the family rites, a certain Wang has allowed his adolescent daughter to die of hunger after the death of her fiancé. In *La Tentation de l'Occident*, and also in his article, Malraux's criticism is precise; he is chiefly concerned with particular doctrines, like the prescription for family rites. Then it becomes generalized, and more emphatic in *Les Voix du silence*: 'The Tahitians were less cruel than the sages of Confucianism, who promulgated so many atrocious laws.'[24]

In short, the work of Malraux implies a fairly unfavourable view of Confucian philosophy. The doctrine of filial duty and the Confucian rites seem to have brought the Chinese more harm than good. Malraux nowhere mentions Confucius' exhortations to benevolence, and he shows the altruism of Confucian man towards his fellows through the mouth of a terrorist attempting to justify an act of violence.

If Malraux has reservations about Confucianism, is it because he has been influenced by contemporary opinion? During the first half of the twentieth century, China has seen the birth of a new young élite which has felt the influence of Western culture, and wishes to transform their ancient civilization at any cost. This new élite blames Confucianism for having corrupted Chinese society and enfeebled the whole country.[25] Through his contacts with Chinese intellectuals, Malraux could not help knowing how they felt about Confucius. This analysis has already shown that he based his opinions on a social ethic which mainly reflects the extreme doctrines of certain Confucians.[26] I think that if Malraux had been more thoroughly informed, and that if the twentieth century had not been a period of contestation, he would feel more sympathy for the thought of Confucius; for this encourages – as Malraux himself has always encouraged – a belief in the altruism of which men are capable.

In contrast to Confucianism, Taoism is a very intellectual philosophy, more concerned with the metaphysical problems of man on earth. In fact, at the beginning of the century, Malraux was among the many young French intellectuals to be attracted to the philosophy of Lao-tse. China as he saw it was inconceivable without Taoism; for him this philosophy represented the country's most essential characteristic.[27]

Malraux's preference for Lao-tse rather than Confucius is marked in his work. Thus he singles out the *Tao-te-king*, Lao-tse's esoteric book, from among the important Chinese philosophical writings, and passes over in silence most of the Confucian works. He explains the Taoist maxims in much more detail than he devotes to the principles of Confucianism. When he has occasion to criticize Taoism, he does so more impartially. Indeed it is questionable how far Malraux was familiar with the different aspects of Taoism. A reading of his works suggests that what he knew best was the thought of Lao-tse, the founder of this movement in the sixth century BC.

Through the old mandarin Wang-Loh, Malraux tells us that 'spiritual uncertainty all the world over'[28] has excited a renewed interest in Taoism among the Chinese. The young feel the need to acquire the culture of the West, but they cannot shake off the ancient Chinese thought. They turn to Taoism, because it seems 'to justify their desires ... and give them a greater strength'.[29] But is this fresh interest in the Taoist school as significant as *La Tentation de l'Occident* seems to suggest? Does Taoism respond to the aspirations of the young Chinese intellectuals? Does it offer a remedy which can deliver twentieth-century man from his metaphysical anxiety? The answer, I think, is rather in the negative, for the basic preoccupation of the Taoists is the preservation of life; they are concerned to avoid the evil and dangers of the world we live in.[30] Moreover, in the first half of the twentieth century, the young intellectuals of China have been busy with the problem of reconstructing their country. Metaphysical anxiety, in so far as it exists, has taken second place to patriotism. It is difficult to see what Taoist doctrines can help to reconstruct the country. However that may be, Taoism has a particular attraction for Malraux, and he has shown a warm interest in certain of its ideas.

China introduced him to a vision of the universe different from that which he had known in the West. According to the oriental idea, suggested by Ling to his friend A.D., the universe – far from being a crushing, and hostile force – is only 'the result of two opposing rhythms which penetrate everything that exists'.[31] Ling goes on to explain that these two rhythms suggested by the Taoists 'interpret, in the human context, the opposition between the masculine and the feminine principle'.[32] The Chinese, in his understanding of the world by its rhythms, strips it of its mystery, and makes it human and natural. Beside the feminine and masculine rhythms, the Taoist recognizes the rhythms of life and death which never cease to transform the universe. This sage is detached from temporal things, because they are 'negligible phenomena, born yesterday and already as good as dead'.[33] In speaking of these successive rhythms, Malraux employs a poetic expression: 'waves in the ageless rivers'[34] and the Stream and the River are favourite images for the Taoist.

The notion of the universe is of great importance in Malraux's work. He sees man at odds with it in a long struggle, for he feels the continual need to create and to 'submit the world' to his will. Thus he discovers 'in his action a pride all the greater because he thinks he is possessing the world more completely'.[35] So nothing creates a wider gap between the Oriental and the Westerner than the way in which they respectively view the relation of man to the universe. In contrast to the Greek idea where man is distinct from the world, the Chinese feels himself bound to it.[36] Moreover, since man and the world have the same origin, they are equals, and not rivals, as they are in Christianity. One should note that the idea of man at one with the universe is the result of a late development of Taoism. It comes from the school of Lao-chung, and one finds it notably in the philosopher Hsiang-kuo. Because of man's close relationship to the universe, as Taoism sees it, man can really be transformed by it. (The universe is called the 'Great Transformer'.) Ling refers to this idea right at the beginning of his correspondence with A.D., when he says that 'the world changes you far more than you change the world'.[37]

Has the oriental conception of man's relation to the universe exercised an influence on Malraux? One might suppose that in creating certain of his heroes – particularly in his first two novels – he has partially adopted the Taoist vision of the world that transforms mankind. But in general he seems to lean towards a slightly different conception, since the struggle between man and the universe emerges as one of the most striking *leitmotifs* of his work.

In speaking of the origin of the universe, Malraux alludes – albeit indirectly – to the Tao, quoting the definition given in the first chapter of the *Tao-te-king*,[38] But when he speaks of the Tao, Malraux prefers current expressions to Chinese words; he calls the two opposing rhythms of the universe the 'masculine' and the 'feminine', and not Yin and Yang. In the same way he designates the Tao by the term 'principle', which is only one of its many definitions. For these reasons, the true Tao of the Chinese is not very easy to recognize in *La Tentation de l'Occident*. In fact, Malraux gives us the impression that he has left out the most essential doctrine of this philosophy.

Malraux certainly refers to the Taoist notion of knowledge, but not very clearly. The Taoist distinguishes between two very different kinds of knowledge; that of Tao, and that of human affairs. For Malraux the universe appears to be the only knowledge worth acquiring,[39] but the Taoists regard the origin or the principle of the universe – the Tao – and not the universe itself, as the supreme knowledge. For the Tao is disinterested by reason of its abstract nature, but the knowledge of those mundane matters that Ling is speaking of is not disinterested at all: 'Nothing is less disinterested than the desire for knowledge.'[40] To attain the higher knowledge, Ling says that one must 'lose consciousness of the external world'.[41] This tallies with Chuang-tseu's advice to 'fast in the spirit', and to 'remain in a state of forgetfulness'.[42] Ling associates this method with a 'particular way of breathing'.[43] However, to tell the truth, the Taoists practise this exercise in order to prolong life, and not to discover the rhythms of the universe or to 'enter into communion with the principle', the Tao.[44]

The genuine Taoists appear passive and even negative in their attitude to the knowledge of human things, for they preach a doctrine of 'studying little and wanting little'.[45] They have the same attitude towards culture and towards action. Malraux refers to the 'anti-cultural' outlook of the Taoists in the conversation between Wang-Loh and A.D. The Chinese sage says that 'Taoism has helped [the young Chinese] to detach themselves from a powerful culture'[46] which has added 'the possibility of pleasure to the continual creations of mankind'.[47] The Taoists are anti-cultural because they regard culture as the source of all the evil in the world: it awakens *desire* in a man. This doctrine of 'anti-culture' had a certain attraction for young French intellectuals like Malraux, who were ill at ease in European civilization, and wanted to be free of it.

If Malraux shares in some respects the anti-cultural attitude of the Taoists, he does not share their prejudice against action. In contrast to Paul Claudel, who found merit in the principle of non-action, Malraux considers it – if not a vice – at least an obstacle which hinders the development of modern China. Under the influence of this doctrine, the Chinese despises force, which he regards as a 'vulgar auxiliary'.[48] The man we should respect does not give way to pointless agitation, because 'nothing inclines him to action. He does not even dream about it'.[49] One asks onself whether the dilemma of 'being' or 'doing', to which Malraux gives such emphasis, does not find an echo in the confrontation of East and West. Just as the Oriental is drawn towards 'being', so the Westerner is drawn towards 'doing'. As a result the West often shows itself incapable of understanding the passive attitudes of the East.

In his two novels about China, Malraux gives us several examples of this, where the Western advisers very often criticize the capricious tendencies of the Chinese. Gérard, in *Les Conquérants*, goes even further; he concludes that 'China has no knowledge of the ideas which lead to action'.[50] Contrary to what is believed in the West, non-action – according to the *Tao-te-king* – does not signify complete inactivity; it rather implies a reasonable and necessary action with a precise end in view. Moreover, the Taoists only condemn action which is violent and impulsive; they very particularly value the act of self-control, incarnated in the character of Tchen-Dai. The reader is told by Garine that Tchen-Dai 'is only capable of one sort of action – that which demands a man's victory over himself'.[51] Critics of Malraux – like David Wilkinson – see in this a proof of Nietzsche's influence.[52] No one has suggested the possibility of a Taoist influence.[53] In order to create the spiritual leader of the right wing of the Kuomintang, it was logical that Malraux should be closely inspired by Taoist ideas. Moreover Tchen-Dai also personifies the idea of non-violence – which is directly bound up with non-action – in his policy of maintaining a passive attitude towards the English. He would like to get the better of England 'without violent measures, without fighting'.[54] His unshakable faith in the final victory of China appears to be based on the Taoist notion of the ultimate victory of the weak over the strong.[55] Tchen-Dai confidently asserts that 'China has always absorbed its conquerors. Slowly, it is true, but it has always done so'.[56]

The Taoist doctrines mentioned here are taken from the *Tao-te-king*. They have interested and influenced Malraux in the first place, no doubt, because they posed the problem of man's relation to the universe in a different way; then because they gave him a better understanding of what he had glimpsed during his visits to the Far East (among other things the problems connected with the Chinese attitude to non-action and non-violence; and finally, perhaps, on account of his own conceptions of knowledge and culture.)

Be that as it may, Chinese philosophy, and more particularly, as we have just seen, the ideas of Confucius and Lao-tse, have had a definite influence on Malraux's thought. The influence can be felt throughout his work, but it naturally appears more evident in *La Tentation de l'Occident*. The young European intellectual wishes to free himself from his *nouveau mal du siècle* with the help of certain concepts of Chinese thought, just as the young Chinese wishes to get rid of his superannuated culture with the aid of certain ideas borrowed from the West. Unfortunately neither was ready for an harmonious exchange between the one culture and the other.

Does Malraux still believe today that European civilization ought eventually to borrow some element from China? Perhaps it has already done so?

GIRIJA MOOKERJEE

*

MALRAUX AND THE HINDU VISION

I turn over the pages of an old diary and my mind's eye recreates a day which I cherish as a high point of my life. There was spring in the air and André Malraux's directive to clean all historic buildings had brightened up Paris and brought forth beauties hitherto hidden beneath dirt and smoke.

On 8 May, the whole Indian community in France thronged Orly airfield for a glimpse of Panditji – Jawaharlal Nehru – who had never met General de Gaulle before, and had left the Commonwealth Prime Ministers' Conference in London for a day, landing in the Queen's snow-white private plane in Paris. There was Ambassador Raghavan, Counsellor Sait and ladies in flowing silken saris. Indian children waved flowers and tiny saffron-white-and-green flags. Waiting on the red carpet were Premier Michel Debré, Foreign Minister Maurice Couve de Murville, Geoffroy de Courcel, representing General de Gaulle for this occasion, and André Malraux, Minister for Cultural Affairs, who had been personally acquainted with Pandit Nehru for nearly thirty years.

At the rather informal *déjeuner de quatorze couverts* in the Elysée, the General and the Reformer sat facing each other. Lively discussions focused on problems of the Third World. President de Gaulle spoke with authority as Head of the French Community. Jawaharlal Nehru represented the view of the new nations who supported Algeria in the UN. The talk touched upon Soviet affairs and the emergence of China as a major power, and both leaders examined the question of mutual cooperation in the field of economics and culture.

I watched André Malraux as he listened attentively to Nehru's reminiscences of Gandhi, and a few lines of *Les Conquérants* crossed my mind: 'If Gandhi had not intervened, India, which has taught the world its most important lesson, would be nothing but a country in revolt.' This appreciation of Gandhi was a revelation to me and my whole revolutionary generation, since Malraux had expressed it even before the Mahatma launched his epoch-making campaigns of disobedience in India with the historic salt march to Dandi in April 1930.

Sitting in front of me at the banquet table set with exquisite porcelain and golden cutlery, he seemed to me a kind of Trimurti, a Trinity – the persuasive minister, the accomplished writer and the daring fighter in the Far East and on the battlefields of Spain and France. Ever since he went to China in 1927 and witnessed the Canton uprising, and throughout the Spanish Civil War up to the end of the Second World War, which he experienced as a colonel in the French Resistance, André Malraux had devoted himself to the defence of just causes, whether in far-off countries or near at home. He was never afraid to risk his life for a cause he thought just. And it became clear to me that this man had never volunteered as a defender of a narrow doctrine, nor for personal interests or a bare theory.

Earlier, André Malraux had acted as President of the International Anti-Fascist League together with Romain Rolland, who is well known all over India for his fine biographies of Ramakrishna and Gandhi. And it was in this capacity that Malraux went to Berlin in the company of André Gide to deliver to Hitler a protest against the implication of Dimitrov in the burning of the Reichstag. Shortly afterwards Malraux made the acquaintance of Nehru in Brussels during a session of the League. When the two met again, after an interval of a quarter of a century, the anti-colonialist had become the Prime Minister of India and the former *maquisard* appeared in the guise of Minister for Cultural Affairs in the Government of General de Gaulle.

Reflecting today on the banquet in the Elysée and on Malraux's visit to Delhi in 1959, which served as a preliminary to Nehru's visit to France, I understood that India could not fail to make a lasting impression upon him because he found himself in harmony with the Hindu ideal of the Perfected Man. Indian thinking rejects purely intellectual endeavours. One of the focal points of Indian culture is true engagement in selfless action to further moral and social improvement. Malraux considered the *Upanishads*, philosophical texts of 800 BC, as the Indian Bible; he called the *Gita* a New Testament and regarded the *Ramayana* as the *Iliad* and *Odyssey* combined. His depth of knowledge made it easy for him to follow Indian ways of reasoning and his sincere search for the truth about life and death met here with answers which Europe was not able to give him. Malraux discovered in India a 'culture of the soul' which was in no way strange to him. In Madurai he found aspects of Chartres, and even Bombay, which appeared to him like 'a bazaar that thinks itself a town', had for him the features of eternal India when he landed at the India Gate after visiting the cave-temples of Elephanta.

Malraux's Indian voyage finds its place in the *Antimémoires*, a recognized modern classic, written without vaunting his own achievements by simply bringing out his innermost thoughts and reflections from the depth of memories of a life lived in many continents and under many unusual circumstances. True, in *L'Espoir* and *La Voie royale* he had described his own bewilderments about life and death and about the enigmatic destiny of man. But in *Antimémoires* he summed up his deepest views of them, and good Cartesian that he is, he also managed to arrange them into a literary pattern. In this book he writes of human grandeur and of man's cruel destiny in a universe which, through centuries of vicissitudes, has not yet yielded its secrets to man. And though it is difficult, impossible even, to devise a classification for the *Antimémoires* and give it a tag acceptable to institutional and professional judges of literature, yet it is a work of imperishable worth, and for us Indians it is almost a testament of faith in the greatness of our country and her perennial search for noble objectives of life, in harmony with devotion to the advancement of the social good.

In this remarkable book Malraux has succeeded in painting a picture which reflects the glow of the spirituality and nobility of some of this century's most remarkable men, among them Jawaharlal Nehru and General de Gaulle. Human grandeur is not the innate greatness of all human beings but of a few only, who shine forth in their integrity, intelligence and heroism. Malraux thinks that heroism makes this world and its uncertain and undefinable destiny bearable and directs these heroes to an invisible goal which can be called social justice.

In his superb delineation of Pandit Nehru, Malraux portrays him as the embodiment of the most effective political idealism the world has ever known. This is the agnostic Pandit who wanted to create a 'just state by just means'. Justice, the fight for justice, just causes and the recognition of the primacy of justice are the ideas which move Malraux most, and he elevated them to the central theme of his actions and writings.

And the more I meditate about Nehru and Malraux the more I am convinced that they are strangely akin. Both are promoters of social justice: they are Marxists with reservations, and they uphold the integrity of the individual. In spite of his faith in socialism Nehru never believed in conformity, and he certainly did not desire a world in which uniformity was the rule. He had a strong feeling for the unusual, and he was aware of the difference in men. He wanted to maintain the sovereign right of the individual in a society patterned on socialism, and he was preoccupied to the end of his life with the problem of how to harmonize the individual and the group.

Malraux's qualified Marxism is in complete harmony with Nehru's interpretation. In his first meeting with General de Gaulle in the rue Saint-Dominique, described in the *Antimémoires*, Malraux points out that his conception of social justice is more Jacobin than Marxist because it does not exclude man's fullest personal liberty in an industrial world. It was also in this conversation that Malraux propounded the view that Communism is in essence a reflex of pure nationalism and that what is known as liberalism is not a political reality but a political sentiment shared by different political parties whatever their national ideology.

General de Gaulle for his part explained to Malraux his own political concept during this meeting. He boldly announced that nationalism and 'the idea of the nation' are two different things, and that it is by treating them separately that a statesman might be able to obtain the best results for the largest number of people. This statement had very much impressed Nehru who despised narrow nationalism but was at the same time a devoted Indian national.

It was natural that nationalism and Marxism should figure largely in the discussion between Nehru and Malraux when they finally met in 1959 in New Delhi. Both leaders showed a preoccupation with the dangers of limiting the freedom of the individual in the march of technological events. Both were perturbed to perceive growing centralization in states patterned on Marxist ideology and to observe the enslavement of the individual to the prosperity and the amenities of civilized life. Both showed awareness that humanity seems for some reason to lack a sort of spiritual element which would restrain the immense power given by science to modern men.

At the banquet table in the Elysée the importance of man's inner values to curb technological misuse came up in discussion. The President and the Pandit silently agreed. These two men, both of them great interpreters of contemporary history, complimented each other and exchanged beautifully styled addresses. With extreme courtesy General de Gaulle praised Nehru as the embodiment of the mystery and poetry of India. Later the conversation turned to art.

Malraux tried to draw attention to the 'Trésors d'Art de l'Inde', the Indian art exhibition under the common patronage of the Indian and

French governments, for which I was General Commissioner in collaboration with the élite of French museology. Nehru was eager to get
a glimpse of the exhibition before beginning his afternoon talks with the
General. A smile invited the company of Malraux. A wink of the
Ambassador told me to go along.

'La fête de la sculpture indienne' in a French setting – the outcome
of the meeting between Nehru and Malraux – was a superb exhibition
and a dazzling personal experience for all lovers of beauty and art. Our
museums had supplied antiquities of priceless value which had never
before left Indian soil. Among the graceful torsos and statues of gods
Malraux found himself in his proper surroundings. He casually shed
the polite reserve of the Minister and displayed a knowledge of Indian
art and aesthetics which completely bewildered Nehru. Malraux dealt
with problems and puzzling questions with ease and agility, through
far-reaching and unexpected comparisons; his bold imagination
transgressed the limits of time and space.

Later, when I came across narrow-minded criticism of Malraux's
ambitious *Musée imaginaire*, I remembered him moving among the
Indian sculptures in Paris. Undoubtedly, his incredible insight must
be incomprehensible to the dry *'rat de bibliothèque'*, and this reminds me
of the rejection of a somehow similar genius, Leo Frobenius, whom
Malraux made a central figure in *Les Noyers de l'Altenburg* and who was
cast out because he had the far-sightedness to put Africa on the map at
a time when the philologist still confined his outlook to the achievements
of classical Greece and Rome.

As we walked through a hall dedicated to proto-historic specimens,
we discussed some aspects of Indian art – the Indus civilization, for
instance, still a riddle, although we know that it had a very high
standard of aesthetics and public sanitation foreshadowing modern
town planning as early as 3000 BC. Among objects dating from the time
of Alexander the Great's advance into India we discussed the Emperor
Asoka, who experienced moral conversion on the blood-stained battlefield of Kalinga and henceforth eschewed war and conquests and
evolved *vijaya dharma*, the policy of winning the hearts of his opponents
by persuasion and gentleness.

Malraux, who is preoccupied with the phenomenon of eternal
change, studied intensively a serene *Avalokitesvara*, an emanation of the
Buddha of contemplation. This bodhisattva merged in China with the
Mother of the Western paradise.

In the Japanese edition the body contours of the Kwanyen vanish
completely through stylized lengthening. It is important to notice that

in Greek conception everything is lively movement and of this earth. With the process of time Buddhist art becomes increasingly motionless.

Then we went on to debate the controversial origin of the *Buddha-murti* and the Apollonian impact on Indian art. I recollected a last conversation with the venerable Walter F. Otto who sustained Malraux's observations. He emphasized that the world of Homer shunned death as the absolute alien, and experienced the divine as the fullness of life on earth.

Hindus, commented Malraux, value even daily performances ritually and they are not afraid of the aftermath. Man's being is his eternal becoming. Hindus make no difference between the creator and the created and see in God not the 'Wholly Other'. Hindus are non-dualistic, they see God in man. Hinduism seemed to him humanism, a kind of 'inner' humanism as it is concerned with the quest for the perfection of man. The *Gita* prescribes *nivrtti marga*, the path of renunciation and introspection, for the student and the retired man. But during his best years man has to choose *pravrtti marga*, the path of unselfish action. Vivekananda, the brilliant nineteenth-century reformer, Gandhi the *satyagraha* and the poet Rabindranath Tagore agreed on the duty of social participation without being involved in society.

We concentrated again on Indian art and Malraux tried to analyze and summarize changes in modes of thinking expressed in the various styles. Gaily looking at a procession of rain-producing elephants on a *jataka* slab, a story-telling frieze, Malraux conjured the elephants hewn out of living rock he had seen in Mahabalipuram and he referred to the elephants carrying the Mailasa Nath, the famous Siva-shrine of Ellora. 'Indian rock-architecture is sculpture in gigantic proportion.' He reflected a little while in silence and, turning to Nehru, quoted a Buddhist saying which he later chose as an introductory quotation to his *Antimémoires*: 'The elephant is the wisest of all the animals, the only one who remembers his former lives.'

We were standing in front of a small showcase containing examples of contemporary village art, terracottas which may be seen by the hundred in the temple bazaars. Nehru made the following comment: 'Our villagers go on fashioning their deities of burnt clay and believe in their potency after consecration. When the festival is over special *mantras* [prayers] release the celestial bliss from the effigy. Subsequently, the image is regarded as a soulless piece of pottery and broken or immersed in the village pond.'

'Art is not an adornment of civilization. It is expression of its highest qualities. The dreaming sculptures of Hindu temples seem to contain celestial values,' added Malraux, 'the smiling bodhisattvas invite comparisons with the Angel of the Annunciation in Reims.' Malraux, who always sees through things and discovers behind them impressions he had experienced somewhere else and at different times, compared the Gandhara bodhisattvas with the divine messengers adorning the central porch of Reims Cathedral, where most French kings were crowned. Into this portal the Dauphin entered; out of it went the annointed King of France.

One had to be Malraux to be able to solve the much disputed riddle of the surprisingly luminous expression of the Gothic statues of Reims. He traced it back to the meeting grounds of Indian and Hellenic thinking, to the world of Plotinus, who met Indian philosophers during his stay in Alexandria. Plotinus taught in the *Enneads* that the Soul and Being are linked in a comprehensive reality. As this conception was strange to Greek philosophy it has been deduced that he was influenced by the Indian gospel of the oneness of *atman* and *brahman* as revealed in the texts of the *Upanishads*. These ideas were diffused a thousand years later by the Dominican friars preaching the *unio mythica* at Paris and Strasbourg universities and it was during this period that the cathedral of Reims was rebuilt and embellished with the sculptures.

His profound knowledge of his own French and Latin culture gave André Malraux access to the Indian world, and Indian art helped him to re-evaluate Western thinking and see it in new dimensions. Visiting the temples between Kasi and Conjeevram after his conversations with Nehru in the Indian capital, he was fascinated by the sacred art of the Hindus, assuring those who look at it that it involves a secret world which it conveys without unveiling. He participated in silent communion with the *lila* of *brahman*, the graceful appearance of the Indian gods on earth, and he confesses in his writings that he was fully at home 'in the nocturnal garden of the great dreams of India'.

It was in India that I last met Malraux. He was passing through Delhi on his way to Bangladesh. His sad expression reflected the loss of those who had been dearest to him. But when I brought up our meeting in the Elysée he immediately cheered up and confessed: 'I was so happy there because I sat near the men I esteemed most, the General and Nehru. And when I came here as the representative of General de Gaulle to see Nehru here in Government House, as you know, our conversations led to the visit to Paris and I was able to convince him that an exhibition of Indian art would be highly welcome in France.'

The fighting in Bengal was over and I could not help thanking him again and again for all that he did for India and Bengal in their hour of crisis. The author of *Les Conquérants* was the first abroad to grasp the ethical implications of the Indian freedom struggle and he gave this idea new prominence in his *Antimémoires*; 'Everyone knew that Gandhi's ultimate aim was the purification of India, whose independence was only its main consequence.'

With the same conviction in support of a just cause he sided with the Mukti Bahinis, the guerrillas of Eastern Bengal, and this at a time when the whole world ignored the brutal massacre at the Meghna as painfully revealed by the Anderson reports. I can affirm that it was neither simulation nor pose that led Malraux, at the age of seventy, to offer himself as a volunteer to the fighting forces of Bengal. The lives of millions of men and women were at stake, and the cultural heritage of such brilliant writers as Nazrul Islam and Rabindranath Tagore.

André Malraux, with his love of justice and his deep perception of beauty – the keynotes of his writings and his life – is fully in tune with the Hindu ideal of the man in quest of perfection and in search of eternal truth. He is in complete agreement with Nehru, who told him that we have to stand steadfast on earth but must raise our heads high, and with General de Gaulle, whom he quotes in *Les Chênes qu'on abat* . . . : 'When everything is going wrong and you're searching for your decision, look towards the peaks; there is no congestion there.' This beautiful and touching advice of the General might have been formulated by an Indian.

TADAO TAKEMOTO

*

MALRAUX AND JAPAN: AN ENCOUNTER UNDER A CASCADE

It cannot be said that Japan alone has a claim to the genius who has contributed so much to the resurrection of the voices of past civilizations: besides Japan, during the years between 1923 and 1932, André Malraux travelled extensively in Cambodia, Persia, Afghanistan, Pakistan, India, Mongolia, China and even in the ancient kingdom of Sheba in the Yemen. At first glance, the cultural and spiritual baggage he brought back from those travels seems to be crystallized above all in *Les Voix du silence*, and may give the impression of a Spenglerian variation on the plurality of cultures. Why then does Japan stand out particularly?

Is it not significant that, of all the bodhisattva images, it was the one from the wall painting of the Golden Pagoda in the Horyuji Temple that was chosen for the frontispiece of *La Métamorphose des dieux*, just as later the only Oriental painting to appear in the Malraux Exhibition at the Maeght Foundation was one of Takanobu's portraits. And after all, *La Condition humaine* ends, not with the scenes of bloodshed in Shanghai, but with a serene scene on a hillside in Kobe. It is certainly impossible to talk about Malraux's encounter with Japan without using the word 'serenity', though for him serenity may not be Japan's monopoly, for he had already discovered its meaning in China as early as 1925 – 'This purity, this disaggregation of the soul in the bosom of eternal light . . .' he calls it in *La Tentation de l'Occident*. But what one can say is that his encounter with the Japanese civilization, more than with any other, has widened his understanding of the concept of serenity.

The word 'serenity' was first voiced by Malraux in *La Tentation de l'Occident*, although at that time he had not yet visited Japan. In spite of the fact that he writes only about China in that work, Japanese spirituality is so superbly suggested that a Japanese reading it may feel as if it is Japan he is writing about. Nevertheless at that time his evocation of Japanese spirituality was not absolutely perfect: it was only in *La Condition humaine* (1933), after his first visit to Japan, coming from China and Mongolia, that he touched upon the narrow line which separates the Chinese and Japanese spiritual attitudes. The author himself was to write in the spring of the following year: 'My aspiration is to push the tragic away. Then in this way will serenity become more piercing than tragedy.'

Forty years later, in *La Tête d'obsidienne*, Malraux wrote about Takanobu's portrait of Shigemori: 'What this expresses supremely is not the interrelation of superb black planes, nor the signs of a face: it expresses a sense of ritualistic death – *hara-kiri.*' These words take on their full meaning when one remembers the scene in *La Condition humaine* in which Kama, the Japanese lavis painter says to Baron Clappique just before the revolution: 'Impending death will allow an artist to put enough of his fervour and sadness in everything, so that the forms he paints are revealed, as well as what they hide.'

It is by no means only a Japanese, and an artist, who might be ascribed these words, for after all the aim of all great religions is to elucidate the meaning of life through the approach of death. Then what was Kama's meaning here, and why did he have to be a Japanese and a painter of lavis? It is perhaps because Kama expresses the Bushido belief that the supreme form of life is the act of self-sacrifice – which is the basis of the Samurai code of honour. Here is an example of spirituality without faith, but without a certain upward aspiration.

Has Malraux discovered other key-words, apart from Bushido, to express his views about Japan? On each of his four visits there he proclaimed that the 'way of the Samurai' was the secret of the Japanese soul. But whilst the admirer himself has scarcely changed, the object of his admiration has. No doubt the 'Japan converted to the West' in Malraux's own words, was moved to see Malraux admiring the 'Eternal Japan', but on the other hand it is not without some dismay that my country has listened to this praise. In the post-war 'democratized' Japan, where the so-called progressive intellectuals are the leaders of public opinion, the Japanese who could be said to truly understand Malraux were to be found among those who had to remain silent. Among these was the greatest literary genius of this century, the novelist Yukio Mishima.

At the time of Malraux's last visit to Japan, Mishima had already taken his own life, but though the two great writers never actually met, the impact of Mishima on Malraux started a new phase in the latter's relationship with Japan: the phase of mystery. There are undoubtedly certain similarities between *The Sea of Fertility*, the last *roman-fleuve* by Mishima, who chose death by the sword in November 1970, and some of Malraux's early novels dealing with the theme of purity of action. But, further, the *leitmotif* of Mishima's novel is the metaphysical problem of Time for the agnostic, a problem which is at the centre of Malraux's preoccupation with the meaning of life.

Since the English translation of Mishima's *Sea of Fertility* is not yet completed, it would not be very useful to discuss it extensively, but it seems important to emphasize a point which posterity will not fail to notice: referring to their respective experiences in India, André Malraux – in his *Antimémoires* – and Mishima – in *The Sea of Fertility* – give the measure of their earnestness in their attempt to elucidate the meaning of transmigration. Since from the agnostic standpoint the concept of life beyond is not denied, and since, on the other hand, the self has ceased to be the means and end of everything, there is no longer any necessity for the soul to be restricted to 'here' (i.e. to the flesh).

One can wonder whether for Malraux the second life is merely episodical. We must remember that the legend of the ascetic Narada which is told at the beginning of the first volume of *La Métamorphose des dieux* is inseparable from the basis of Malraux's aesthetics, which is that from the standpoint of truth all is *maya* – appearance is illusion. Reading *Lazare*, one of Malraux's latest books, we may ask ourselves whether the question underlined by the writer's father in the book left by his bedside when he had committed suicide, was not a question even more shattering for his son: 'And who knows what we shall find after death?'

As far as the problem of transmigration is concerned, it is India and not Japan which provides the common ground between Malraux and Mishima. They both raise the same question about the existence of the transmigrated soul. But while Malraux would induce from it the idea of man's destiny, it seems that the word 'destiny' is oddly lacking in Mishima. Is this difference perhaps due to the fact that while Malraux belongs to a civilization which considers Limbo as part of the Revelation (we must not forget that the *Antimémoires* are but the first chapter of a work entitled *Le Miroir des limbes*), Mishima belongs to a civilization for which Limbo is Illumination. 'For', Mishima writes, '*it is only through the existence of Limbo that the chance for Satori will come*' (Mishima's own italics). It is precisely from this point that by preaching deliverance for transmigration, Mahayana – a branch of Buddhism which aims at transcending its ordinary rules of discipline by opening out the paths of feeling and intellectual speculation – and particularly Zen, begins. But again this approach belongs to India, not to Japan.

What does belong to Japan, however, is the spirit which endeavours to achieve – by means of a disembowelling sword – an Illumination as glaring as the one Sakyamuni experienced under the bo-tree. It was after Mishima's suicide, an event which shocked the whole world, that Malraux added a chapter on Japan to the revised edition of the *Antimémoires*. In it he describes a visit to the famous 'dry' Garden of the Seven Stones in Kyoto, in which he has a very significant conversation with a Japanese professor of aesthetics whom he calls 'the Bonze'. 'Remember', says the Bonze, 'that *hara-kiri* is not suicide: *hara-kiri* is sacrificing to the altar of the ancestors.' Then he produces a small oblong package tied in the red-and-white string, which indicates that it is a present, but instead of giving it to Malraux he unwraps it, revealing an exquisite Buddhist statuette. He does not give it to him, but, after Malraux has turned to go, the Bonze burns it in a corner of the garden, holding it by the legs. This scene and the Bonze's words, seem to have lighted a fuse in Malraux's mind, bringing images of sacrificial acts which run through the whole tradition of Chivalry in the West and are symbolized above all in the burning of Joan of Arc. And he ends up with these words which seem to be a homage to Japan: 'The blue flame of the statuette, symbolizing the invincible permanence of Japan, was rising like a flame struck from a flint in that solitary garden which for centuries had been free even of plants'.

Through the Bonze, Malraux says: 'One must establish communion with what is beyond Nirvana. . . . Nirvana is the highest temptation. The absolute is what is *beyond*.' And these words find an echo in a sentence of Mishima's book in which the hero, who chooses death by the sword at the age of twenty, is entranced by the bright sun rising above the Ganges: 'What Isao had always imagined *beyond* his self-destruction by the sword was nothing but that sun.'

'If we try to lead a pure life, we will reach a presentiment, of another life, won't we?' This is the question Mishima asks on the death of his hero. Leading a pure life and committing suicide are probably inseparable – at least in Japan. The expression 'hurry to death' can be found only in Japan. Mishima also writes in the same novel: 'If one dies early, it will be impossible to die late, and if one dies late, it will be possible to die early.' And later: '. . . what is important is only this: foresight by action, by death.' Here, at last, it is no longer India, be it

Hinduism or Indian Buddhism: the inseparability, the concept of a pure life and the act of self-destruction as a means of attaining that Sun is totally Japanese.

'We shall meet again. Indeed we shall. Under a cascade.' These words are uttered, on the closing pages of the first volume of *The Sea of Fertility*, by Kiyoshi Matsugae, the first young man to achieve transmigration. After delivering this mysterious message, he dies of love and despair, and Honda, who witnesses his death and the miracle of transmigration – which occurs four times throughout Mishima's work – will later indeed meet his friend under a cascade, and remember the words of Seson, author of *The Thirty Odes to Vijnaptimatrata*: 'To be endlessly transmuted just like a wild torrent'.

I am far from saying that this purely Japanese way of dying is Malraux's own vision of death. We must remember that he has repeatedly emphasized that what is important in the metaphysical problem of the significance of life is 'death' and not 'decease'. At the same time we must recognize that traditional Japan, even within its own Buddhism (except for the sect of Shingon esoterism), has never successfully expressed that metaphysical question, and there is no country which has delved more deeply into it than India. But contemplating death and deciding to die are not the same thing. Japanese spirituality recognizes the intensity of life at the moment the decision is taken to die, and it knows no other colour but white, no other sound than that of a unicord, no other accessory but one flower, one stone. *How man can enter into relation with his own condition through this monosyllabic whisper*, which in Japan can be heard from a stone garden to a tea-ceremony, is an attitude with which Malraux identifies particularly.

From this point of view it is very significant that Malraux, on his last visit to Japan, travelled as far as Kumano and Ise, two sanctuaries of Shintoism. It was my good fortune to be the companion of this ambassador of the *Mona Lisa* for three weeks all the way from Tokyo through Hakone, Kyoto, Nara, Uji and the Kii peninsula to these shrines deep in the mountains. The journey was a modest but extraordinary pilgrimage. During it he made unexpected discoveries. I have the feeling that he had had a foretaste of the meaning these new discoveries would have for him when he was moved by the painting of *The Nachi Cascade* at the Nezu Gallery. In several of our museums Malraux obviously enjoyed looking at some works by Zen artists such as Mu-Ch'i, Liang K'ai and Sengai (he is to write on Zen painting for the first time in the last volume of *La Métamorphose des dieux*). He compared the portrait of Yoritomo with that of Shigemori (it was the third time he had seen the former and the fifth time he had seen the latter). In Kyoto he visited the Stone Garden of the Ryoanji Temple and the Sand Garden of the Honenin Monastery, and in Nara ancient temples such as the Horuji and Todaiji temples. Eventually he arrived one day at Kumano, deep in a forest of black Japanese cedars, where at last he was able to see the Nachi Cascade which he had hitherto known only from the painting. To reach the gigantic cascade Malraux had to go down the long stone stairway, dragging his legs and leaning on Madame Sophie de Vilmorin, and finally stood before the Torii, the holy portico of Shintoism which gives the cascade its holy character. Never shall I forget the image of André Malraux contemplating in total stillness the falling waters breaking through the mass of ancient cedars, nor his whispered words: 'Rarely have I been moved by Nature . . .'

But it was afterwards, when we visited the Ise shrine, that I heard him express the deepest emotion the cascade had stirred in him. Our visit there took place just after the reconstruction of the shrine had been completed (the shrine must be reconstructed every twenty years in accordance with a tradition which has been observed for the past two thousand years). We visited with due respect the Inner Shrine which is 'the very centre of Japanese spirituality' in Bruno Tauto's words, and walked back along the front approach, made of white gravel, when suddenly Malraux, putting his hand on my left shoulder, pulled me back and made me turn round: 'Look at that,' he said. I looked and saw a single pine branch stretching from the forest on the left-hand side right across the approach, and behind the branch, like a white curtain, tranquil, the Sanctuary of the Inner Shrine, and further up, towering behind it, the forest of cedars. 'You see, those cedars cut vertically the horizontal line of that pine branch, its *brisure*. The trees are standing erect from the ground: this is the real vertical axis of Japanese civilization as revealed in the *Bushido*!' 'But,' I asked, puzzled, 'haven't you already discovered such a vertical axis in the famous *Winter Mountain Scene* by Sesshu, and found in it a force which breaks the arabesque of Ukiyoe engravings?'

'What is so overpowering here, however,' he replied, 'is the very force which breaks the *brisure* itself. I first discovered it in the painting of the *Nachi Cascade*, and then I came to discover it in the real cascade. In Europe the painter who first broke with the convention of arabesque was Titian, and Rembrandt followed him. In Japan it was Sesshu. But now that I have seen the Nachi Cascade, I can understand that there exists one direction – the vertical one – which is opposed to both the arabesque and the *brisure.*'

And he added gravely, 'The cascade and the trees of Ise have the same importance: their combination constitutes the meeting-ground on which Japan discovers the sacred without a cave [*le sacré sans la grotte*]. Could we not say that the cascade is in some way the "sacred" of the sun? It looks as if the Nachi Cascade falls towards the earth, but as an image it is ascending at the same time!'

The 'sacred without a cave' – that is, light without shadow. I thought Malraux must have had in mind the meaning of the 'Rock Door of Heaven' in the Japanese myth.

Just at that moment a beautiful black butterfly appeared from somewhere and stopped by the feet of Malraux, who was standing still. I somehow shuddered. But he said, smiling: 'The left wing is a little damaged,' and continued to talk obsessively.

Undoubtedly that black butterfly symbolizes Malraux's encounter with Japan – I wonder *from what chrysalis* the butterfly transmigrates – and also the inverted image of those ancient cedars as well as the mysterious voice which seemed to rise from behind those trees: 'I was just dreaming. We shall meet again. Indeed we shall. Under a cascade.'

PART III

*

THE ETHICS OF IMAGINATION

FRANÇOISE DORENLOT

*

UNITY OF PURPOSE THROUGH ART AND ACTION

Translated by Robert Speaight

'It was called *La Lutte avec l'Ange,*
and what else am I undertaking?'[1]

History and existence teach the fragility of all speculative logic. Nevertheless, once a judgment has been made, the tendency of the human mind is to question it no longer. It requires real courage to model one's life on the facts of experience. This is especially true in the case of a public figure, where political passions are involved. One is then accused of going back on one's principles, or even of treachery. To found an opposition newspaper and then, twenty years later, to become a minister lends colour to the belief that one's commitments are contradictory. To pass from the Revolution to the *Musée imaginaire* looks like a break in one's philosophy of life.

However, even a superficial examination at once reveals a common element in these four options. None of them could be described as quietist; all of them have mobilized the energies of André Malraux to the full. And a second reflection leaps to mind. With the moral and intellectual authority which he enjoyed, the author of *La Condition humaine* could not have exposed himself to the fire of criticism without a very strong conviction.

Every book of Malraux's, from *La Tentation de l'Occident* to *Lazare*, shows a lively distrust of intellectual games. 'Idle thoughts, orchards eternally reborn, which the same fears always kindle like this evening's sun',[2] exclaims Vincent Berger, pondering alone in the Alsatian countryside, after listening to the contradictory debates of the intellectuals of Altenburg. The phrase leaves one in no doubt that thought is impotent to solve the problems of existence. In this universe of fiction the characters, like their author, base their action on feeling born of experience. Never on an ideology, never on an *a priori* concept. In the factual context which is our lot – *la condition humaine* – Malraux untiringly pursues whatever answers are possible to a purely practical question: 'How can one try to live?'[3] A well-known formula, taken from *L'Espoir*, defines the connection between life and thought. 'Tell me, Major, how can one make the best of one's life, in your opinion?' askes the aesthetician Scali; and the ethnologist Garcia, a subtle analyst of human behaviour, replies without hesitation: 'By converting as wide a range of experience as possible, my friend, into conscious thought.'[4] An empirical thought is necessarily a thought in motion, and its persuasive power is undeniable.

On the creative level it was Malraux's 'Indochina Adventure'[5] which inspired not only *La Tentation de l'Occident* and *La Voie royale*, but also *Les Conquérants* and *La Condition humaine*. To the revolutionary struggle we owe *Le Temps du mépris* and *L'Espoir*, and to Malraux's experience with the tanks in 1939, *Les Noyers de l'Altenburg*.[6] Taken as a whole, the *Antimémoires*, *Les Chênes qu'on abat . . .*, *Les Oraisons funèbres*, and *La Tête d'obsidienne* are the result of Malraux's encounter with the great figures of history. The filming of *Sierra de Teruel* based upon *L'Espoir* led to *l'Esquisse d'une psychologie du cinéma*. Nearly twenty years' familiarity with works of art explains the article of 1937 entitled: 'La Psychologie de l'Art'.[7] We know how many books, over the following years, were fed on Malraux's constant preoccupation with art.

The transposition of 'experience' into literature – and by that I mean essays on art as well as fiction – was often accompanied on the active level by a corresponding commitment. Encouraging the Young Annam movement and writing *Les Conquérants* and *La Condition humaine* expressed an identical concern. So did taking on the presidency of the Anti-Fascist League and combatting anti-Semitism, writing *Le Temps du mépris* or *L'Espoir*, and defending the Spanish republic. All expressed the same thing. Malraux renounced the revolutionary ideal to which Marxism alone gave concrete form in the context of our times, on account of Stalinism no doubt, but even more, perhaps, because his personal experience in France and Spain had shown him that Communism realized neither the 'trust' nor the 'fraternity' on which he had so deeply counted. This explains, on the one hand, why he rallied to de Gaulle and, on the other, why he transposed his disappointed hopes into art. Here he discovered a communion that was invulnerable because it was lasting.

In this dual and simultaneous orientation Malraux is exceptional, if not unique. For if there is no hiatus between art and action, it is because, for him, the two are basically analogous. In the one as in the other, by the simple fact of his self-expression, man transforms a

destiny to which he *submits* into a destiny which he *dominates*. That is
to say, he transforms this destiny into *awareness*.

'It is very rare for a man to be able to endure – how shall I say it?
– his condition, his fate as a man,'[8] observes Gisors. In fact every
character in Malraux is haunted by his condition, which can be
summed up in a single word: 'alienation', or 'humiliation', according
to the ground on which one stands – the ground of ideas or of sensibility.
Since we experience our lives before we reflect upon them, it is the
feeling of humiliation that we find most frequently described in
Malraux's novels. This feeling releases the springs of awareness and
gives rise to every reaction. For Garine, his trial (*Les Conquérants*), for
Perken, his impotence (*La Voie royale*), for Kyo, the status of a half-
caste, for Hemmelrich, dependence on his family (*La Condition humaine*),
for the Spanish people (the real hero of *l'Espoir*), poverty, for Vincent
Berger, Shamanism (*Les Noyers de l'Altenburg*), etc. To mention every
'humiliated' character would be to mention practically all, from the
most intellectual to the most primitive. In the first place, humiliation
is endemic to human nature. Before elucidating in *Les Voix du silence*
the meaning of his title, *La Condition humaine*, Malraux already had the
intention of it as early as 1929. In a lecture called 'La question des
Conquérants', he raised the opposition between objectivity and
subjectivity, and illustrated it by Kyo's experience as he listens to his
own recordings, which he does not recognize. 'We hear our own voice
with the throat and the voice of other people with the ear; on a more
serious plane, we are aware of others by means which are not those by
which we have awareness of ourselves.'[9] Quite strikingly, the problem
of incommunicability appears time and again, and recently in almost
identical terms, as we can read in the last pages of *Lazare*.[10] It is not
so much that people are different, but their memories and the way they
imagine things vary so widely.

Similarly, on the social level, the 'poor man' is excluded from the
life enjoyed by the rich. From Hong in *Les Conquérants* to Barca in
L'Espoir, the humiliation of the proletariat matters less than the
humiliation of the man who 'has nothing any more to look at' – such
as the prisoner.

We must not forget that the novel which follows *La Condition humaine*
is entitled *Le Temps du mépris*. More limited in its range, it contains
the same denunciation of crimes peculiar to our time. Again, the
concentration camps fill Malraux with horror, and it is to them that
he devotes the final pages of the *Antimémoires*. Listen to this judgment:
'The attempt to force human beings to despise themselves. That is

what I call hell.'[11] Physical suffering may be horrible, but for Malraux it affects the individual less than the solitude which goes with it, and the fact that he is powerless ever to reverse his situation.

Nevertheless it is not with torture but with imprisonment that Malraux obsessively associates the feeling of humiliation. Each of his novels contains, in fact, either scenes or accounts of imprisonment. Doubtless the theme was imposed on him by the nature of the subject; its fascination is so pronounced as to become a torment[12] – especially in view of the interest the novelist repeatedly shows in *Robinson Crusoe*, *Don Quixote*, and *The Idiot*. For he mentions these works in three places, first in a speech to the Congress for the Diffusion of Culture in 1936, then in *Les Noyers de l'Altenburg* in 1943, and in the two successive versions of the *Antimémoires* in 1967 and 1972. In these stories of men lonely and condemned he sees 'the revenge of solitude, the reconquest of the world by the man who returns from hell'.[13] 'Hell', in the context of these works, and of torture, must be understood in a metaphysical, not in an ethical, sense. In his preface to Manès Sperber's book, *Qu'une larme dans l'océan . . .*, a remark of Malraux's reveals a great deal about the psychic and metaphysical universe inhabited by the author of *La Condition humaine*. 'In this manichaean book, history serves Evil present in all its mystery. Originally the meaning of the word Satan was not the Adversary, but the Accuser. It is the meaning of the world (and not Good), which is the contrary of Evil; and here it is less a reality than a quest.'[14] In his writings and in his commitments Malraux urges us to revolt against Evil (Hell), and he fights it in order to replace it with 'the meaning of the world'. All thinking hinges upon 'the death of God' and the impossibility of coming to terms with it. Hence the overwhelming importance of death and time. 'What weighs on me,' says Perken 'is – how shall I put it? – my *condition humaine*, my limitations; that I must grow old, and that time, that loathsome thing, must inevitably spread through me, like a cancer.'[15] Parallel to physical decline there is 'an inner process from which few men escape'[16] – death in life, renunciation of the hopes one had when one was young; the state that Malraux attributes to his old men, Gisors, Alvear, and recently Méry, the disturbing character introduced in the second edition of the *Antimémoires* and reappearing in *Lazare*.

Time, to be sure, is death, which is another humiliation. The characters and their creator care little about death, which nonetheless, in so far as it 'transforms life into destiny', overwhelms them. If it is true, as Gisors believes, that 'every man dreams of being God',[17] how absurd is this immutable sentence 'that weighs upon you like a prison regulation'.[18] Also, to all appearances, 'man is a chance element, and fundamentally speaking the world consists of oblivion'.[19] Even supposing that the universe had a purpose,[20] the tragedy of alienation would not be lessened, for man has no knowledge of the laws that govern it. In this respect, his superior awareness is a vain advantage. The supreme humiliation lies in not being able to modify a situation imposed on one, in a slavish submission to it, so that man appears vulnerable whichever way you look at it, whether the universe has a meaning or not. For the agnostic, destiny can only be contingent and absurd, and thus an incarnation of 'Evil'. The hero of *Les Conquérants* observes that man can live in the acceptance of absurdity, but not in absurdity itself.[21] So what conceivable defence is there?

Against social humiliation there is revolution. Kyo espouses it to 'conquer dignity for his people', and for Barca in *L'Espoir*, 'brotherhood is the opposite of vexation'.[22] Malraux leaves two of his characters, Klein in *Les Conquérants* and Alvear in *L'Espoir*, to explain the revolutionary impulse, although their political options are different. What emerges is its mystical value.

'A man who has been unjustly sentenced . . . is bound to stake his hopes on some new order. . . . Among other functions, the revolution plays a part that an "eternal life" used formerly to play.'[23]

Gisors, the former professor of sociology, makes the same analysis: 'A civilization becomes transformed, you see, when its most oppressed element – the humiliation of the slave, the work of the modern worker – suddenly becomes a value; when the oppressed ceases to attempt to escape his work, and seeks in it his *reason for being*.'[24]

Malraux's personal attitude to the revolutionary question is complex. He celebrated the 'lyrical illusion' while at the same time distrusting its doctrine and practical application. The ideology of Marxism has never captured him. Certainly not during the time of the Rassemblement du Peuple Français (a movement initiated by General de Gaulle in the hope of calling together all Frenchmen and Frenchwomen, regardless of their political beliefs), when the dialectic between capitalism and the proletariat seemd to him outdated,[25] and when, as he saw it, the evolution of history showed Marx to be wrong and Nietzsche to be right. 'It is not Marx, with his philosophy of international Communism, who has triumphed today; it is Nietzsche who said that "the twentieth century will be the century of national wars".'[26] And just as clearly, during the pre-war years, you have only to read his speeches in 1934, 1935 and 1936, and to scrutinize *Les Conquérants*, *La Condition humaine* or *Le Temps du mépris*, to realize the antithesis between his way of thinking and historical materialism. When the pressure of events made Malraux an ally of the Communists, he paid tribute to their discipline and their energy 'in the service of social justice', but he contested their methods, which were so opposed to the aim they were pursuing. 'If the men on whose side I am fighting don't trust me, why go on fighting, my son?'[27] declares Magnin in *L'Espoir*; and Magnin is a character whose objectives make one see him as an incarnation of Malraux himself. 'Trust' was precisely what Malraux, in 1934, applauded in the Soviet revolution;[28] and so, when the necessities of war no longer obliged him to make common cause with the Communist Party, Colonel Berger – now become Malraux once again – drew away from it. 'The tide had receded.'[29]

In breaking with the Communists Malraux remained strictly, and paradoxically, true to himself. He was not slow to emphasize this: 'André Gide and I happened to be requested to deliver to Hitler protests against the condemnation of Dimitrov, who was guiltless in the Reichstag fire. When today Dimitrov is in power and has the guiltless Petkov hanged, who has changed – Gide and myself or Dimitrov?'[30] The argument is irrefutable, and Malraux was perfectly right when he was questioned about his changing political alignments and replied: 'It is not I who have changed, but events.'[31] Since, for him, the root of the problem has always been the metaphysical alienation, it was doubtful if any historical action – even, as in the case of Communism, the appeal of brotherhood – would have succeeded in overcoming it. Garine – in Trotsky's phrase the 'second self' of the writer[32] – admits in his disillusionment: 'One cannot cast the revolution into the fire; all that is not the revolution is even worse; one has to admit it, even when one is disgusted.'[33] Garine's critical sense is acute, but it does not prevent him dying in the service of the revolution, nor Malraux from comradeship in arms.

But the outline of the revolutionary question, as it is raised in the life and thought of Malraux, is one example among others; the intention of this outline – superficially drawn, since several chapters in the present book are devoted to various forms of the man in action – has been to show an essential aspect of the way the author of *La Condition humaine* looks at things: the coexistence of the most lucid realism and the most romantic exaltation. Bound as he is to work within the context of the relative, this idealist is never altogether happy with it; and he transforms necessity into conviction for so long as he reconciles his aim with the means he employs to reach it. If we examined his other positions we should come to the same conclusions.

Let us very briefly explain that it was also the case with his devotion to de Gaulle, born of his disenchantment with Communism. In 1945 he made the following, almost cynical, declaration to Roger Stéphane: 'Since there can be no question of adapting ourselves to Russian socialism, we shall try to adapt ourselves to Anglo-Saxon socialism.'[34] In discussing the post-war political situation in the *Antimémoires*, and his intervention at the congress of the MLN (Mouvement de Libération Nationale), he states that the only alternative open to a movement born of the Resistance was obedience to Moscow or General de Gaulle's will to independence. Hence his choice. The 'legendary' attributes of the General naturally exercised their charm upon Malraux, for he was more sensitive to the 'qualities of a man' than to his political label. His lecture on 4 November 1946 is very revealing: 'It is a matter of absolutely no importance to any one of you students, whether you are Communist, anti-Communist, liberal, or anything else, because the only real problem is to know – beyond these structures – in what shape we can recreate Man.[35]

Since the present book contains a chapter on Malraux and de Gaulle and another on Malraux and myth, we shall not discuss these questions in detail. One should emphasize, however, the remarkable power of the imagination which tends to magnify the subjects of its choice. To represent a 'romantic reality'[36] is naturally a proof of creative genius; it is also to reveal the secrets of one's thought. The insistence on identification with a collective will, the fierce desire to animate the chosen ideal with a concrete presence, derive from the mind's incapacity to harmonize with any truth whatever. The young European in *La Tentation de l'Occident*, after making his diagnosis of the profound malaise which afflicted European consciousness at the beginning of the twentieth century, arrived at this conclusion: 'For the man who desires to live beyond his own immediate pursuits, a single conviction may organize the universe.'[37] In the opening pages of *Les Noyers de l'Altenburg*, Malraux distinguishes two kinds of individuals: those 'living from day to day for thousands and thousands of years', and the 'intellectual whose reasoning, however elementary, affects and directs his life'.[38] One remembers Tchen and his thirst for 'certainty'. 'For people who live as we do there must be a certainty. Something must be *sure*. Must be.'[39] Without this certainty which he turns into a religion, and charges his 'disciples' to transmit, he would go mad. The longing for a faith is at the root of his despair. 'What is the good of a soul, if there is neither God nor Christ?'[40]

Lack of belief on the personal plane and the absence of spirituality on the collective plane haunt Malraux far more deeply than historical situations. From the 'death of God' – the premise of *La Tentation de l'Occident* and 'D'une jeunesse européenne'[41] –stem all the questions that Malraux asks himself about man and history and the meaning of the human adventure. In his essays and speeches he addresses his public as a moralist, and brings up again in various ways the question raised in 'D'une jeunesse européenne': 'What concept of Man can a civilization of loneliness create out of its anxiety?'[42] The central theme of his 1946 speech on Man and Artistic Culture, is formulated as follows: 'The problem facing us today is to know whether or not, on this old land of Europe, man is dead.'[43] In 1969 his last political speech to the Union des Jeunes pour le Progrès repeated the question. 'I said in May that the crisis of youth was first of all a crisis of civilization. It is within this crisis that you are called upon to act, it is this crisis that will determine what you do.'[44] In the novels the continuity of these preoccupations, though clear enough, does not appear on quite the same level. The earlier novels tend to describe the efforts of particular individuals to achieve harmony with the world outside, and with themselves. Beginning with *L'Espoir*, the questions are no longer raised in quite such personal terms. Man has supplanted the individual. Notice incidentally that this is the moment when creative fiction exhausts itself. Art, which had been Malraux's initial involvement, began to preoccupy the novelist more and more. 'I have entered art as a man enters religion,' he said in 1945.[45] The long researches, which he had never abandoned, brought out certain convictions in him; it is these which led him, on the one hand, to write his well known essays, from 'La Psychologie de l'art' to *La Tete d'obsidienne*, and on the other hand to take on the duties of Minister for Cultural Affairs. Once again, ethics and metaphysics merge.

> If I can say, when I die, that there are 500,000 more young people who, thanks to what I have done, have seen the opening of a window through which they will escape the harshness of technology, the aggression of advertising and the need always to make more money for their recreations, most of which are trivial or violent – if I can say that, I shall die satisfied, I can assure you.[46]

Not only do the Maisons de la Culture bring a discovery of art to those who would not otherwise be aware of it, but they also answer a definite need of our time. Cities of artistic interest receive more visitors than Rome in the Holy Year (every twenty-fifth year). Stripped ourselves of all transcendental values, we expect from the arts of yesterday an answer to our questions. Hence the 'invincible dialogue' of the 'voices of silence'. 'In many respects, the imaginary museum is the resurrection of the invisible.'[47] If it were no more than that, art would be the affirmation of liberty, the domination of 'fatality'. Malraux's predilection for painting and sculpture can be explained precisely by the fact that these are concrete objects, and therefore a tangible presence of ideal values.

So the human condition is not only Möllberg's 'bottomless pit of nothingness',[48] nor the implacable hegemony of torture, as we are shown it in *Les Conquérants, La Voie royale, La Condition humaine, Le Temps du mépris, Les Noyers de l'Altenburg,* and *Antimémoires,* and more discreetly in *L'Espoir.* Its shape appears in Grabot's millstone, in the courtyard of the insurgents, in the prison of the partisans, in the ditch where the tanks, with their blind crews, plunge into the darkness of the night. We see it in the friendship between Perken and Vannec, in the murmur of self-sacrifice among the revolutionaries, in the blows struck against the walls of Kassner's cell, the long procession of Spanish peasants looking for their dead or wounded airmen, in the rush of the German soldiers towards their Russian enemies to save them from the gas.[49] The dumb heroism of the peasant women in Corrèze is another authentic witness.[50] If the history of our times can lead Malraux to say 'the shadow of Satan has reappeared over the world',[51] it can also inspire his funeral oration over Jean Moulin.

Malraux does not tire of scrutinizing the other side of the human condition which gives us grounds for hope. The mystery of human reactions touches him as closely as the mystery of our dereliction. In *La Tentation de l'Occident,* where for the first time in twentieth-century literature, the 'forces of the absurd' are denounced, he also recognizes another tendency in man. 'And yet, what sacrifices, what unjustifiable acts of courage, lie dormant in us!'[52] – three short lines in a text of 218 pages. As the years went by, the qualities in man impressed themselves on Malraux's thinking, and faced him with the same problem as death and Evil. 'The mystery of greatness, be it never so humble, is no less profound than the mystery of death';[53] 'the existence of love, art, and heroism is no less mysterious than the existence of evil'.[54] The noblest character in Malraux's fiction, Katow, explains why devotion to something inspires respect, and why it can become a passion. 'If you believe in nothing, and *especially* because you believe in nothing, you're forced to believe in the virtues of the heart when you come across them, make no mistake about it.'[55] In fact, Malraux's fascination with any act that transcends the conditions of its performance – like his revolt against the absurd – is the consequence of his unbelief: '. . . for if it is true that for a religious spirit the camps, like the torture of an innocent child by a brute, pose the supreme riddle, it is also true that for an agnostic spirit the same riddle springs up with the first act of compassion, heroism, or love.'[56]

If Malraux is captivated by the privileged expressions of the human spirit – art, holiness, and heroism – the simplest reactions to what threatens the individual, or the race, with destruction never cease to excite his wonder. *L'Espoir* ends with a magnificent paragraph celebrating a new and almost miraculous harmony between man and the world around him. 'For the first time Manuel was hearing the voice of that which is more awe-inspiring than the blood of men, more enigmatic even than their presence on earth – the infinite possibilities of their destiny.'[57] Malraux's astonishment is evident in all his essays on art, and it is the basic subject of *Les Noyers de l'Altenburg* and the *Antimémoires*, where it is pervasively felt or suddenly perceived. In the latter book, as in *Lazare*, there unfolds a series of questions, stated or implied, about 'the mystery of life' – '*l'énigme fondamentale de la vie*'.[58]

Neither an atheist nor a believer would stop to ask them, but Malraux, the agnostic, cannot avoid his obstinate quest for something to deliver him from contingency. The passionate analyses of the 'imaginary museum', as we know, are far more concerned with penetrating the metaphysical significance of works of art than with evaluating their aesthetic properties. But in the last resort, art, the supreme proof of man's 'quality', 'resolves nothing, all it does is to transcend'.[59] As a result, from whatever angle you look at it, the question of life's meaning remains untouched. As Malraux observed to Nehru: 'If art is to play the part that we see it playing today, the question must be unanswerable.'[60]

The persistent concern for 'the questions which death raises about the meaning of the world'[61] is deeply felt even in the novels. These are not only stories but dialogues, and it is this third dimension which gives them their considerable power to move us. Perhaps the influence of Dostoevsky, in whom Malraux recognizes the first novelist in modern times to put the essential questions, can be seen here; for Dostoevsky had given flesh and blood 'to a meditative interrogation which runs, like an underground stream, through his characters'.[62] A better expression could not be found for the problems which haunt the universe of Malraux. Certainly the dialogues between Perken and Vannec, Gisors and Ferral, Gisors and May, Tchen and Kyo, Garcia and Hernandez, Scali and Alvear, Ximenes and Manuel, seem at the outset to belong to an external literature, for they go far beyond their immediate context. Personalities and situations may change, but the question remains essentially insoluble. For the existential philosopher and novelist this is perfectly logical, given the 'structure' within which we are forced to live. 'Our civilization, alike in its sciences and its thought, is based on these questions, and it is beginning to recognize one of its secret voices in the expression of interrogation.'[63]

Malraux's thought has not basically varied since the period (1927) when he declared his 'conscious intention to show his striving though he had no doctrine'.[64] Nevertheless, in the course of his 'encounters with man' one element has been transformed. The absence of 'doctrine' has acquired a value in itself – to such an extent that in distinguishing two contradictory faculties in man, the demoniac and the 'divine', Malraux attributes to the latter 'the ability to call the world in question'.[65]

How then can we subscribe to his own judgment on his life – 'my vain and turbulent life'?[66] Turbulent, yes; vain, assuredly not. Both in what he has written and what he has done, he gives to us, his readers – 'atheist about everything, even perhaps about ourselves'[67] – 'a consciousness of our own hidden greatness'[68] – faithful to the aim he set himself in the preface to *Le Temps du mépris*, which was more exactly the aim that he attributed to art.

Here we should recall that, with the exception of his two archaeological expeditions (Banteay-Srei and the Queen of Sheba), no action was undertaken in his own interest. From the newspaper *L'Indochine* to the Maisons de la Culture, his activity has been directed to a useful end. 'I have a tendency to think myself useful'[69] he says in the *Antimémoires*. Since there is no question of considering him presumptuous, this attitude shows a compulsive need to ally himself with other people, either by a community of feeling – justice and liberty – or by attachment to a person, such as General de Gaulle. It is an almost vital need to break the 'hell' of loneliness and solipsism by action or creative work. The striking phrase – 'I became wedded to France'[70] – reveals this desire to identify himself with a cause. Here, as he frequently does elsewhere, Malraux reminds one of some of his characters who, from Garine to Vincent Berger, fuse together their personal lives and their commitments. He thus illustrates very clearly his definition of humanism: 'Humanism does not consist in saying "No animal could have done what we have done," but in declaring: "We have refused to do what the beast within us willed us to do, and we wish to rediscover Man wherever we discover that which seeks to crush him to the dust."'[71]

The life and the works perfectly coincide: *La Condition humaine*, the *Antimémoires*, *La Métamorphose des dieux*, are all 'chapters of a single life',[72] forcing conviction upon the reader. After all, it is Malraux who said of T. E. Lawrence, that 'the greatness of a living personality lies precisely in the link between thought and action'.[73]

JOHN LEHMANN

*

THE MYTH AND THE WRITER

It is not easy to write about a novelist, one's own contemporary, whom one has known personally at most stages in his career, and who has a unique, almost hypnotic power of fascinating friends and admirers with whom he enters into conversation – I all but said those to whom he addresses his monologues. As soon as I began to re-read the novels, however, I found myself engaged again, not only with the philosophical problems they raise, but with the (to me) even more interesting problem of Malraux as mythomaniac. And, in this connection, I have found it instructive to compare what I thought about the novels before the Second World War began, and what I think now.

André Malraux has, in my opinion, written three major novels: *La Condition humaine*, *L'Espoir* and *Les Noyers de l'Altenburg*. He has also written three lesser, I would say botched, novels: *La Voie royale*, *Les Conquérants* and *Le Temps du mépris*. His other fictional works, *La Tentation de l'Occident*, and the surrealist essays, *Royaume farfelu*, etc, seem to me of altogether minor importance.

La Condition humaine was first published in 1933, *Le Temps du mépris* in 1935, and *L'Espoir* in 1937. That is, all three novels were written and published during the period of left-wing fervour and militancy of the Thirties, the time of the Popular Front and rapidly growing inter-national intellectual solidarity against the advance of Fascism. *Les Noyers de l'Altenburg*, always considered by Malraux himself as only the first part of a greater work to be called *La Lutte avec l'Ange*, was written during the war, and did not see the light until 1943, outside France, and 1948 for the first time in France (Editions Gallimard). It was with some difficulty that I finally persuaded the author to let me publish it in English translation as *The Walnut Trees of Altenburg* in 1952. In any case, it represents a Malraux with a very different *Weltanschauung* from the pre-war novels.

La Condition humaine bowled me over when I first read it, first of all for its descriptive and imaginative power, and then for its deep commitment to the cause of the liberation of the masses by a revolution that would enable them to find their human dignity as individuals, perhaps paradoxically by violent mass action. The extent and danger of that paradox was not evident at the time – at least to the whole-hearted sympathizers with the anti-Fascist cause.

Le Temps du mépris, little more than a *récit* or *nouvelle*, disappointing even at the time for lack of the authentic Malraux creative power, seems even more so now that the topical appeal of its total commitment to the revolutionary Communist cause has evaporated, and cannot any longer obscure the serious artistic deficiencies.

L'Espoir was written at the height of the Spanish Civil War, long before the final defeat of the Republican cause and the disillusionment with the Communist role on the Republican side which followed it. It was heady stuff at the time for those committed to left-wing ideals, with its theme of 'organizing the Apocalypse' and its great descriptive scenes of action and suffering on the Republican side. Today, in spite of the many absorbing and unforced discussions of the philosophical background to that cause which appear in it, I cannot help feeling pretty strongly that it suffers from its unswerving commitment to an ideal that history has shown, not to be a sham but to have concealed too many uncomfortable truths. There seems to me no doubt that it was written too close to the actuality for detachment or perspective, not surprising in view of the fact that Malraux himself helped to organize the Republican air force and took a leading part in raising funds in the democratic countries. Again, and partly for the same reason, it suffers from a multiplicity of characters insufficiently differentiated, and a fragmentation of incidents.

Only *La Condition humaine*, I now feel, stands up today as a balanced and powerful work of outstanding originality. Malraux's sympathies are clearly with the Chinese revolutionaries; and yet the novel is designed to portray the varying attitudes to the revolutionary situation of characters of very different background and conviction – even among the revolutionaries themselves. The young Chinaman of Japanese education, Kyo, has joined the Communist cause, not because he is a proletarian seeking emancipation from his intolerable slave condition, as Katow is, but because he is inspired intellectually by the idea of human dignity; and it is significant that though he is in a sense the central and most fully explored character – perhaps because Malraux, of middle-class origin himself, can most easily identify with him – and though he makes the heroic gesture of refusing to betray his comrades to König, the police chief, in return for his life, the most heroic act of all is given to Katow, when, in the penultimate prison scene, he offers his cyanide pill to two of his fellow prisoners who fear the horrible death that awaits them more than he does himself. Katow transcends his human condition by dedicating his life to the struggle to emancipate his *class*; Kyo transcends it by sacrificing his life for an ideal of human brotherhood which is beyond his class background. Tchen, again, has a subtly differentiated motivation; assassin and terrorist – and therefore not a disciplined party Communist – his life, with all its bitterness and hatred of the class enemies, is given meaning by violence; and Malraux's unmistakable suggestion is that violence is in any case necessary to his temperament, even though in the situation in which he acts it is in the service of the revolutionary struggle.

Against these revolutionaries, effectively deepening the perspective in which we see them, Malraux places several other major characters. First, Kyo's father, Gisors, the contemplative teacher whose pupil Tchen has been in his earlier youth. Gisors is obviously sympathetic to the revolutionary cause, but believes in love without violence, and is separated from the scene of action by his vice of opium smoking; which is at the same time more than a vice, rather his own deliberately chosen and traditionally Chinese way of transcending the human condition. He is a link not only with Kyo and Tchen, but also with two other leading characters, Clappique and Ferral. Baron Clappique is perhaps the most interesting and unexpected creation in the novel: neither, strictly speaking, on the side of the revolutionaries nor of the oppressors, he lives by fantasy and the gift of making a mythical image of himself. He transcends his condition, one might say, by never acknowledging it. What makes Ferral tick, on the other hand, is simply the will to power. He is the representative of Western capitalism, the seemingly omnipotent financier who pulls the strings behind the scenes and is responsible for Chiang Kai-shek's betrayal of the Communists. Without the will to power, which is revealed as dominating his sexual life as well as his business dealings, Ferral is nothing; and Malraux, by a fine stroke of irony, shows him cheated of his power at the end by the Paris bankers behind the consortium for which he has acted.

It can thus be seen that *La Condition humaine* is far removed from the simplified and incomplete drama of *Les Conquérants*, and a far richer intellectual achievement than *L'Espoir*, where, for example, no attempt is made to explore the minds of the anti-Republicans gathered under Franco's banner.

There is one element in all Malraux's pre-war novels which I have never been able to take without a qualm: his continual insistence on the concepts of Destiny and Fate, always repugnant, I believe, to Anglo-Saxon taste, for the rhetorical and sententious note they strike. One should not, however, for that reason refuse to examine them more closely, for they are central to Malraux's thought. The most explicit statement of the concept of Destiny does not in fact occur in his work until *Les Noyers de l'Altenburg*, where, in the section devoted to the Altenburg colloquy, Vincent Berger (surely the character Malraux most closely identifies with himself) says:

> We know that we did not choose to be born, that we would not choose to die. That we did not choose our parents. That we can do nothing about the passage of time. That between each one of us and universal life there is a sort of . . . gulf. When I say that every man is deeply conscious of the existence of fate, I mean he is conscious – and almost always tragically so, at certain moments at least – of the world's independence of him.

Nearly all the major characters in the novels are aware of this Existentialist predicament (and I think it worth remarking in passing that Malraux is without doubt the precursor of the Existentialism that in the Forties became so manifest in the work of Sartre and Camus). Destiny, appearing as an absurdity in human existence that must somehow or other be overcome in order to make it meaningful, is something that all his heroes have to struggle with. Allied with it, again and again, is the concept of *fraternité virile* and *amour viril*. It seems to me that this concept, appearing as it does so often in Malraux's work, has all too rarely received the attention it deserves, perhaps because the author himself has given the impression of being shy of elucidating it.

In another writer, a reader liable to jump to conclusions might assume from such an obsession with *fraternité virile* a more than intellectual bias towards his own sex. In the case of Malraux, of course, we may dismiss any conclusion of this sort at once; but it is surely not unfair to observe that heroic action or adventure is always undertaken by men, sometimes alone but with the aim of helping their fellow men, sometimes together – but never with women. In fact women, with only two or three not very persuasive exceptions (e.g. Kassner's wife), play hardly any part in the novels. The concept of *amour viril* has, one might say, an Homeric ambience. And, when it is first adumbrated in *La Voie royale*, it appears linked with the idea of death; that is, it is an attitude especially strong among men who are obsessed with death in one way or another. It is interesting in this connection also to note the recurrent appearance of what one could call the Socratic relationship: the association of a young man with an older man at whose feet he sits in an intimacy rather closer than that of mere disciple – Gisors and Tchen, for example.

The Nietzschean will to power; the concepts of Destiny and Fate in their Existentialist context; and the necessity in action of *fraternité virile*; these seemed to me in the Thirties the chief philosophical themes that dominated Malraux's thinking, themes which I now see as far more important than the Marxist framework of ideas which he appropriated for a time. But the immense influence that he has exercised over his own generation (and it would seem also over succeeding generations) is surely due, not to his treatment of these themes alone, but to the fact that the novels in which he dramatizes them are the crystallization of a myth he has acted out, at least in part, in his own life.

Three other outstanding writers come to mind, whose careers have followed a not dissimilar parabola: Byron, Rimbaud, and Lawrence of Arabia. And I find it significant that the last two at least are particularly dear to Malraux. What is also noteworthy is that all three had strong temperamental leanings towards their own sex, Rimbaud and Lawrence most unmistakably, while Byron, famous as the great lover of women in his lifetime, in the light of modern research is now known to have been strongly attracted by boys and young men as well as women. In fact he is on record as declaring that his feelings for his own sex, at least in the guise of passionate friendship, meant more to him than any other relationship in his short life. All three, in fact, found *amour viril* in one form or another, a necessity in their lives.

Byron projected himself in the ultra-romantic figure of Childe Harold, a rebel against the corrupt and reactionary society of his time, and a voice that calls to the Greeks to revive the glories of their past. In the end, he is forced to *become* Childe Harold by the power of his own legend: he takes up arms for the Greeks and dies for the cause (even if not actually on the battlefield). But what would have happened if Byron had survived? Surely we have an inkling in that very different, great unfinished poem *Don Juan*, in which the heroic attitudinizing is already gone, and is in fact lightly mocked. Byron would have had to find a way to compromise with a more humdrum world, perhaps as a radical member of the House of Lords and satirist of the conceits of his time; for the legend has to vanish at the will of the myth-maker, in order, paradoxically, to live on.

In Rimbaud's case, the visionary young poet knows that he cannot sustain the image of precocious genius, rebel against the literary establishment of his time and all comfortable bourgeois values, into middle life; he disappears into Africa, to earn his living as a hard-headed colonial trader.

T. E. Lawrence again projects himself, with consummate skill, as a legendary figure, the leader of the Arabs in their insurrection against the Ottoman Empire, and when the war is over finds himself confronted by the same problem. His solution is to vanish into the anonymity of the Royal Air Force.

In Malraux's case, the strands are complex, but the pattern is basically the same. From the first, he had wished to present himself as a man of action: to begin with, as an explorer. *La Voie royale* is the story of a Frenchman, Claude Vannec, who sets out for Cambodia in order to discover forgotten and ruined Khmer temples, and bring their sculptures back to Europe by hook or by crook – and enrich himself by selling them to dealers. In the course of his journey he meets another adventurer, Perken, a Dane who owns a huge estate in a remote part of Siam, and who needs money to buy machine-guns to protect his local powers. They join forces, and in fact should, I think, be considered from the novelist's point of view as two aspects of one character. The theme is basically the struggle of the will against destiny: Perken is cheated of success in their adventure – *after* they have discovered some priceless sculptures – by a simple accident which results in his death, the Absurd thus triumphing in the end. The difficulty of taking this adventure as truly heroic lies, of course, in the fact that the aim is pure spoliation for commercial gain. And precisely the same difficulty arises in connection with the author's own adventure out of which the novel is created. In his early twenties Malraux himself set out for Cambodia to find and hack out sculptures from ancient temples, and was eventually arrested for looting historical monuments. With a mythomaniac's instinct already highly developed, Malraux managed to cast a cloud of obscurity over this episode; but there seems little doubt about the essential facts, however one may judge them. He was, after all, not the first archaeologist to consider that he had a right to the finds he made.

*La Voie royale** is not only interesting as Malraux's first attempt of any importance to embody in fiction his obsessional theme of the struggle of man's will against Destiny and the Absurd, but also for two other

* Though not published until 1930, it nevertheless seems certain that it was started, and temporarily abandoned, before the writing of *Les Conquérants*, published in 1928.

reasons. First, his lifelong preoccupation with ancient art and its significance in man's contemporary life, which was many years later to become dominant; and, second, for the fact that at one time he toyed with the idea of presenting it as the first in a series of novels with the general title of *Les Puissances du désert*, surely an indication of his already deep fascination with Lawrence of Arabia.

The explorer, facing hostile nature and unsophisticated peoples – peoples who seem to have scarcely more individual meaning than the insects of the jungle – is thus Malraux's original legend-making conception of himself. But before *La Voie royale* was completed, his preoccupation was changing to revolutionary action. He appears to have been in Indochina again in 1925–6, and to have taken some part in the political struggle there. The new incarnation of the legend emerges in *Les Conquérants*, in my opinion an even more unsatisfactory novel than *La Voie royale*. It is best to see it as Malraux's first raw attempt to present himself in the thick of revolutionary events, and to breathe into the Communist struggle the internal drama of his Existentialist preoccupations. As I have tried to show, in *La Condition humaine*, the masterpiece which follows it, the novelist gets the better of the myth-maker. It is not until *L'Espoir* that the novelist and the mythomaniac converge again. Though the actual extent of Malraux's active military involvement in the Spanish Civil War, through his organization of the Republican air force, remains in detail uncertain (again the mists have descended), his presence and engagement are incontestable as a leader in the drama he is making his novel out of. The very uncertainty may have magnified the shadow of the legend; though the thought occurs to one that he may have experienced a certain frustration in not being able to play as large a part in the Spanish Civil War as Lawrence played – or is portrayed by himself as playing – in the Arab Revolt.

Now it seems perfectly clear that after writing *L'Espoir*, and directing the film of the book himself just before the final collapse of the Republicans, Malraux, like so many other intellectuals who had been inspired by the ideals of the Popular Front, experienced a profound revulsion against the Communist International and the political attitudes it demanded of the anti-Fascist movement. It is plain enough, at least by implication, in *Les Noyers de l'Altenburg*, and has been confirmed by Malraux's own admissions. The War of 1939–45 only suspended the solution to the problem with which this disillusionment faced the mythomaniac. It is true that Malraux's wartime activity keeps up a certain legendary quality: his capture by the Germans in a tank battle; his escape to Vichy France; his second escape and Resistance activity;

his loss of the notes for *La Lutte avec l'Ange* to the Gestapo (remember Lawrence again, and Reading station); his final incarnation of Colonel Berger (taking the pseudonym from the hero of *Les Noyers*) fighting with the resuscitated French army in the last battles of the war. But when the Armistice came, he was faced once more with the unresolved problem of the future of the legend, the same problem which, *mutatis mutandis*, had faced Rimbaud and Lawrence and would, I believe, have faced Byron. Even the most heroic soldiers and Resistance leaders have to lay down their arms and don civvies when peace comes.

Malraux's solution was swiftly arrived at. It was as startling at the time as it was seen to be characteristic afterwards. There was only one Man of Destiny visible in France in the aftermath of the war, only one man in whom the mystique of the heroic will appeared to be incarnated. Malraux declared unreserved allegiance to de Gaulle, and remained loyal to him to the very end. Thus the man of action died to be reborn as politician and civil servant; but the rebirth took place in circumstances, unlike Lawrence's which consisted of total self-humiliation, that related, to some extent and in a different key as it were, to the former legend. If de Gaulle was, in a sense, Malraux's Abyssinia, it was an Abyssinia, unlike Rimbaud's, in the full glare of publicity. No fiction followed, and in the books on art which he began to write he was able to pursue, in immense detail and ramification, the idea which had already surfaced more than once in his fiction: that the creation of works of art is man's surest answer to the Existentialist predicament.

The first thing that strikes the reader about *Les Noyers de l'Altenburg* is, as I have already suggested, the total absence of political engagement. On the contrary, the recurrent theme is the endurance of man as a human being with his age-old, unchanging needs, occupations, and basic human responses, through all historical changes, through wars and revolutions and also through the disputatious theorizing of intellectuals who are vain enough to believe that they are capable of influencing the fundamental human condition. A change indeed from the heroic dreams of a revolution that will give back to each man his human dignity, to find Malraux concluding, through the person of Vincent Berger, that though to an intelligent inquirer into the metamorphoses of civilization, 'humanity's successive psychic states are invariably different', nevertheless there is something, below the level of the intellect and the various formulations of state and religion, fundamental and unchanging about man. Vincent Berger has a blinding flash of intuition about this as, at the end of the colloquy, he finds himself face to face with the centuries-old walnut trees – the *noyers* of the title – in the grounds of the priory:

The magnificence of the venerable trees was due to their great bulk, but the strength with which the twisted branches sprang from their enormous trunks, the bursting into dark leaves of this wood which was so heavy and so old that it seemed to be digging down into the earth and not sprouting from it, created at the same time an impression of free will and of endless metamorphosis.

Malraux has always claimed that *Les Noyers* is only a fragment or sketch which was likely to be changed when *La Lutte avec l'Ange* (an image which first appeared in his essay on Lawrence) was continued and completed. Nevertheless, the book appears to be very carefully designed as a self-sufficient entity. It opens, as it closes, with a section about the 1939–45 war, presented as personal experience of the narrator as a tank commander who is taken prisoner by the Germans and herded with the other French prisoners in Chartres Cathedral. Within this framework are three longer episodes, each describing experiences of the narrator's father, Vincent Berger. The first is concerned with his adventures as trusted adviser to the Young Turks in their revolt against Abdul the Damned. In this episode one is bound to see Vincent as a transposed image of Malraux himself: Vincent has a passionate interest in Nietzsche, he is drawn to regions of the world spiritually remote from Europe, he finds fulfilment in conspiratorial revolutionary action – and in 'war comradeship, friendship'. And he returns to Europe a figure enveloped in legend. At first it may seem that these adventures have little to do with what follows; but it is important to remember that Vincent ends by being *disillusioned* with his conspiratorial activity, and when he comes back it is for stage II of his spiritual education. This takes place at the ancient priory of Altenburg in Alsace, where Vincent's brother Walter has established an annual gathering of European intellectuals. Obviously based on the famous *décades de Pontigny*, at which the young Malraux himself made a sensational impression between the wars, the episode is a firework display of ideas on the theme chosen for the colloquy: 'Is there any meaning to the idea of man?' They are handled by Malraux with brilliant dialectical skill. And yet the tone is unmistakably, though never crudely, ironic; an attitude all the more remarkable as it is difficult not to see the various strands of Malraux's own thought embodied in the different participants. All through he emphasizes, with a few light touches, the alienation of the intellectuals from life as it is lived: while the argument inside the room is at its most heated, he notes, for instance, that men from the village were loading tree-trunks outside, just as they had done in the Middle Ages.

After Vincent's personal revelation in the presence of the ancient walnut trees, the section ends with the ominous words: 'There had been no war in Europe for forty years' – prelude to the third section, where Vincent, as an Alsatian enrolled in the German army, finds himself on the Eastern Front, facing the Russians. This section is famous for the description of the gas attack (so oddly included in the *Anti-mémoires* seeing that Malraux never experienced it), one of the finest set-pieces of dramatic description in the whole of his work. But as remarkable to my mind as the gas attack itself, is the description of the talk of the soldiers before it takes place: an absolutely authentic mixture of fantasy, folklore, distorted facts picked up in bars and newspapers, and earthy commonsense. Neither ideology nor flag-waving patriotism here. The point of it is crystal-clear: man's feeling for man, as in the poems of Wilfred Owen, beyond the war-makers and the warring ideologies, emerges in the ultimate horrors of war experience as the most powerful element in human nature.

Malraux was not, of course, alone among novelists in emphasizing this lesson of war. What is remarkable is that it should be Malraux, previously so deeply committed to the necessity of revolutionary action and the justification of the means by the ends, who should finally have stated, in fictional form, and with such overwhelming dramatic effect, that the ends never justify the means.

Les Noyers de l'Altenburg was thus, as I have already suggested, a renunciation of the former bases of the legend even before his activity as an underground anti-Nazi leader. It is difficult to resist the thought that he may have dreamed that the completed *Lutte avec l'Ange* would be his *Seven Pillars of Wisdom*; but, Gestapo or no Gestapo, one can also see, what he saw so clearly himself, that, in the form in which he had cast it, it would never do as a first volume. If there had been no de Gaulle, perhaps he would have hidden himself away and re-written it as a greater masterpiece than *La Condition humaine*. Or would the impulse to devote himself to the study of the meaning of art have been too insistent to be denied even before de Gaulle? Nowhere, previously, had he expressed his conviction about art more forcibly than in the 'colloquy', directly after the definition of Destiny I have already quoted:

To me our art seems to be a rectification of the world, a means of escaping from man's estate. The chief confusion, I think, is due to our belief – and in the theories we have propounded of Greek tragedy, it's strikingly clear – that representing fatality is the same as submitting to it. But it's not, it's almost possessing it. The mere fact of being able to represent it, conceive it, release it from real fate, from the merciless human scale, reduces it to the human scale. Fundamentally our art is a humanization of the world.

Malraux as a young musketeer or marquis.

Malraux with his son Gauthier, at Cap d'Aïl, *c.* 1942.
Malraux, *c.* 1951, with his daughter Florence, who was later to marry the film director Alain Resnais.

Josette Clotis, mother of Malraux's two sons, at Cap d'Aïl, *c.* 1942.

Malraux with his two sons Gauthier and Vincent, looking at his collection of Hopi Indian dolls.

Statue on the central pavilion of the temple at Banteai-Sïey.

The temple of Banteai-Sïey in Cambodia.

The young archaeologists – Malraux and Louis Chevasson in Saigon, 1924.

OPPOSITE Malraux in 1933 at the time he was awarded the Prix Goncourt for *La Condition humaine*.

LEFT Malraux with Eisenstein in Moscow, 1934. The Russian film director was then considering filming *La Condition humaine*.

RIGHT Malraux, Meyerhoff and Pasternak in Moscow, 1934, during the International Congress of Writers.

BELOW Malraux with André Gide (*right*) at a meeting in aid of the victims of Fascism, Paris, 1935..

ICI FUT ARRÊTÉ
LE 7 JANVIER 1945
PAR LA 1ᴵᴱᴿᴱ D.F.L. ET LA
BRIGADE ALSACE-LORRAINE
L'OFFENSIVE ENNEMIE SUR
STRASBOURG

OPPOSITE Malraux in the *maquis*, *c.* 1943–4.

TOP Malraux, Albert Camus (*left*) and Jacques Baumel at the offices of the paper *Combat*, 1944.

LEFT Malraux on his return from the Alsace–Lorraine campaign, 1945.

ABOVE Plaque commemorating the stopping by Malraux's brigade of the German offensive on Strasbourg.

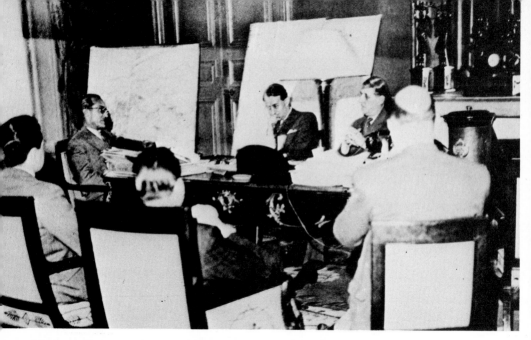

Meeting in the rue Saint-Dominique during the first government of General de Gaulle, 1945. Malraux was then Minister for Information.

General de Gaulle with Malraux as his Minister for Cultural Affairs at the Opéra, c. 1959.

Working with Nehru in New Delhi, 1958.

Meeting with Chou-en-laï, Peking, August 1965.

Looking at the Nochi Cascade.

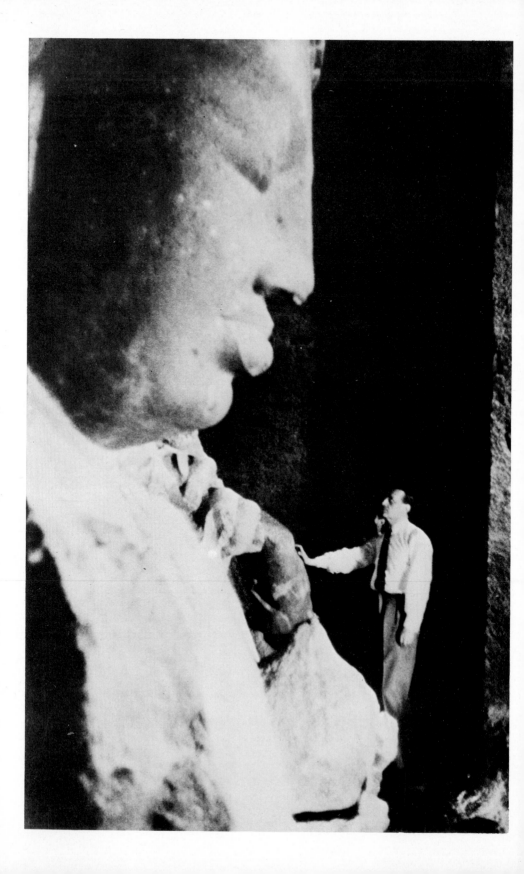

ABOVE With Chagall, looking at the ceiling of the Paris Opera House which he commissioned from him.

OPPOSITE Malraux at Elephanta, India, 1958.

With Le Corbusier after decorating him with the *Légion d'honneur*.

Malraux at Braque's funeral.

ABOVE *Malraux's* Musée réel: In the 1930s with his 3rd-century Afghan Boddhisattva.

ABOVE A pastel by Picasso.
BELOW The entrance to Malraux's house at Verrières-le-Buisson; a Dogon mask on a table by Higuily.

Malraux's Mexican bull; traditional art.

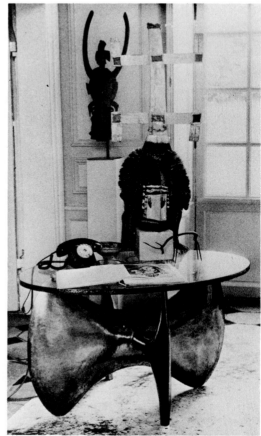

OPPOSITE Malraux with Jacqueline Kennedy in Washington, January 1963.

Notes from Malraux to various members of his staff at the Ministry.

Doodles of a Minister for Cultural Affairs.

At his favourite restaurant, Laserre.

It may seem that I have treated André Malraux in these pages, mainly devoted as they are to a study of his fiction in relation to his mythomania, not only as a novelist of ideas but as a novelist only of ideas. This is certainly not the impression, the conclusion I want to leave. I have said that to the Anglo-Saxon reader his obsession with the concepts of Destiny and Fate, and the rhetorical flourishes which this obsession so often inspires throughout the novels, all this essential element is distasteful, even sometimes embarrassing. We are more than a little inclined to accuse him of sententiousness and humourlessness. I have tried to show that the obsession goes much deeper than the rhetoric with which it is sometimes expressed, and that we should recognize the validity of a tradition foreign to our own. But Malraux would not have achieved his undoubted international status if he had not been able to capture the imagination of his contemporaries by other, more basic literary skills as well. Above all, his mastery of the French language. No one can read a few chapters of one of the great novels without realizing the richness, the colour and intellectual precision of his vocabulary. And, allied to this, his superb capacity for creating dramatic atmosphere. I think in particular of the gas attack I have just mentioned; of the scene in the prison at the end of *La Condition humaine*, where the captured revolutionaries await a death which is to consist of being thrown into the furnace of a railway engine; of the episode in *L'Espoir*, where Manuel visits a hospital in which a wounded young airman keeps up an endlessly repeated hoarse screaming. But it is not only in these scenes of *terribiltà* that he excels, but also in pure descriptive atmosphere, as in those extraordinary pages that lead up to the dis-covery of the ruined temples in *La Voie royale*, in which he makes the putrescence of the jungle a vast symbol of the forces of decay and death. Nor should one forget those other scenes of action in which he gives one the feeling that one is present, with all one's senses and nerves alive. From all that he has written, one cannot fail to notice that he takes an especial delight and pride in scenes of action in the air. The episode of the attack on the hidden airfield in *L'Espoir*, for instance, is hauntingly memorable, and it is hard to believe that it is not based on personal experience; far more significant and more dramatic to my mind, than the often quoted description of the flight to Prague in *Le Temps du mépris*. Kassner is a rather boring character, and once he has been released from his Nazi prison (so oddly controlled, not by the Gestapo or the ss but by the sa) one does not care very much whether he reaches the Czech airport or lands in a turnip field, miles away, upside-down; but in Magnin's flight with the peasant to find the hidden Fascist aeroplanes the tension is superbly developed and maintained: one is in the air with them, one's sympathies totally engaged. And, finally, the power which he displays supremely in *La Condition humaine*, a power which recalls Dickens and Dostoevsky, of creating an enveloping atmosphere for a whole novel. Every time I read that novel, I am more impressed by the way in which Malraux suggests that the action takes place in a brooding and sinister darkness in which the city glows dully like a dying coal, sinister with the imminence of terrible events and brooding with the restless, doom-laden self-questioning of the chief actors; a darkness penetrated by the recurrent thematic 'noises off': vibrations coming as if from the depths of the earth, ships' sirens and hooting of the picket boats, the sudden bursts of firing from the invisible armoured train and the thudding of the hidden printing presses.

MANÈS SPERBER

*

MALRAUX AND POLITICS

FAME AND SCORN

In France, the years between the First and Second World Wars were the years of the committed writer. They were a period of renown for authors who openly used their talents and social positions to support aesthetic, social or political movements. Ever since then, André Breton, Georges Bernanos, Louis-Ferdinand Céline, Louis Aragon, Drieu la Rochelle and André Malraux – the youngest of them all – have had a lasting influence, not only on their immediate contemporaries, but also on later generations. Each of these names stands for a typical case although and because it is unique. That applies especially to Malraux. He became famous when he was still very young, and from the outset his literary fame was linked to his reputation as a political militant and as a *maître à penser*, a pioneering thinker of the young Left.

Even so, few writers have been attacked quite so often and quite so maliciously as André Malraux. Attacks on Malraux multiplied after he had come out in support of post-war Gaullism; but even before that time he had been the target of a systematic campaign of denigration, conducted against him by the Communist Party, because of his role in the anti-German Resistance movement. Towards the end of 1944, Malraux had successfully opposed the impending takeover by the Communist Party of some of the most important Resistance groups. The hostile campaign against him eventually also affected non-Communists, who accused him of treason against the cause of the Left. Stalinism was just then at the height of its power. A great many left-wing intellectuals, together with opportunists of every description, used the occasion to curry favour with the Communists. The slightest occasion was enough to make them join in the chorus of the slanderers and defamers who denounced Malraux (as also Sartre, for a time, along with many others) as a 'hyena of the typewriter in the service of Wall Street'. To quote only one of these libellous allegations, which was highly characteristic as well as particularly stupid, they maintained that Malraux had become a deserter from the very air squadron which he himself had organized in Spain, explaining that this alleged desertion occurred just at the moment when the Republican government ceased to pay him in dollars.

In the early 1950s Malraux gave up all political activities in order to devote himself exclusively to his wide-ranging studies of the philosophy of art. That did not stop the polemics against him, but they gradually lost their cutting edge. In 1958 he was again put in charge of a ministry. Immediately afterwards, attacks on him redoubled once again. He was attacked in particular for his Gaullism, although he did not in fact become a member of the Gaullist Party. Practically all the initiatives and measures which he took as Minister of Culture were, at least in the beginning, ruthlessly criticized and maliciously scorned. Even rather bourgeois newspapers abroad published extensive reports designed to demonstrate that the Minister of Culture, the former writer André Malraux, had become an inefficient reactionary and a merely pathetic buffoon. This hate campaign expressed, among other things, the almost total opposition of both the intellectual Left and the ultra-Right to the person of General de Gaulle, to his policies as well as to all his collaborators.

Then, in 1967, there appeared wholly unexpectedly – despite several prior announcements – Malraux's *Antimémoires*. As a result, even the author's hitherto most irreconcilable critics stopped their attacks. The book was discussed in countless long reviews. Hardly any of them subjected the author to political criticism. Malraux was lauded to the skies as if he had suddenly undergone a complete transformation and had once again become the old, that is to say the young, Malraux. Those who had never tired of asking how one could possibly account for his treason, meaning his loyalty to de Gaulle and to the latter's tortuous policies, behaved all of a sudden as if the whole issue had been, or had become, irrelevant.

This astonishing reaction suggests a confusion on several levels. For we may discover that the many former admirers of the young Malraux were no less mistaken about his real political views than his present political opponents are who can see nothing but his supposedly fanatical Gaullism. In other words, it may emerge that Malraux was never a Communist and thus could not have become a renegade. It may even turn out that Malraux's Gaullism, though meaning all sorts of things, has very little political meaning and no ideological meaning at all. Nevertheless, some facts are indisputable. Malraux stuck to General de Gaulle even at moments when this loyalty forced him to support, or countenance silently, all sorts of policy twists which he would otherwise have disparaged or even actively opposed. That caused him at times to shift his political position from one day to the next. For de Gaulle, though upholding his ultimate goal, pursued it with the often changing stratagems, with the cunning propaganda and the sudden reversals of policy which are the hallmark of the Machiavellian opportunist.

Where then does Malraux stand politically? I shall return to this question in a roundabout way. For it can be answered only in the light of all that he has done and represented in the course of his long, militantly active and highly creative life.

Only two facts should be mentioned at the outset. In contrast to most French writers, including anti-Fascist and Communist writers, Malraux refused to publish anything in France during the years of the German occupation. The novel *Les Noyers de l'Altenburg*, which he wrote at that time, was first published in Switzerland, and only after the war in France.

Malraux never altered or suppressed even a single page of any of his books which were reprinted in new editions. He has stood by everything that he ever published. That will not surprise people who understand his work and the inner logic of his development. But it must be stressed just because there have been many instances in recent decades of authors who later denied their one-time self and subsequently acted as their own censors. One need only recall Sartre's ban on further performances of his political play *Les Mains sales*, or the elaborate changes which Aragon lately introduced into his trilogy *Les Communistes*.

THE COINCIDENCE

André Malraux was born on 3 November 1901 in the centre of Paris, in the Butte Montmartre. His father chased after fortune with intermittent success. He was several times reduced to bankruptcy and eventually committed suicide. (It is instructive to take note of the fact that many writers come from families which suffered economic and social degradation. This incisive experience seems to further the growth of both an extreme form of social sensitivity and an urge for creative overcompensation.)

At the outbreak of the First World War, Malraux was not yet quite thirteen years old. By the time the war ended he had become a precocious young man. The defeated countries were shaken by revolutions which destroyed mighty empires and seemed, at long last, to turn nightmares into realized wishdreams. There followed, in victorious France, *les années folles*, the crazy years. The survivors sought to drown their memories in a desperate all-pervading zest in living. They sought to blot out the memory of the ten million needlessly murdered war victims and to forget themselves and their tragically lost and wasted years. Everything exotic acquired a special magnetism, for instance the art of the Far East, which at that time was rediscovered and imbued with a topical significance.

Sick as it was of its own suicidal frenzy, Europe abandoned its conviction that other civilizations could neither teach it lessons nor set examples. Too much had happened or was happening – the Russian revolution and the upheavals in the defeated countries and, in the victorious countries, the gnawing doubts as to whether their triumph had been not only too costly, but perhaps altogether futile. All this, though not only this, drove a new generation to try to see itself and its own world with the eyes of others and to look on its own civilization as merely one among many conceivable civilizations; as a mere transient episode that might even never have been.

Europe – you have left me surrounded by nothing but an empty horizon and the mirror held out by despair, that ancient teacher of desolation. Maybe it, too, will perish of its own being. Far away in the port a siren howls like an abandoned dog. The voice of vanquished cowardice. . . .

These lines come from the first important essay, which the then twenty-four-year-old Malraux published in the form of a correspondence under the title of *La Tentation de l'Occident – The Temptation of the West*. A more appropriate title, in more than one respect, would have been *The Temptation of the East*.

In his adolescence Malraux turned to art with a truly passionate interest. He was a tireless visitor of museums, exhibitions and art collections, so that even before he had turned twenty he had acquired a special knowledge of the palaces and temples of Indochina which survived from the past or had been newly dug up. Convinced that he would know where to discover unsuspected or neglected treasures, he boldly decided to undertake archaeological digs of his own. In making this decision, he was mainly motivated by intellectual curiosity and ambition, but he also intended to take the most precious pieces of the sculptures he hoped to discover back to Paris, where he planned to sell them so as to get rich quickly and become materially independent.

By December 1923, a very youthful André Malraux had succeeded in unearthing statues buried in the jungle. After all sorts of obstacles he managed to transfer them to a port. The young dreamer, it turned out, had worked intelligently and carefully. The dismayed subalterns in Indochina and the higher civil servants in Paris had only one way of washing their hands of the whole affair; they disavowed their young compatriot and handed him over to the courts.

It was the time of China's national, anti-imperialist revolution. Supported by the Soviet Union and assisted by Russian advisers, Chiang Kai-shek's armies marched from victory to victory. Their irresistible advance stimulated our imagination and encouraged the hope that the frustrated world revolution would come back to the heartland of Europe by way of China.

It was the brief, illusory interval between the post-war period and the new pre-war period. The relative stabilization of the capitalist economy, together with its rationalization and the frenetic advance of industrial technology, produced a boom in which general living standards went on rising. Nobody in the Western world believed that revolutionary movements could revive in the foreseeable future. In the Soviet Union, too, the emphasis was on reconstruction. The mixed economy which Lenin had inaugurated under the name of NEP (New Economic Policy) was ill-suited to arouse the enthusiasm of a new generation.

That was the moment in Malraux's life when coincidence assumed a major significance. Thanks to a coincidence, which nobody had intended and which came about as a result of purely personal circumstances, Malraux was detained in Indochina. He had appealed against a two-year prison sentence and had to remain to prepare for his trial. Initially out of sheer sensationalism, and later for political reasons, the colonial Press made him the target of a pernicious campaign of denigration. So as to counter this campaign and also for reasons of his own, Malraux involved himself with growing vehemence in the fight against the conditions in the French colony. The young Parisian, whose thinking had been chiefly dominated by aesthetic ideas, became embattled in the struggle against the exploiters of distress, the insatiable profiteers, the colonial administration and its pen-pushing parasites who tried to disguise and embellish these conditions in the name of French civilization. He found kindred souls, not only among the native intelligentsia, but also among Frenchmen. One of them was Paul

Monin, a young lawyer and politician who had frequently and coura-
geously pleaded the rights and the cause of the oppressed. Monin had,
moreover, close connections with the Chinese inhabitants of Saigon,
and through them with the Kuomintang. In the years 1924–5, Malraux
edited, jointly with Monin, the paper *Indochine* and wrote for it forty
long articles which are worth reading even today.

Malraux had gone to Indochina in order to unearth the bas-reliefs
of the buried temple of Banteay-Srei in Cambodia. He did not suddenly
turn into a political revolutionary at the age of twenty-five. Yet the
more he saw of the appalling conditions in which the indigenous
population, especially the intelligentsia and the peasants, were condemned to vegetate or even to perish, the greater became his conviction
that it would henceforth be impossible for him to live and behave as if
these wrongs and misfortunes did not exist.

Malraux had remained an enthusiastic supporter of the aesthetic
permanent revolution to which, incidentally, he owed his early
maturity. But thanks to his enforced stay in Indochina, he developed
simultaneously into an anti-colonialist rebel. In this, as in many other
respects, he was a pioneer. His increasingly sharp conflict with the
ruling classes was inspired, not by the short-term or long-term interests
of the French or European proletariat, but by the then merely incipient
contest for the freedom and identity of the Third World.

PASCAL AND CHINA

This may explain why Malraux's first novel, *Les Conquérants*, centred on
an important episode of the Chinese revolution during the period when
the author was still in Indochina. The form of the book made many
readers and reviewers mistake it for autobiographical reportage, and
this in turn helped to promote the legend of the significant role which
Malraux is supposed to have played in China – a legend from which
the author has never been able altogether to dissociate himself. Even
a man with so penetrating a mind as Trotsky believed that Garine,
the European revolutionary and hero of the novel, was Malraux himself. The notion thus spread that André Malraux had been politically
active in Canton and other Chinese cities, that he had closely cooperated
with Chiang Kai-shek, and that the latter had finally put him in charge
of Kuomintang propaganda.

Even a superficial glance at his biographical data should have made
it easy for anybody to discover that Malraux had no part in the military
or political actions of the Chinese revolution. That emerges plainly
from the easily accessible chronology of his various journeys and his

prolonged residence in Indochina and Paris between 1923 and 1926, to say nothing of the fact that he was still extremely young and unknown. All this should have sufficed to destroy the legend, but the penchant for preferring legend to truth is not the monopoly of simpletons or imaginative youths. There is, however, an additional reason why even a man like Trotsky failed to reject the transparent fabrication about Malraux's first novel. One of its special merits is its distinctive form of realistic imagination. Its realism conveys such a perfect impression of immediacy that the reader is driven to identify the extraordinarily lifelike fictive hero with the author himself, while mistaking the partly fictitious and partly real events of the novel for the author's own experiences.

Malraux's third novel, *La Condition humaine*, takes the reader back to China. The time is the year 1927, during which the victorious leader of the Kuomintang succeeded in achieving a twofold conquest of Shanghai. Having put the enemy troops to rout, he wrecked the military and political organizations of the Shanghai Communists. He then proceeded to exterminate all their leaders, who had just been on the point of trying to seize power for themselves. Almost all reviewers described *La Condition humaine* as a masterpiece, and in December 1933 its author was awarded the Prix Goncourt for it. Trotsky wrote about this novel too, and he once again overrated Malraux's own part in the crucial events of the time: 'In 1926, Malraux was in China; he worked there for the Kuomintang-Comintern; he is one of those who must be held responsible for the strangulation of the Chinese revolution.' In addition, Trotsky criticized Malraux for his allegedly inadequate or even wrong application of Marxism to the problems and actions of the Chinese revolution. The old revolutionary made this charge mainly because *La Condition humaine*, though somewhat less so than *Les Conquérants*, seemed to justify Stalin's policy in China, which Trotsky had rightly attacked from the very outset.

Les Conquérants describes the rebellion of the Chinese coolies who struggled for their dignity as working men, for their future as revolutionaries and for China's national independence. Among them, as one of their leaders, is Garine, a typical Malraux creation as well as the typical hero of the post-Dostoevsky philosophical novel. He knows precisely against what and whom he is fighting, but he rarely knows for what and for whom he is risking his life and whom he should regard as his true comrades-in-arms. He turns to impersonal action as a way of self-affirmation, as a way of affirming the meaning of his being in the daily and endless struggle against the threat of nothingness. Even at the hour of triumph, he still doubts that he will ever be able to overcome his own limitations and to transcend the confines of the *conditio humana*, man's enslavement by the conditions of his life. Perhaps Garine also doubts that victory is inevitable, and he certainly has his doubts about the meaning of victory. Malraux's first novel merely hints at all that, but Trotsky was particularly sensitive to hints of that nature and used them as the focal point for exposing the author's and his novel's 'political weakness'.

Gravely ill, Garine eventually makes his way back to Europe. He thinks: 'We shall conquer Shanghai within a year'; yet the author and his readers know that although Shanghai will indeed be conquered, it will almost immediately afterwards be turned into a mass grave of the revolutionaries, so that the very victory ends up in the most blood-stained defeat of the Chinese revolution. The novel is thus impregnated with the premonitions of disaster to come, and Trotsky, for all his political criticism, praised it highly.

As a tragedy, *La Condition humaine* is to prose what *Antigone* is to drama. In the end, nearly all its heroes die as the victims of unbearable tortures. In his dread of their common fate – tortures and death by fire – a young comrade gets from one of the novel's heroes the saving poison with which the latter could have protected himself from unspeakable torment. This act of sovereign humanity represents at the same time the most convincing achievement of human dignity. The novel puts greater emphasis than *Les Conquérants* on the brotherly solidarity of dignified men.

Among the survivors, there are May, the wife of Kyo, one of the revolutionary leaders, who at the crucial moment deceived him and now tries to take his place in the seemingly hopeless struggle; Gisors, Kyo's father, a professor of philosophy, who seeks refuge from his own insight and mourning in carefully dosed bouts of opium smoking; and Clappique, a crooked adventurer who, having failed from weakness, ends up by betraying the revolutionaries. What else remains in the city of Shanghai after the annihilation of the revolutionary forces? How much does the reader retain of it all? Nothing, it seems, except the certainty that the ultimate condition of human existence is as immutable as Blaise Pascal put it in this allegory: 'Let us imagine a number of men in chains, and all condemned to death, where some are killed each day in the sight of the others, and those who remain see their own fate in that of their fellows, and wait their turn, looking at each other sorrowfully and without hope.'

A return, in other words, to the point of departure, to the everlasting beginning which is an end. The bold plans and the even bolder risks end in torture and death. Everything that had been staked and squandered, that had been won and yet forfeited, was destined to lead the survivors back to one simple truth. Man may be allowed from time to time to batter at the walls; but in doing so he only experiences over and over again that the walls – and only the walls – are unassailable.

Was that the message which the thirty-two-year-old author wanted to bring home to his readers half a year after Hitler's advent to power? Perhaps so. But no doubt he also wanted to affirm the opposite. He set out to affirm his conviction that the best in man is inviolable. The best, in this context, includes man's potentially inexhaustible solidarity and fraternal friendship. It includes man's capacity to maintain his dignity, in the teeth of life's degradations, humiliations and disfranchisements, so that man's ever threatened and always dubious existence derives its ultimate meaning from his ability to maintain his dignity for its own sake.

La Condition humaine is a novel filled with stirring actions, with allegories on multiple levels and surprising hints, which every reader will take in his own way. The novel deals with events that took place more than forty years ago in a foreign city in a far away country. Yet, like all literary masterpieces, *La Condition humaine* retains a topicality which never fades and which, in a sense, is created afresh by each generation. It has that peculiar kind of topicality in which the time-lessness of true civilization achieves its varying forms of expression.

Was this novel solely concerned with a revolution which drowned in its own blood? Apparently so. It seems to be a novel in which politics dominates everything and determines the motives of every character until it turns into tragic fate. Yet in actual fact politics, in this novel, is merely the dialect of concreteness. As used here, this term is analagous to the term 'the dialect of the organs' which Alfred Adler coined in his *Individual Psychology* to characterize the manner in which mental disturbances are expressed in physical symptoms. For the philosopher-novelist of our day, politics is thus the raw material which can be handled and formed into events and experiences. Yet, at the same time, politics is also the writer's dialect of concreteness which enables him to depict his characters both in their isolation and metaphysical doubt and on their activating social existence which impels them into enthusiastic and often destructive acts of collective struggle, such as rebellions.

Trotsky set out to discover the extent to which *La Condition humaine* treated and interpreted the Chinese revolution in orthodox Marxist terms. Malraux, by contrast, conceived his novels as a quest for the meaning of an extreme form of political involvement – a meaning which may conceivably reveal itself only to those who created it beforehand. Malraux sought, not to explain, but to illuminate the contradiction between our hopeless individual isolation and our indissoluble collectivity; between life within the limits of time-bound conditions and the inevitable death which banishes us to the realm of timelessness and thus to absolute social suspension. That is the problem for Dostoevsky as much as for Malraux and the philosopher-novelists of our time – whether they express it in the dialect of political reality or in metaphysical allegories such as the paradigmatic novel which the young Albert Camus published under the title of *L'Etranger*.

'Why China? Why not the class struggles in Europe, in France, here in Paris, for example?' That was the question addressed to the novelist in the 1930s by workers from the Renault factories. In his reply, Malraux abstained from stressing the advantages of distantiation by transposition and explained that the situation in China and the initially victorious but later cruelly repressed revolution there had thrown the most vivid light on these very phenomena which he, the French novelist, had to use as the subject matter of his writing if he was to remain true to his task.

Why? Not least because he had personally witnessed how the heirs of an ancient culture had become the victims of colonial masters who exploited, oppressed and humiliated them to the very denial of their being.

The youthful André Malraux thus picked China for the scene of his first two revolutionary novels because he grasped, at that early period, the social, psychological and metaphysical problems of the men of the Third World which Franz Fanon, in a grossly exaggerated manner, was to pose at a much later stage. It would be interesting to investigate the link between the over-sensitivity with which Malraux, fifty years ago, reacted to the distress of the Third World and the systematic, arbitrarily exaggerated touchiness with which some Western youths today react against everything that could throw doubt on the claim and hopes of that Third World.

PILGRIMAGE INTO NOTHINGNESS

In 1930, in between his first novel, *Les Conquérants*, and the third, *La Condition humaine*, which is in a way its sequel, Malraux published a wholly unpolitical book – *La Voie royale*. It describes the archaeological adventure of a young Frenchman in Indochina who resembles the author in more ways than one. In *La Voie royale* Malraux first formulated his concept of art as *anti-fatum*; in epic form he described the interplay between nature and civilization, between the destroyer death and indestructible artistic creation. Remarkably enough, Malraux was not yet thirty years old when he expressed his views on this far-ranging theme, yet they contained in essence all that he was later to write on the philosophy of art in *Psychologie de l'art*, *Les Voix du silence* and *La Métamorphose des dieux*.(He worked on these books between 1947 and 1958.) If matters had gone according to biographical and literary logic, *La Voie royale* would have been Malraux's first novel. It is all the more revealing and significant for an understanding of the writer's development that this book, which was wedged in between two 'political' novels, seemed somehow to be displaced.

The seeming displacement becomes meaningful when one recalls what I said above about the process of concreteness. In writing *La Voie royale* or his last novel, *Les Noyers de l'Altenburg*, or, for that matter, his books and essays on the philosophy of art, Malraux merely employed a different dialect of concreteness for his approach to the same fundamental problem which reached its political concretion in his novels.

Was Malraux a Marxist when he wrote *Les Conquérants*? Was he no longer a Marxist when he wrote *La Voie royale*? And did he once more become a Marxist when he wrote *La Condition humaine* and, again later on, in 1935, when he wrote *Le Temps du mépris*? And once again, two years later, when he published the great novel of the Spanish Civil War, *L'Espoir*? Did he once more cease to be a Marxist when he wrote *Les Noyers de l'Altenburg* between 1940 and 1942, and later on his works on art mentioned above?

The problem of Malraux's 'Marxism' overlaps with another set of questions that has threatened to banish his political biography into the limbo of twilight. Was Malraux a Communist in the 1930s? Did he cease to be a Communist under the German occupation when he became the leader of a non-Communist resistance group and later on the commander of the Brigade Alsace-Lorraine? Was he or did he turn into a nationalist or even a reactionary in 1945, when he became a minister in de Gaulle's government, or soon afterwards when he became one of the leaders of the RPF, the movement created to bring the General back to power? From 1958 Malraux remained a minister for eleven years, and de Gaulle's unconditionally loyal supporter in fact as well as in appearance. Did he become a renegade when he turned to the Right? Did he perhaps even become a Fascist?

These two sets of questions are of course interrelated. The strange dichotomy of his literary output and his changing roles in the political struggle of our time are two closely linked problems.

It should be recalled in this context that Malraux republished his books – a very few stylistic changes apart – in exactly the form in which he had written and published them during his revolutionary period. That does not fit into the picture of a renegade. But how then can one explain his political career?

The first answer that comes to mind is intrinsic to the story of his life and work as outlined above. Malraux never renounced Pascal's question. On the contrary, he frequently transplanted it into the realm of politics and into those of his books which could be regarded as Communist. As he put it in his *Antimémoires*; '[I think of] death as it manifests itself in everything that is beyond man's control, in the ageing and even the metamorphosis of the earth ... and above all the irremediable, the sense that "you'll never know what it all meant". Faced with that question, what do I care about what matters only to me?'

When Malraux wrote this passage he was sixty-five years old. Yet the twenty-five-year-old Malraux had thought the same and had expressed it in a similar way. Even in that respect he was and remains a typical hero of our time. Throughout his ever-changing life, he manifested a truly astonishing constancy which was continually menaced yet always preserved. The continuity in his thinking and feeling came up against deadly challenges but it had the permanence of an obsession which stays the same, irrespective of the dialect of concreteness which it uses to express itself. In seeking to discover the value of artistic creation, the meaning of a work of art and its lasting effect, Malraux poses the same question that drove him into revolutionary action and made him the author of exemplary revolutionary novels. This problem can be stated as follows: Is it possible for man to change from a tool of destiny into its master? Is it possible for the lump of clay in the potter's hand to turn itself into a potter with power to form the clay?

The basic question which André Malraux poses in the above quoted passage from his *Antimémoires* and which, in his own view, is central to all his writing is: How does one live in the knowledge that one must die? If the future is in any case mortgaged to death, what point is there in actions which can achieve their objectives only tomorrow or the day after tomorrow? Why should one struggle to improve man's living conditions when one knows that, no matter who triumphs, ultimate defeat is inescapable because in the end death remains the only victor? On the other hand, how can one bear life as an individual, as an ephemera endowed with the intimation of an immortality that cannot be, without seeking escape in actions which may help one to forget that one is merely a dead man on leave?

When the young André Malraux changed from the dandy he pretended to be (though he was actually a man of letters obsessed by art) into a revolutionary partisan of the insulted and injured, this was perhaps an attempt to escape from the Pascalian dilemma. Pascal, we know, did not escape into action. He wrote of the wager according to which it is always more prudent for us to stake everything on the chance that God is, than to entrust ourselves, without God, to that instrument of destruction called life that has neither permanence nor consolation. Pascal's enlightenment illuminated the road, not to dusty death, but to true faith. Malraux, and others like him, especially men who came after him and began to write under his influence, such as Sartre and Camus, were different. They never forgot that they were caught in the net of an ubiquitous absurdity which, like a giant clown without consciousness and without conscience, pretends to be omnipotent. Ultimately, life threatens to remain an absurdity which parodies reason and injures self-confidence, unless creative or destructive man imposes on it a meaning which, once generalized, may overcome man's own transience.

Here, we come close to the swing of the pendulum which determines Malraux's pilgrimage. It leads him from the unbearable metaphysical awareness into actions which, as long as they continue, can rescue the individual from his isolation. Yet, once he recognizes the tragic vanity of action, he returns time and again to metaphysics. In Malraux's case, metaphysics, in its most adequate form, assumes the character of an all-inclusive act of questioning, a 'global interrogation'. From time to time he escapes from this pendulum movement, from this pilgrimage without a Mecca, by means of his philosophical interpretation of art as the *anti-fatum*, a force capable of conquering fate.

BETWEEN ACTION AND CREATION

Even so, for Malraux action has retained an irresistible temptation. Intellectuals tend to be attracted by activism thanks chiefly to the unique prestige which action has gained among them since the French Revolution and, more specifically, since the Russian Revolution. Most of us know the sensation of disgust aroused by words which, just because they remain ineffective, make us more acutely aware of our impotence than inaction would. In that kind of situation the daydream of action and its seemingly unlimited effectiveness tempts us most strongly. Let us call this kind of dream, which we dream with open eyes, the myth of efficiency. Both within the Communist and the Fascist movement, and indeed, in every extremist movement, intellectuals have sought the chance of lending power to their words, of securing their efficiency. Henceforth they would not merely pillory and incite, nor merely denounce or praise, but actively intervene and so, at long last, come to grips with reality.

Even if and when man has become mature and has freed himself of practically all his illusions, he still preserves certain enclaves in himself within which he cherishes hopes which can never be fulfilled but to which he can now and then abandon himself. Up to the very last minute of his life everyone can be tempted. Malraux is, without a shadow of doubt, unusually intelligent, clear-sighted and discerning. Yet, for all his verbal skill and obsession with words, he never ceased to believe in efficiency. He went on believing in it as unquestionably as an ugly woman does who, even against her will, still believes in the possibility and actual existence of absolute beauty. To that illusion Malraux succumbed on several occasions. In the 1920s, when he founded the paper in Indochina, he hoped to achieve with it far more than was possible. Chiang Kai-shek's victorious campaign and Stalin's triumphs certainly impressed him far more strongly than his sceptical mind should have allowed. In the same way, he enthusiastically took up the legends which, with assiduous skill, were systematically woven and spread round T. E. Lawrence. In fact, he regarded the legendary Lawrence of Arabia as an example worthy of emulation. Lawrence seemed to demonstrate that an intellectual could, in certain circumstances, become exceptionally effective. He had only to be cruelly ruthless with himself and truly determined to display the same kind of boundless courage that certain individuals have who wholly lack the gift of realistic imagination.

Malraux was determined to live according to this concept of efficiency. He became the spiritual and organizational leader of the French intelligentsia in the struggle against Fascism. He was on the spot when the time had come to help the Spanish Republic. He procured the planes for the international air squadrons which, under his command, intervened in the battles of Badajoz, Teruel and other places. He did not write hortatory poems. He rarely signed protests and proclamations. He threw himself into the midst of the battle: first in Spain; then as a volunteer in the armoured corps of the French army; after that in the Resistance – the so-called *maquis* – and finally, again at the front in Alsace at the head of his brigade.

Fascist intellectuals, too, waxed enthusiastic over the power of action; one need only think of the ageing Gabriele d'Annunzio. Malraux's own interpretation of the meaning of action, the love of battle and of the loyalty of comrades-in-arms is expounded in his most mature novel, *L'Espoir*. This novel describes the early phases of the Spanish Civil War and the military operations on land and in the air. At the same time, it describes complex mental processes in the course of which the anti-Fascist volunteers from all over the world rediscover themselves and one another. Finally, it describes the Spanish peasants who were hardly politically-minded and were still revolutionary. If anything, *L'Espoir* is even less 'heroistic' than Malraux's China novels, but he himself has remained heroistic up to the present day.

If that seems hard to explain in the light of his deep scepticism and tragic humanism, it becomes explicable as soon as one discovers that his cult of the hero bears an extraordinary resemblance to that cult of genius that was the hallmark of the early German Romantics. For Malraux the history of art is, up to a point, the chronicle of sublime strokes of genius. Only a genius succeeds in assimilating everything that preceded him only in order to break away from it and soon afterwards become himself a creator. Out of the salvaged remnants of the wrecked tradition and the innovations which correspond to his own being, the genius creates works of art which inaugurate a new phase and a completely new style. In the light – and often in the shadow – of this genius, dozens or even hundreds of gifted artists then continue to work until a new genius once again overthrows everything and leads art along a new untrodden path. This is how things look from a bird's eye view. Looking at a city from high above or afar, we only see its highest towers and skyscrapers. One may thus be tempted to conclude that they alone matter. It is superfluous to disprove this deceptive impression.

No matter what serious art and trickery Malraux employs in his *Antimémoires*, he does not succeed in demonstrating by means of quoting their own words that Nehru, Stalin, Mao Tse-tung or de Gaulle are historically great in the Hegelian sense of world history. He fails to persuade the critical reader that the Long March owed everything to Mao Tse-tung's planning, achievement and personal victory because, in the same breath, so to speak, he describes the efforts, sufferings, bold initiatives and countless sacrifices of the ordinary soldiers who paved Mao's path to glory. Both in structure and in content the *Antimémoires* are a work of an almost confusing multitude of levels. And in this work there appears an insuperable barrier between the two aspects of Malraux's personality. On the one hand, there are the experiences of

Malraux the soldier, the partisan, the wounded captive and, finally, the
prisoner, that is to say, the experiences of one man among the many.
On the other hand there are the experiences and remarks of Malraux,
the minister in de Gaulle's government, on the occasion of his travels,
official meetings and in more or less official speeches.

In 1969, after de Gaulle's retirement and Pompidou's election, Malraux
returned to private life and to his working desk. In 1971 he published
Les Chênes qu'on abat . . ., his last dialogue with the late President, his farewell to an honoured friend and, at the same time, his farewell to politics.
There followed *La Tête d'obsidienne*, a book on the philosophy of art
which, in part, centres on Picasso; *L'Irréel*, the second volume of *La
Métamorphose des dieux* and *Lazare*, a dialogue with and about death,
which is to be followed by *L'Intemporel*. Malraux thus found the way
back home to artistic creation as a permanent rebellion against death,
which means against non-being.

   In the middle of this phase he took his initiative in favour of Bangladesh. The seventy-year-old Malraux volunteered for service at the front
in the civil war. Was that not a political demonstration? Undoubtedly
it was. But more than that it was a commitment to that tragic humanism
which he formulated in his youth and to which he has remained faithful
throughout his life in his works and in his actions.

E. H. GOMBRICH

*

MALRAUX'S PHILOSOPHY OF ART IN HISTORICAL PERSPECTIVE

In the Third Part of Malraux's *Les Voix du silence* – to my mind the most persuasive and important section of the book – the conclusion is put forward that 'the artist builds up his forms from other forms; the raw material of an art that is emerging is never life, but an art preceding it'.[1] What Malraux here says of art also applies to other manifestations of human life. Civilization is composed of a web of traditions which reach back into the distant past. It is one of the paradoxes of Malraux's position that he would not seem to have drawn this inference from his study of art. Nurtured, as he is, on the extremist philosophies of Nietzsche and Spengler, he likes to dramatize the discontinuities of human culture, the revolutionary ruptures with the past which separate one culture from another and leave us no choice but to contemplate their radical otherness in the guise of a myth that is really of our own making.

It is difficult for a professional historian to follow him here. For why should that continuity of forms which Malraux likes to celebrate not also extend to intellectual as well as artistic creations? Indeed it is tempting to make this point by a *demonstratio ad hominem*. In trying to place Malraux's philosophy of art in its historical perspective I am not out to belittle its status. On the contrary, I hope that his 'Museum of the Mind' – as I should like to render his *Musée imaginaire* – will become both more intelligible and more accessible once its historical background has been sketched in.

Surveying the library of the mind, the literary heritage of Rome, that great and humane teacher of Latin oratory, Quintilian, who wrote in the first century AD, comes to speak of Ennius, the earliest of the great national poets of the Roman world who lived some three hundred years before him: 'We worship Ennius as we worship those groves which have become sacred through their very age, where the grand and ancient oaks are not so much beautiful as numinous.'[2]

The reaction of the Roman critic from a sophisticated age to the rugged grandeur of what had become the archaic diction of Ennius illustrates a response to the art of remote periods which has recurred quite frequently in the Western tradition. Seen in this perspective, André Malraux stands as the most recent in a long line of critics who are captivated by that numinous quality which ancient utterances or creations so frequently assume in our civilization. Quintilian, like Malraux, might have conceded that there was nothing sacred in a knobbly old oak tree; in other words, and again like Malraux, he might have said that the awe inspired by vegetation really sprang from a myth, just as he realized that his response to Ennius was due to distance. But neither he nor, as we know, Malraux, would have wanted for this reason to forgo the experience which archaic poetry or nature can arouse.

Indeed it is tempting at this point to recall the pages of *Les Noyers de l'Altenburg* which describe the narrator's father entering just such a grove after the end of the great *colloque* on the Concept of Man:

The richness of these age-old trees came from their bulk. But the effort with which their twisted branches sprang from their huge trunks, the way in which this heavy old timber burst into dark leaves so that it seemed rather to be sinking deep into the earth than tearing itself out of it, all this suggested the idea of endless strivings, and endless metamorphosis . . .

. . . the tortured trees with their burnished leaves and their ripening nuts silhouetted against the sky, burgeoned into eternal life in all their solemn mass, overhanging the young branches and the dead nuts of winter.[3]

At another time Malraux has told us explicitly how open he is to that suggestion of divinity that emanates from old trees. In the *Anti-mémoires* we read of a sacred tree he visited with an African queen:

The Queen's fetish was a tree like a giant plane. They had cleared the ground around it, which made one realize that it dominated the forest. From the writhing ganglions of its roots there rose tree trunks, straight as walls, together forming a colossal shaft which, some thirty metres above, curved royally outwards. . . .

What I was looking at was not a marvellous tree, a King of trees – although it was that – but a tree that conjured up a whole world into which it magically compelled the living as the Gods of Egypt compelled the dead.[4]

As if to confirm the fusion in Malraux's thoughts, as in those of the cultivated Roman, of ancient trees and ancient art, we encounter the same link in *La Tête d'obsidienne*, where the author is meditating on an elongated fetish 'which resembles a branch, like the angels of the Autun tympanum'.[5]

Those subtle critics of language, the ancient teachers of oratory, had a word for that cluster of emotions – the word we translate as 'the sublime'. The unknown Greek author of a treatise on the sublime which goes under the name of Longinus characteristically finds this precious and elusive quality in the words of power uttered by the creator in the Hebrew scriptures: 'Let there be light and there was light.' This numinous quality which is thus attributed to the sacred texts of an alien cult cannot be achieved at will. If you try to make your speech sublime you will only make it bombastic. For the sublime is not so much an aesthetic as a psychological category. It is, in the famous formulation of Longinus, 'the echo of a noble soul'. We relish the sublime precisely for that reason. It brings us face to face with great minds. It will satisfy those who seek not beauty and contrivance but an encounter with greatness. In fact Longinus is emphatic on the point that polish and flawless perfection counteracts sublimity. He thus sowed another seed which produced a rich critical harvest, particularly after the rediscovery of Longinus and the various translations of his treatise in the late seventeenth and eighteenth centuries. A certain suspicion began to cling to the idea of beauty in art. Was there not a higher and less accessible value – the value of sublime? Malraux has no doubts on this score. He sees the significance of modern art starting from Goya[6] in its rejection of beauty and pleasure, and he connects the rediscovery of earlier exotic styles with this revaluation of old values.

I believe we can still learn something about this momentous development by following up the clues offered by the sublime. Perhaps the most penetrating psychological analysis of human aesthetic reaction is to be found in Edmund Burke's *Philosophical Enquiry into the origin of our ideas of the Sublime and Beautiful*, of 1756. The boldness of Burke's conceptions commands respect even though we may find him over-ambitious. What he attempts is no more and no less than a system of aesthetics based entirely on naturalistic premises. Briefly he proposes the hypothesis that the sentiment of beauty if rooted in the instinct of the propagation of the species, in other words in sex, while the sentiment of the sublime is rooted in the instinct of self-preservation, in other words in anxiety. It may well be argued that the identification of our enjoyment of beauty with the erotic response, so natural for a critic writing during the age of the Rococo, contributed to that conscious or unconscious devaluation of beauty of which I have spoken. The eighteenth century was a century of guilt feelings, whose spokesman was Jean-Jacques Rousseau. The charge of corruption, of decadence, of the debasing influence of an art pandering to the superficial pleasure of a licentious public, could only serve to raise the stock of the sublime, for there was no guilt in feeling dread and awe.

It is true that Edmund Burke looked for this experience primarily in nature rather than in art, but even so his analysis affords sufficient parallels both backwards to Quintilian and forwards to André Malraux. Discussing the sublime effects of obscurity in the second part of his treatise (Section III), he writes: 'Almost all the heathen temples were dark. Even in the barbarous temples of the Americans at this day, they keep their idol in a dark part of the hut, which is consecrated to his worship. For this purpose too the Druids performed all their ceremonies in the bosom of the darkest woods, and in the shade of the old and most spreading oaks.'

Once more a transition suggests itself from here to a revealing passage in Malraux's *Antimémoires* where he traces his ideas about art back to his first sight of the Great Sphinx of Gizeh before the site was tidied up and sterilized by archaeologists and thus still spoke 'the solemn language of ruins'. He had asked himself what there was in common 'between the message of the medieval half-light filling the naves and the imprint the Egyptians left on their vast creations, in short between all the shapes which embody something of the ineffable'.[7] We know Burke's answer to this question. Obscurity arouses fear and is therefore sublime. Malraux's intuition was less psychological. He suddenly conceived of two contrasting languages, the language of everyday appearances and the language of Truth, of the Eternal and the Sacred. The Sphinx as an embodiment of mystery also embodies that unknowable truth that is revealed through her very metamorphosis. It is that intimation of the supernatural that the eighteenth century sought in nature.

Not only in nature, though, but also in the manifestations of the human mind. Malraux writes in *Le Musée imaginaire*[8] that the idea of interpreting a style as the expression of a civilization belongs entirely to the twentieth century. He is right that as far as the visual arts are concerned the idea has only recently become a cliché. But after all it was that great proto-Romantic Johann Gottfried Herder who, in 1773, published a collection of folk songs under the programmatic title *Stimmen der Völker in Liedern* (The Voices of People in Song).

Why folk songs? Because in the creations of the untutored 'folk' we hear the voice of natural man, uncorrupted by reason and artifice. The German language identifies the primitive or savage with the *wild*, and Herder seized on this usage to expound this theory of poetry:

The *wilder*, that is the more vital, the more spontaneous a nation is (for the word means no more than that), the wilder, also, that is the more vital, more spontaneous, more sensuous, more lyrically active will be their songs if it has any songs at all. The further removed their modes of thought, their language and their literature remains from artifice and logic, the less their songs will have been composed for paper and become dead literary exercises ... the longer a song is to last, the stronger, the more sensuous must these arousers of soul be to defy the power of time and the changes of centuries....[9]

The pamphlet in which Herder published these subversive thoughts also contained an essay by a young student of law he had befriended in Strasbourg, Goethe's prose hymn on the Strasbourg Minister. It is in this essay that we find the first impatient denunciations of the 'effeminate' 'beauty mongering' which blinded people to the greatness of medieval architecture, and a first intimation of the cult of primitive art which Malraux, like others, regards as a twentieth-century novelty:

In this way the savage may use weird lines, horrible shapes, strident colours on a coconut, on feathers or on his own body. However arbitrary these forms, they will harmonize without his knowing anything about the laws of proportion, since it was one single emotion that fused them into one significant whole. This significant art is the only true one.[10]

Though Goethe probably spoke without actual knowledge of the work of American Red Indians, knowledge of the arts of the globe was expanding in the eighteenth century, and lovers of art were beginning to reflect on that widening of horizons which Malraux also wants to locate in our own era.

Before the end of the eighteenth century there appeared that embarrassingly named collection of essays on art, the *Outpourings from the Heart of an Art-loving Monk* from the pen of W. H. Wackenroder. A much lesser mind than either Goethe or Herder, Wackenroder was, for all his sentimentality, more radical than either. In his essay 'On two miraculous languages and their mysterious power', he thrusts aside the 'benefaction' of human speech to celebrate the message of 'the invisible that hovers around us', conveyed by the two languages of Nature and of Art. Inevitably we hear again of the rustling of the trees in the woods and other natural events which arouse in us dark intimations inaccessible to well-weighed words. And in another essay he drives to the conclusion that foreshadows the claims of the *Musée imaginaire*:

We, the sons of this century, have been granted the advantage to be standing on the summit of a high mountain, with many countries and many ages lying quite open before our eyes and at our feet. Let us, then, make use of this good fortune, and let our eyes serenely roam over all ages and nations, endeavouring all the while to sense in these manifold works and emotions only what is *human*.[11]

Almost the only word in this passage which immediately betrays that Malraux cannot have been its author is the word 'serenely'. Wackenroder's pieties makes him trust in the deity, while Malraux's heroic despair has no room for serenity in his view of man's changing destiny.

Even so, it is important to note that Wackenroder's acknowledgment of global art should not be considered an isolated freak. Throughout the nineteenth century artistic horizons were widening, but this process first affected two arts which happen to interest Malraux very little and have not found admission to his Museum of the Mind – architecture and decoration. Nobody who remembers the variety of styles exemplified in our nineteenth-century cities will doubt the world-wide ecclecticism prevalent at the time.

But the real breakthrough to a global viewpoint first happened in the art of ornament and decoration, and here, as so often, it was triggered by a nagging dissatisfaction with the state of European design. The Industrial Revolution had debased the standards of craftmanship and created a deep-seated malaise that first found its expression in England. The Great Exhibition of 1851 was both the result and the cause of thoroughgoing heart-searching, for it looked as if the decorative instinct of savage nations were far superior to the taste of Western manufacturers.[12] Indeed, if the *Musée imaginaire* has a real predecessor it is Caxton's Glass Palace in South Kensington, with its dazzling display of the products of India, Africa and America, which deeply impressed the crowd of visitors. It impressed precisely because it enforced the conclusions that artistic talent had nothing to do with representational skill. On the contrary, the very dexterity of Europeans in imitating natural objects, flowers or animals, appeared to militate against the effectiveness of their design which, as it was increasingly emphasized, should lack all illusionist features and rather emphasize the flat surface. Here, indeed, is an important root of that revaluation of non-illusionistic art which Malraux has overlooked. One quotation must suffice. It comes from an essay on 'The Critic and Artist' by that influential spokesman of the *fin de siècle*, Oscar Wilde: 'By its deliberate rejection of Nature as the ideal of beauty, as well as of the imitative method of the ordinary painter, decorative art not merely prepares the soul for the true imaginative work, but develops in it that sense of form which is the basis of creative no less than of critical achievement.'

It was in this way, I believe, that the ground was prepared for that reversal of values that Malraux celebrates in his writings: the rejection not only of beauty but of truth to appearance. Nor is he concerned with decoration or indeed with 'abstract' art: what interests him is the acceptance of non-illusionistic representations, particularly of the human figure.

It is only natural that in his accounts of that revolution Malraux concentrates on its French antecedents, notably on the contribution of painters such as Cézanne, who accustomed the public to a different scale of values.[13] It may be worth while therefore to redress the balance a little and to draw attention to other sources.

Characteristically it was a student of decorative art, the Austrian Alois Riegl, who first explicitly rejected the notion that changes of style could be described in terms of progress and decline. He wrote for specialists, but his doctrine was spread among artists and critics by Wilhelm Worringer, whose *Abstraction and Empathy* came out in 1908.

As far as this doctrine is remembered at all, it lives on in Bernard Berenson's glorification of the 'life enhancing ideated sensations of tactile values' which the sensitive observer is supposed to experience in front of a Renaissance painting. Worringer did not deny the possibility of such aesthetic enjoyment, but he rejected any attempt to judge all styles by this standard. A positive relation to nature, such as it is expressed in classical and Renaissance art, he thought, could only develop in societies which felt safe in their existence. Most peoples lacked this sense of security. To them nature, reality, space itself was threatening. Their art, therefore, could not be an expression of love and confidence, but rather of an anxious withdrawal. It is this flight from reality that is manifested, according to Worringer, in the creation of abstract forms. Quoting the Latin tag that 'fear created the Gods' Worringer wishes to add that fear also created art. We are back, on a different level, at Burke's identification of the sublime with dread. It is this dread or awe which Worringer sees expressed in all non-classical styles, and since ours is said to be an 'age of anxiety' his message was soon taken up by his contemporaries among German artists. Expressionism had found its ancestry in all styles of the globe founded on 'abstraction'.

It was in another of Worringer's books published before the First World War, *Formprobleme der Gotik* (1911), that art lovers first encountered those impressive and expressive photographs of details of medieval works of art which dramatize their contemporary appeal. The technique caught on, as did Worringer's approach, and after the 'latency period' of the war a spate of more or less scholarly art books began to flood the market which exploited this feeling of immediacy that could be achieved by cunningly lit and cleverly cut shots of medieval, exotic or primitive sculpture, particularly of heads.

When, in the early Fifties, Malraux's *Psychologie de l'art* first came into my hands I therefore experienced something like a *déjà vu* sensation in turning its pages. While still a schoolboy in the Twenties I had been much impressed by books of this kind, which may well have had their share in propelling me towards the history of art. My studies had thoroughly weaned me of this approach, which now appeared to me somewhat hysterical and sensationalist. It was with considerable surprise that I discovered in reading Malraux that he shared the conviction at which I had arrived – the conviction that these photographic techniques falsified the works they purported to reproduce and imparted on them an 'unjustified but aggressive modernity'.[14] Another surprise awaited me though when I saw that Malraux somehow accepted and even relished this falsification as part of that metamorphosis that turned the art of the past into an indispensable myth.[15] In an age when man had begun to realize – if I can thus summarize Malraux's views – that God is dead, it is the art of the past which in this transformation preserves for him that sense of the numinous which is his birthright.[16] Harking back to the earlier pages of the present essay we might say that the mysterious and unintelligible works of art of the past have joined the sublimities of nature in offering a screen for the projection of our deepest fears and longings. Communion with art, like communion with nature, is really a form of self-communion.

I have no doubt that we can learn a great deal from Malraux's diagnosis, but I do not think that we cannot go beyond it. The historian who is interested in the psychology of art is surely entitled to ask why it was that art assumed this function at a given period. More exactly perhaps, we should ask who it was who experienced this particular metamorphosis with such intensity. For one thing is clear – when Malraux uses the term 'we' to characterize 'our' response to the art of the past he is really talking of a tiny circle. It is to be feared that the overwhelming majority of people in our age never look at works of art in museums or in art books. Of those who do, again a large majority are quite unaffected by the attitudes described by Malraux. That rejection of beauty and sensual pleasure, that contempt for a faithful rendering of natural appearances, that worship of creative otherness which Malraux attributes to 'us' is – or should I say was? – the preserve of a mere handful of people. What were their motives?

In a paper on 'Psychoanalysis and the History of Art',[17] I once attempted to lay bare at least one hidden strand in this development which Malraux has not mentioned – I mean that tendency of the sophisticated to be repelled by what has come to appear to them as cloying, indulgent and emotionally cheap. We have seen how early the erotic sensualities of the Rococo became identified with the corruption of society and drove art-lovers into the arms of the sublime. There is a strong social element in this situation. The fear of sharing a debased taste with the despised bourgeois or petit bourgeois has put a premium on a preference for what is disturbing, shocking and difficult. True, in pursuing this type of analysis we must not fall into the trap of dismissing the modern revolution as mere snobbery. The *kitsch*, the sentimental trash of the department store, does indeed represent an unprecedented debasement of art precisely because it combines manual dexterity with meretriciousness. As a matter of fact the verdict of the rising generation on the art of the Salon and of the best parlour is much less severe than it was in my youth and in that of André Malraux. Even so, no historian of twentieth-century art can afford to neglect the forces of repulsion that drove the pioneers of the new movement towards new artistic explorations. Malraux is right when he links the emergence of his Museum of the Mind with this revolution, though he somewhat overdramatizes its novelty.

Perhaps it is only in one of his most recent books that he fully reveals who he means and has meant when he uses the term 'we'. *La Tête d'obsidienne* of 1974 combines a deeply felt tribute to Picasso with a restatement of Malraux's ideas about art occasioned by the great exhibition organized in Malraux's honour at Saint-Paul-de-Vence by the Maeght Foundation. Malraux's interpretation of art as a triumph over death finds much scope in these reminiscences and meditations, which open with an account of his visit to Picasso's home after his death. We must leave it to future historians to sort out how much in the 'flashbacks' telling of conversations with Picasso is Malraux and how much may be authentic, but what these Platonic dialogues reveal is the degree to which Malraux made himself the spokesman of what he took to be Picasso's philosophy of art – a philosophy based on contempt

for the purveyors of pleasure and on a constant striving for new transformations which are seen as the very essence of art.

Maybe this fusion of Malraux's interpretation of art with the oeuvre
of the master of metamorphosis can also assist the historian to locate
the source of Malraux's 'myth'. No artist in all history exhibited that
range of styles and of skills that marks the fabulous oeuvre of Picasso.
For him every new move was indeed also the rejection of an earlier
manner of which he had grown tired. A virtuoso of the first order, he
was able to evoke images of haunting beauty classical no less than of
terrifying mystery and ugliness. Neither the rendering of natural
appearances nor the creation of abstract structures presented any
problem to him. If he did not cultivate a fully non-figurative style it
was, one may surmise, because what he was looking for in the images he
created was precisely that expressive intensity that we experience most
readily in front of a living organism, however distorted. When Malraux
reports him as saying that what he was looking for was 'the mask',[18] it
was perhaps an expression of that desire for a mysterious numinous
physiognomy which his generation had discovered in the ritual masks
of tribal Africa.

There are such heads and physiognomies in Picasso's oeuvre, sometimes achieved with the simplest of means, as in the *papiers déchirés*
which appeared to look at us with haunting magic. But there is an old
Latin proverb that tells us *si duo faciunt idem non est idem*. It is one thing
for Picasso to reject his skill and to explore the expressive possibilities
of chance formation, it is something very different for a tribal artist to
carve a mask according to a strict tradition.

The myth Malraux distils from his Museum of the Mind is really that
mankind might be seen as a super-Picasso, ever creating new forms and
rejecting others, each creation implying a negation of something else.
It is this conception that permits Malraux to appreciate both the stark
shapes of primitive idols and the stupendous virtuosity of masters such
as Titian, Chardin and above all Goya and Manet. But this approach
presupposes precisely that all artistic creations of the past are to be seen
as the products of the same kind of choice which is inherent in all
Picasso's creative whims.

Malraux tells us that Picasso remarked: 'It is a good thing that
nature exists, so that we can violate her,'[19] and though I cannot find
this utterance very attractive it does throw light on his oeuvre. To look
for the same kind of aggressive defiance in the non-naturalistic styles
of the past is to do violence, not to nature but to history. Yet Malraux
cannot give up this interpretation, because he has made it the corner-

stone of his philosophy. For him 'the human power to which art testifies is man's eternal revenge on a hostile universe'.[20] We recognize echoes of Worringer's ideas, but now they have been absorbed into a wider vision of man, defiantly asserting himself in the face of blind 'destiny'.

The words 'negation' and 'refusal' punctuate his glorification of the hieratic styles of the past, and he is convinced that we all share this taste for negative virtues. 'The rejection of the illusion', he writes, 'rarely leaves us indifferent.'[21] If he is right in attributing this bias to us, it would do little credit to our sense of discrimination. Purely negative criteria are poor criteria in art. Anyone may like the device of rhyme in poetry, or abhor it as trivial jingling, but it really will not do to extol all rhymeless poetry of the world for its heroic refusal to indulge in an artifice that was not known.

It is at this point that Malraux's reading of the 'message' of art impinges on the psychology of image making. It is strangely inconsistent for Malraux, who knows that images derive from images, to follow Riegl and Worringer in dismissing the idea that the remoteness from natural appearances which we find in most artistic styles of the globe can have anything to do with lack of skill in rendering the visible world. He is right in insisting that while there may be clumsy works of art there can be no clumsy style. But the issue of skill and will cannot be resolved by any facile formula. No doubt the master of the Lindisfarne Gospels had no longing to go out sketching and to paint the cloud formations which fascinated Constable. No doubt also Constable would have been unable to paint the crosspage of the Lindisfarne Gospel.

So much is trivial. What is not trivial is the question of what is involved in making an image that strikes the beholder as a faithful rendering of natural appearance. To assume that anyone could have done that but refrained, as Picasso refrained, because he wanted to 'violate' reality is to fly in the face of all evidence. After all, the apprentices of the classical tradition spent years in the cast room and in the life class to master the human figure and the laws of perspective. Neither were the skills of landscape or still-life painting ever acquired overnight. Whether the toil was worth while is a matter of opinion. That it was a toil is not; and though there are no clumsy styles there are styles – as there are musical instruments – which demand a smaller repertoire of skills than others. The main reason why the rendering of nature has come to look trivial and even easy can be stated in Malraux's terms: we are constantly surrounded by images, photographic, painted or printed, in which three-dimensional reality has already been reduced to two dimensions, and those with a knack can pick up these formulas and reproduce them without too much trouble. It does not follow that all the image makers of the globe who practised different methods did so because they rejected appearances for the sake of a higher, invisible reality.

Once more I think that Malraux has seen an important point in the role of art in our civilization; he is right, no doubt, that far more people have come into contact with religion through works of art than in any other way. Temples and cathedrals, cult images and biblical illustrations keep alive a tradition that might otherwise be in danger of breaking off altogether. Naturally he is right again in insisting on the dominant role of religion in past societies, but once more he is turning a historical fact into a myth if he wants us to believe that men and women in the past were always cowed and overawed by the mystery of their existence. Anthropologists who have visited the tribes who carve these frightening masks tell us of much laughter and horseplay. Nor need we assume that all the art of these or other civilizations is really concerned with the 'sacred' because it exhibits an unnaturalistic style. It has been suggested that some, at least, of the female figurines which have been called 'mother goddesses' were really dolls, toys for children.[22] The voice we have lent to their silence would have struck their owners as strange indeed. If we experience it as 'sublime' and hear what Longinus called 'the echo of a noble soul' – a collective soul, no doubt – we are certainly, as Malraux postulates, the victims of a myth.

But if we succumb, we do so precisely because we are questioning the work not for what it is but for what lies behind it, for the soul that we seek rather than the form that we see. The history of the 'sublime' may here be particularly telling. For those who communed with the sublimities of nature certainly did so in the eighteenth century in the hope or belief that in nature they could find the echo of the Creator. And even when this hope was fading, the worship of nature offered the nearest substitute to religion. It is in the light of this development that we can appreciate Malraux's attitude to art. To him, remote and exotic images now speak with the voice of the forest, or of thunderclouds. The lover of art is like the child who holds the seashell at his ear to hear the sound of the sea. What he hears is the rush of his own blood, but is not the myth more poetic, more consoling than the knowledge that empty shells are nothing but empty shells?

One can sympathize with this dilemma and still think that it is an unreal one. It arises somehow from the basic assumption that what we must seek in nature or in art is some kind of message, that we must for ever look for a meaning in a universe devoid of meanings. I suspect that this expectation carries over into adult life an attitude that is natural to the child, for whom every object, every toy and every image has indeed an intense feeling tone, an intense personal physiognomy.[23] It has been shown by the psychologist C. E. Osgood and his colleagues that we can make ourselves regress to this frame of mind at will and are ready to give an answer to any question about the feeling tone of any object or quality. In this frame of mind we will not be disposed to doubt that old oaktrees are not only stronger than birchtrees but also wiser, holier and perhaps more fatherly. We will be equally ready to respond in some such way to Easter Island idols or to a gingerbread figure. But are there no other ways to approach art and nature? Can we not appreciate the beauty and intricacy of the seashell instead of holding it to our ear? Granted that both the universe and the creations of man are mysterious, are they not also miraculous in a way that makes us transcend our puny selves? Do they not challenge our thirst for the knowledge rather than for communion?

One of the interlocutors of the colloquy that forms the core of *Les Noyers de l'Altenburg* is made to speak of this wish to understand, but Malraux has seen to it that the dice are heavily loaded against him: 'We art historians, particularly if we are historians of German art, confront the Gothic or the Egyptian man with the disinterested intention of dragging him to the light. What is in question here is the honest will to knowledge: we interrogate him, and we interrogate ourselves.[24]

It is not difficult to recognize in this art historian a disciple of some-one like Worringer, who did indeed claim to have unriddled the psychologies of 'Gothic man' and of 'Egyptian man'. One cannot but agree with Malraux that the claim is ridiculous, because there never were such creatures. But this insight need not throw doubt on the second part of the statement, the existence of an honest will to knowledge. After all it was this will that led to the information about the late Middle Ages and the ancient Egyptians which Malraux also uses. Without it the hieroglyphs would never have been deciphered and would still be regarded in the light of the myth that they embodied some portentous archetypal wisdom.

Maybe Malraux is right that it is not the most learned Egyptologist who can make us love Egyptian art best,[25] but I for one would still entrust myself to his guidance rather than to anyone who wants to arouse my emotional response. Malraux makes much of Man in the abstract, but let us remember the opening words of Aristotle's *Meta-physics*: 'All men naturally desire to know.' True enough, what Aristotle took for knowledge has been partly consigned to the category of myth by science, that science which appears to play so little part in Malraux's image of man. If it did he would have to concede that we do know more about the universe than Aristotle did – and that rational inquiry has also increased our knowledge of man's past.

Not that Malraux is wrong in reminding us that the interpretation the historian imposes on the evidence also changes our perception of the main accents of developments.[26] The historian who regards Mannerism as decadent will also select his facts differently from the one who sees in it a forerunner of modern art. And yet it is a fallacy to conclude that all is relative and that there are no facts to be discovered which would be of use to both historians. We have dispelled a good many myths about the past through our 'honest will to knowledge'. At any rate, what is the alternative? Should we not try to find the truth, should we close our research institutions and make do with those second-hand stereotypes about the 'spirits' of past ages, the tired ghosts of Hegelian philosophies that have seeped into our art books including – regrettably – even into Malraux's own presentation of past cultures? Surely as a champion of change, of the search and the quest, he is the last man to advocate such a submission to mental inertia.

Maybe, however, he fails to see where his paradoxical glorification of the myth would lead: not to an initiation into the sacred, but to the cynicism of the hoax. Two years ago Cornell University in the State of New York organized an exhibition under the heading 'The Civilization of Llhuros'. Its guiding spirit was the American artist Normal Daly, who had picked up discarded machinery and other industrial detritus from rubbish heaps and cleverly transformed these pieces of metal into vaguely portentous objects suggesting implements of ritual and mysterious artefacts of a strange cult. The catalogue and labels expounded an elaborate interpretation based on the fiction that there once had been such a civilization which had been destroyed by an atomic explosion, and that archaeologists and anthropologists had succeeded in reading its script and reconstructing much of its creed and its mores – abounding in sexual practices of the more shocking kind. Needless to say, the whole thing was a transparent spoof; transparent in the sense that the visitor was not expected to be taken in for a moment. He was to look at these mounted screwdrivers or bent aerials 'as if' they were the tragic relics of a vanished world of beliefs. In taking the small step from the sublime to the ridiculous, and back again, he was to be awed and amused in turn, playing the game and watching himself responding to these suggestive forms.

I am not sure that such a game can ever be worth the expensive candle, and I have only referred to it to reveal the danger inherent in Malraux's intellectual position. He himself has amply testified to his genuine love of art. Indeed the value of his writings on art seems to me to transcend his theories precisely because they reveal a man for whom the problems of art are ultimate problems of desperate seriousness. In a world where most academic study of art history has broken up into specialisms, he has challenged us to reflect on the totality of human artistic production and to incorporate it into our image of man. When the books by professionals are gathering dust in libraries he will be read, as we read Ruskin, as a witness to a civilization to which art still mattered.

JEAN LEYMARIE

*

MALRAUX AND THE CREATIVE PROCESS

Translated by Robert Speaight

Malraux was born at the beginning of the century, exactly twenty years after Picasso, under the same Plutonian star, and he remains an important witness to it. Like Picasso he is surrounded by an aura of legend, where strength and generosity play an even larger part than the gifts of genius and the powers of fascination. Nietszche and Vincent van Gogh, burning in the fires that they themselves had set alight, are for Malraux and Picasso the solar planets of humanity. 'My father', says the narrator of *Les Noyers de l'Altenburg*, letting us a little into his secret, 'loved Nietzsche more than any other writer. Not for his preaching, but for the intellectual generosity which he found in him, and this was incomparable.'[1] Vincent's profession of faith, which is the core of the dialogue with Picasso in *La Tête d'obsidienne*, forms an epigraph for the first volume of the trilogy on *La Métamorphose des Dieux*, and clarifies its meaning. 'Both in life and in painting, I can do without God. But I cannot, suffering as I do, dispense with something that is greater than I am; and that is my life, and the power to create.'

It was not long before the unfettered and lively curiosity of a self-taught man drew Malraux towards literature – he had a conjuror's flair for the unusual and the unpublished – and just as intensely towards the plastic arts. He approached them from every side with an enthusiasm that knew no bounds. Following the Armistice, and at the most impressionable age, he haunted the Musée Guimet. Then it was the room in the Louvre, not yet rearranged, where the masterpieces were huddled around the *Pietà* of Avignon. 'Breathless', he tells us, 'from the deep chiming of the bells in my heart',[2] he 'got down on his knees, and striking a light'[3] discovered the hallucinated fetishes from the old Trocadéro. His first friends among the writers and poets, Max

Jacob, Marcel Arland, and Pascal Pia, were also enthusiastic lovers of art, and prophesied for him a future as an orientalist and historian of design. He was not yet twenty years old when one of his strange stories, inspired by the themes which haunted him, *Lunes en papier* (1921), and illustrated by Léger's woodcuts, was published by D. H. Kahnweiler, the famous editor and art dealer. At Kahnweiler's he met several painters of his own generation – Beaudin, Masson, who afterwards illustrated *L'Espoir*, all the pioneers of Cubism, and all those who, in their heroic period, 'patiently or furiously bent over their insulted canvases, made the whole past of the world live for us again'.[4] In the beginning, and working to a careful plan, Malraux went from the studios to the museums. The ending of the war excited him to travel. He plunged into Italy, the native country of his grandmother, and followed where Suarès, equally excited, had gone before. He passed through Germany, where his wife's family had connections, and found it submerged by the wave of Expressionism. He caught the surf of this, and went on to Vienna and Prague – magical cities both; got as far as Greece and, inspired by Gide and Flaubert, reached Tunisia. Then he came back to Belgium, and his Flemish ancestry. His taste oscillated between the fantastic represented by Ensor, to whose house decorated with shells at Ostend he paid an unforgettable visit, and the classical represented by Derain, who then obscured the importance of Matisse and appeared as the rival of Picasso. In March 1922, he wrote the preface for an exhibition by his friend Galanis, the heir to the Mediterranean tradition, and forcefully explained why he had done so 'Comparison is our only guide ... the genius of the Greeks will be better understood by putting a Greek statue alongside an Asiatic or Egyptian statue than by an acquaintance with a hundred statues from Greece.'[5]

Before its elaboration in his books, this revealing confrontation of works separated in time and origin was tested by Malraux on the field. Between October 1923 and February 1926 he made two consecutive visits to Indochina. These were a rough experience – archaeological in one case, and political in the other. His energies were spent in a mission to the borders of China, and this gave an unforeseen expansion to his thirst for *adventure*. From now onwards the ways of art and the ways of action would run together. 'But why Asia?' Valéry was quick to ask him; and Valéry was his sharpest interlocutor, whose thought – at once so close to his own and so different from it – he has so often recalled. 'It is the obsession with other civilizations which gives to my own civilization, and perhaps to my own life, their particular accent.'[6]

Almost all Malraux's forebears had been seafaring folk, or in some way dependent on the sea. In the course of his long voyages, to be followed by so many others, he could watch, open-eyed and astonished, against a background of ocean and stars, the molten flow of the centuries with their train of comets and passage of Argonauts. 'The cosmic forces set astir in us the whole past of humanity.'[7] And his voice, which was to discover its resonance on the public platform, had first of all to fight with the winds and the waves. Giacometti, obstinate landsman that he was, went only once to sea, shortly before he died, to gain a better awareness, in face of its timeless immensity, of how precious and yet how precarious works of art are. It was on the boat, returning from Indochina, that Malraux wrote *La Tentation de l'Occident* (1926), in a style that did not measure up to the flight of his thought. This drew up the balance sheet of his odyssey, a meditation on Europe and China, and on the respective bases of their civilizations, corroded as they were by the universal crisis of values. One of its most insidious symptoms is our present approach to art, which substitutes a soulless and insatiable knowledge for a balanced sensibility. 'The particular pleasure one takes in discovering unknown forms of art ceases with their discovery, and is not transformed into love,'[8] The imaginary museum was in process of construction with its charms and its dangers, and this 'great disturbing spectacle which is beginning to unfold before our eyes'[9] was calling for a master of ceremonies to organize it on a planetary scale. The book shows a subtle penetration of the Chinese mentality, after the manner of Victor Segalen – gardens, eroticism, transmigration, rhythm of the universe – and ends on a haughty refusal of all religious submission, on a bitter and inflexible clearsightedness, worthy of de Vigny: 'I am still on fire in front of you – eager lucidity, solitary and steadfast flame – in the heaviness of this night where the yellow wind cries, as it cried through all those nights of my distant voyaging, and echoed around me the presumptuous clamour of the sterile sea.'[10]

Malraux returned to Paris in the middle of the Surrealist excitement, but kept his distance from it. He made his presence felt at Daniel Halévy's evening parties – for, like himself, Halévy was a disciple of Nietzsche and Michelet – and revealed his magical gifts as a speaker during the 'conversations' at Pontigny. His contribution to one of Grasset's *Cahiers Verts*, 'D'une jeunesse européene' (1927), raised the agonizing question: 'What conception of man will be able to release the civilization of solitude from its anxiety?'[11] In a world which has lost the sense of the absolute, with no ideal worthy of its sacrifice, and that faith cannot justify nor science decipher, three novels inspired by his Asiatic experience attempted to answer the absurdity of death by the intensity of action or the serenity of art. Only in the first of Malraux's novels do aesthetic considerations find no place, but the new type of hero, lucid and resolute, put forward in *Les Conquérants* (1928), for whom 'creation is the only means of self-defence',[12] and who would like to chisel his life and his acts 'as one chisels wood'.[13] is of the same family as the artist as hero celebrated in that epic of conquest, *Les Voix du silence*. 'This hero', explained Drieu la Rochelle in writing of the novel that followed, 'is not Malraux, but the mythical image of himself, more sublime and also more concrete'.[14] The young amateur archaeologist who leaves to discover, by his own efforts, *La Voie royale* (1930) of the temples linking Angkor with the lakes in the basin of the Menam, is torn apart, in spite of his intrepid nihilism, 'by the hunger for eternal things'.[15] He explains to the director of the French Institute in Saigon, who declares himself 'attracted rather than convinced'[16] – for the misunderstanding persisted between Malraux and the official scholars – his personal views on art: and here we can read already the fertile intuitions of metamorphosis, timelessness, and mythical transmutation. 'You could say that in art time ceases to exist. What interests me, you see, is the decomposition and transformation of its works, their deepest life which springs from the death of men. In fact, every work of art tends to become a myth,'[17] And when, after a fearful struggle, he snatches from the horror of the jungle, from its 'imprisoning power',[18] the remains of one of the most perfect Khmer temples, there appeared on one of the smiling and emergent heads 'a very fine blueish-grey moss, like the down on a European peach'.[19] So it was that on the stone of these ecstatic and rediscovered deities, the dust of centuries had deposited the velvet of a fruit. This victory of art, immortal and appetizing, over the putrid forest of the future, is a significant theme in the book.

The title of *La Condition humaine* (1933) indicates, clearly enough, its Pascalian resonance, and here the existentialist anxiety – 'fundamentally, the mind only thinks about man in the dimension of eternity, and the awareness of life can never be anything but anxiety'[20] – is only appeased by the community of the revolutionary struggle, which is also the place where love discovers its fulfilment, or in the refuge of oriental art; in music which sets death at defiance, or in painting which opens up the way to charity, as it does with us. One of the last pages of *Les Voix du silence* distils – beyond its essential context, which is 'the return of Asia into History'[21] – the very core of the book and its deep connection with the essays on art.

I related, formerly, the adventure of a man who does not recognize his own voice when it has just been recorded, because he hears it for the first time with his ears and no longer with his throat; and because it is only our throat that transmits our interior voice, I called this book *La Condition humaine*. The other voices, in art, do no more than ensure the transmission of this interior voice ... the voice of the artist derives its strength from a solitude which summons the universe in order to impose upon it the accent of humanity; and in the great arts of the past there survives for us the interior and invincible voice of civilizations which have seen their day.[22]

As artistic director of Gallimard's publishing house, Malraux made several journeys, between 1928 and 1931, to study the Near and Middle East, and particularly to Persia and Afghanistan – cross-roads of civilizations. He also went round the world, through the whole length of Asia, Mongolia, India, China, Japan, following in the legendary tracks of the silk-merchants, and returned by the United States of America, with their rich store of museums. His aim was the preparation of an Indo-Hellenistic exhibition (1931), one side of which would reveal the glittering achievements of Alexandria; and a so-called Buddhist-Gothic exhibition (1932), based on the recent excavations at Pamir. He wrote two notices on a couple of contemporary artists, one on Rouault (1929) and the other on Fautrier (1932), born colourists and representing, the one from a Christian and the other from a secular point of view, 'the tragic expression in painting'.[23] Behind the God of Rouault, as behind the God of Bernanos, the features of Satan were discerned. *La Condition Humaine* was being published at a time when Hitler was seizing power. *Le Temps du mépris* denounced the Nazi techniques of humiliation and imprisonment; the solitary cell where the musician's only defence against madness are the melodies which he recalls. The admirable preface had the force of a manifesto. 'One would like to think that the word "art" has this among other meanings; an attempt to give mankind a feeling of its own grandeur of which it is unaware.'[24] A grandeur which it discovered and asserted, in the face of mounting danger, better in solidarity than in the cult of self. Between the visit to Berlin where he protested against the arrest of Dimitrov and the brave speech in Moscow on the freedom of the artist, which left Gorki so astonished, came the daring expedition to the Yemen (1934) to discover in the hostile desert the lost capital of the Queen of Sheba. This was the last romantic fling of a man fascinated by archaeology and its forbidden places, and it gave him the experience of the aeroplane both as an instrument and a means of transport. On the way to Arabia, where the shade of Lawrence met the shade of Rimbaud,

Malraux landed in Egypt; visited the Cairo museum 'in its sleeping dust',[25] and discovered the Sphinx, its feet still buried in the sand, like a sentinel of eternity, guarding the tombs and watching over the stars. His thoughts about art as a *presence* and as *another world* were beginning to take shape. During his militant phase with the anti-fascist committees almost all his speeches in Paris or Moscow, London or Madrid, reproduced in *Commune*, dwelt on the value of culture and the specific character of art. 'Art obeys its own logic, and all the more unpredictably because the function of genius is to discover it.' (21 January 1936.)

On the outbreak of the Spanish Civil War, where universal values were at stake, Malraux was at once committed, for he sought in the Revolution that 'subterranean community'[26] which had once been the community of Christendom. Conceived as a classical tragedy and produced by a cinematic artist inspired at once by Tolstoy and Goya, *L'Espoir* (1937) remains among the more poignant and concentrated witnesses to the twentieth century. Its exceptional vibration derives from the perfect coincidence between the inner movement of the novelist's world and the dramatic tension of History. The true hero is the Spanish people, whose future concerns the whole world, but its international protagonists – musicians, engineers, sculptors, art historians, and ethnologists – are men of culture and practical skill capable of assuming what is best in humanity, that is to say, as one of them puts it, 'to translate into awareness the widest possible experience'.[27] In the heat of an action, to which they are dedicated, body and soul, and under the eye of History that 'watches and judges them',[28] they cannot help asking themselves, each according to his character and convictions, questions about the inexorable and perhaps insoluble conflict between being and doing, between the individual and the group, between necessity and freedom. The tensest fighting takes place at Toledo, in El Greco's country, which is both a fortress and a museum, and here their chief concern is to save the works of art whose lasting essence is the foundation of their perishable form. But art has a function that goes beyond them; what is their worth beside hunger and suffering? The aesthetic and political questions are inseparable. 'Have revolutions a style?'[29] somebody asks towards the middle of the book, and if this revolution succeeds, what sort of art will come out of it, for the individual and for the mass? In the last sequence Manuel, who is an organist, enters the deserted town of Brihuega where there is no other sound but the trickle of the springs and the little rivulets over the sharp paving. He withdraws to his room, and on a borrowed gramophone plays a Beethoven record, his wolf-hound at his side, 'stretched out like you

see them on bas-reliefs'. Transformed by the cause which he has just
been serving, he is caught up again by the music which in his passion,
and this is in tune with the passing stream of memory and the un-
ending murmur of the water. 'For the first time Manuel heard a voice
graver than the blood of men, and more troubling than their presence
on the earth – what he heard were the infinite possibilities of their
future.'[30]

For the first time. All change is a birth; and art only exists in manifest-
ing the grave and single instant of beginning.

The soul of Spain is unconquerable; it is a land of violent contrasts;
and it has gripped our own time in the way that antiquity gripped the
Renaissance, and the Middle Ages Romanticism. The unique knowledge of the country which he had acquired through danger and
enthusiasm gave to the author of *L'Espoir* an opportunity for intense
conversations and a close understanding with the painter of *Guernica*.
Certain drawings for this were to illustrate the novel, although the
engravings of Goya's *Disasters of War* would suit it better. What artist
has expressed more vividly the sufferings of a people, its timeless soul,
and its crucifying experience? Malraux and Picasso both turned to
Goya; to those arms outstretched against the night of the *3rd May*, and
facing the sinister yellow torch and the devilish mechanics of the
execution. 'Because of the Spanish Civil War, Picasso has talked to me
about Goya more than about any other painter.'[31] One also understands why Malraux has hitherto devoted his two most important single
essays on the plastic arts to the two Saturnian painters who open and
close what he has called *Le Musée imaginaire* with their screams of death.
They will henceforward be seen together 'in that unpredictable Prado
where Spain awaits *Guernica,* and where the greatest of the Goyas was
awaiting the young Picasso'.[32]

The years preceding the Second World War saw the publication
of luxurious reviews illustrating with the same care the latest forms of
modern art and bringing back to life those of the old masters. They
profited from the technical progress in reproduction, whose influence
on an understanding of the works and the creative process Walter
Benjamin was then engaged in studying. To the latest and most
perfect of these, *Verve,* Malraux gave the early chapters of his *Psychologie
de l'art* (1937–8), which was once again interrupted by world events.

In September 1939, the war surprised him in front of the church at
Beaulieu in the Limousin. This had 'one of the finest romanesque
tympanums, the only one where the sculptor has depicted the arms of
the crucifix, like a prophetic shadow, behind the arms of Christ out-

stretched over the world'.[33] It is the same gesture of despair that you see in the condemned man from the *3rd May*. Malraux, the famous colonel of a squadron in Spain – a unit composed of intellectuals from many countries – now enrolled as a simple private in a regiment of French tanks on his native soil, and found himself among unknown companions whom their officers called 'the men'. This revelation of a basic humanity, felt as an enigma and experienced in danger as a brotherhood, appears in *Les Noyers de l'Altenburg*, the fine transitional novel of his maturity, against the blood-soaked horizon of two world wars. Vincent Berger fights in one of them, and his son – the narrator – in the other. Memories of Asia mingle with the moving evocation of Nietzsche. Walter Berger, Vincent's uncle, tells how he saw Nietzsche, then insane, in the train which was taking him from Turin to Basle, and how the philosopher suddenly began, quite distinctly, to sing his last, sublime poem, *Venice*, while the train, all lights extinguished, passed through the Saint-Gothard tunnel. In his book, written in the darkest moment of the century, and beneath one of the tunnels of History, Malraux, through the voice of Walter who was Nietzsche's friend, asserts his resolutely anti-Spenglerian views on the metamorphic transmission of cultures, and his unshakable trust in the unity of that by which man transcends himself and survives his own mortality. 'The greatest mystery is not that we should be thrown by chance between the profusion of matter and the profusion of the stars, but that, imprisoned as we are, we should produce images which have the power to deny our nothingness.'[34] Such is the conclusion of the great humanist discussion beneath the vaults of the priory at Altenburg in Alsace, where two walnut-trees, a hundred years old, stand before the entrance. The most ancient and perhaps the most universal modes of worship are addressed to trees and standing stones. The wood of these venerable walnut-trees, in which the sap rises inexhaustibly from the earth, is the same as that furnishing the logs one throws on to the fire in winter, and the material for the Gothic statues in the Library. On a calm evening their magnificent branches frame, in the far distance, the spires of Strasbourg; and they become the moving symbols of a continuous creation and of a metamorphosis that has no end.

After fighting under the same pseudonym of Berger in the clandestine maquis of the Dordogne, and then visiting the grotto at Lascaux, which had only just been discovered, the commandant of the Alsace–Lorraine brigade arrived as a liberator in the country that his premonition had already evoked. He was the first to enter the cathedral at Strasbourg, reopened for worship by his orders. He was charged to recover from its salt mine one of the masterpieces of Western art, the reredos of Grünewald, which is the glory of the museum at Colmar. When Roger Stéphane came to interview him at Ilkirch, near Strasbourg, on 2 February 1945, Malraux, who was still in military uniform, declared: 'What matters essentially for me is art. I am steeped in art, as another man is steeped in religion.'[35] It is difficult not to compare this avowal with that of Baudelaire to whom in many respects Malraux is akin. 'To glorify the cult of images is my great, my unique and primitive, passion.'[36] How can one fail to recognize in their mutual enthusiasm a claim which goes beyond aesthetics? 'There is', said Baudelaire, 'a universal religion made for the alchemists of thought, a religion which detaches itself from man, and regards him as a memento of the Divine.'[37]

In November 1946, at the inaugural conference of UNESCO, 'the real problem', explained Malraux, pushing still further his meditation at Altenburg, 'is not the transmission of cultures in their specific character, but to know how the quality of humanism that each of them contains has come down to us, and what it has become for us.'[38] After the tortures, and the concentration camps, and the atom bomb, was a universal and not a syncretist humanism conceivable? Or, if history had gone back to zero point, was art no longer possible, had it destroyed itself?

The three volumes of *La Psychologie de l'art* came out between 1947 and 1949, and created an immediate sensation. They were brilliantly produced with every device in the making up of the pages and orchestration of the coloured plates. They excited the fury and astonishment of Georges Duthuit, the high priest of Byzantinism, and the careful and penetrating commentary of Maurice Blanchot. One is sorry to see *Le Musée, l'art et le temps*[39] excluded from most of Malraux's bibliographies. If, as Malraux puts it, 'our deepest relation to art is metaphysical',[40] the title of his book embraces its contents rather less than it indicates the orientation and psychology, not of the artists themselves, but of artistic creation in general, and it does this upon no predetermined theory. The author's shifting thought on a complex and unstable ground resulted in a revision of the test, and the three volumes, extended and modified, were compressed into a single, large work divided into four parts, *Les Voix du silence* (1951). It was not until 1965 that the opening, and most famous, chapter of this, *Le Musée imaginaire*, appeared in its final form.[41] At the same time Malraux's initial study of Goya's drawings, 'Goya en noir et blanc' (1939) was included in *Le Triangle noir* between the essay on Laclos (1939) and the essay on Saint-Just

(1954). It was amplified under the title of *Saturne* (1950), a monumental study of human suffering, and 'the prophet of the irremediable'.[42] When Goya was compelled by illness to a detachment from current affairs, he was thrown back on his own genius, withdrew from society, probed into his own feelings, and put a question mark against man himself. With his broken voice, and his colour of ashes and sulphur, he was the father of modern painting. One of the essential dialogues in *Les Voix du silence* is exchanged between Rembrandt and Goya, outside the walls of the Musée Napoléon where the greatest Spanish paintings have no place, and where the last phase of Rembrandt is misunderstood. If *Les Voix du silence* has had the same wide repercussion as the fanatical books of Winckelmann and Ruskin, by which Goethe, in the one case, and Proust in the other were so strongly influenced, it is because – apart from their instinsic splendour – these essays are animated by the same 'visionary gleam'.

Malraux did not discover the imaginary museum, but he gave it a name and, for our own time, the active importance of a category. It is more than the physical inventory of real museums and of historical monuments, which have themselves become museums. It is not a receptacle for works of art, but a centre for their transmutation. Malraux creates a mental and flexible space where, *for the first time* in the adventure of humanity, and thanks to the ease of transport and the progress in photography – 'the plastic arts have invented their own printing'[43] – the marvels of the whole wide world and the 'inheritance of the whole of history'[44] are displayed for our fascination. Here it is that the autonomy and universality of artistic creation, art's awareness of its own nature as a strange absolute with no object beyond itself, are realized through *metamorphosis*.

The content of the second chapter, *Les métamorphoses d'Apollon*, was not altogether new, but its title had a fresh relevance to the *Psychologie de l'art*, as this had appeared in its different versions. It showed how the religious arts of antiquity turned their backs on the transcendence which they served and into which they were absorbed, making themselves visible in art alone; just as the Gods, disaffected of their cults, pass from eternity into present time, and are turned into pictures and statues.

The close links between the imaginary museum and the radical development of modern art, and with the prodigious advance in archaeology registered at the same time, made a deep impression on Malraux when he visited studios and studied excavations on the spot. His wide experience of art was equally genuine if he met it in Asia, or fighting in Spain, and he managed to communicate it with an obsessive strength of feeling, and not of demonstration. 'What we write about art invites agreement, sometimes persuades, and proves nothing.'[45] One may complain of the apparently tumultuous disorder of these writings, but this is the result of an authentic and concrete approach, a range of observation simultaneous rather than chronological, and it makes its effect by throwing brilliant lights on the tidal waves. The ideas, with their rhythmical and emotional suggestions, extend beyond their meaning, and if there exists, says Malraux 'an understanding of forms superior to the understanding of ideas',[46] the ideas tend to become clear in the light of the works of art which they evoke and to which they give shape. The insistent repetition of assertions which seem to be already accepted, but which in reality come as a continual shock to established doctrines and prejudices widely held, is due to the need to enforce conviction and to the demands of an incantatory lyricism. One should also remember that *Les Voix du silence* is an extraordinary prose poem, and that all the famous writer's essays on art constitute, according to the critic Henri Peyre, 'the supreme achievement in prose of French romanticism'.[47]

Malraux welcomes the romantic conception of *genius*, but he demands, under the pressure of contemporary art, that 'genius shall create forms'.[48] Creation is not the same as vision; forms stand in opposition to images; they are different from signs, and are not to be explained by dreams; and when they are combined with colour – in the case of Kandinsky, Klee, and Miró – 'we touch upon action in modern painting in what is, for the time being, its extreme form'.[49] The third chapter is of capital importance. It analyzes the process of artistic creation, the syntax by which forms, through their successive stages and the *diagrams* that give them their direction, become style. The two clearest examples and the most typical of modern taste are El Greco and Georges de la Tour. The feverish lighting of El Greco inscribes the baroque design in movement on the Byzantine space which has no depth; and in Georges de la Tour certain volumes appear like surfaces through a geometrical crystallization of Caravaggio's universe. Scholars who are on the track of Malraux's sources and like to quote the lecture by Max Dvoràk in 1920 on 'El Greco and Mannerism',[50] forget to remind us that at the beginning of the century Picasso and the friends of his youth carried El Greco's pictures in procession from Barcelona to Sitgès, as Tuscan painters used to do; and those for whom 'La Tour is the triumph and the justification of the art historians',[51] and who use his name as an excuse to unroll their list of experts, forget that we are equally indebted to Juan Gris for our understanding of the master from Lorraine. For a long time several of his pictures were attributed to the Spanish school. Perhaps the next generation of art historians will include El Greco and La Tour among the overestimated reputations of our time; and Caravaggio himself, resurrected by Cubism, as an heroic accident on the solar highway of painting where an unfading star – the brother of Seurat and Cézanne – keeps watch and ward: Piero della Francesca. (Scali, in *L'Espoir*, is a specialist of Piero.) Reference has often been made to the function of *chiaroscuro* in Malraux's novels, but without sufficient emphasis on its plastic value and spiritual significance. Artistic creation, that the wear and tear of time and the metamorphosis of the way we look at it transform into artistic fiction, is subject to the same breathless inflection and the same imperious palpitation as the inventions of the novel. *Les Voix du silence* has something also of Caravaggio's dramatic effect in the way it throws clusters of light on to the dark stage where the geniuses, each in their turn, glitter and are faded out, and those 'super-artists that we call styles'[52] secrete their masterpieces. 'Every great work is illuminated by the trail of beacons that sweep a path for the history of art and for history in general, and fade away when they desert it.'[53]

Malraux belongs to a period in which theories of culture and systems of forms are both elaborated. The fourth and last chapter, *La monnaie de l'absolu*, is a difficult and sometimes pathetic argument between a dual need – to safeguard the deep resonance of culture and the autonomous voice of art; and this is not entirely comprised in the complex notion of style. The artist or the amateur who would only preserve in the works of the past their specifically plastic qualities 'is a superior type of modern barbarian',[54] since the lesson we learn from the primacy of art is that everywhere, and for a long time, art was something other than art. At this stage of his enquiry, Malraux was still a prisoner of the Hegelian myth. He came up against the problem of *time*, of time in art, and had the presentiment of its polarity which the works that followed were better able to elucidate. He was forced to unravel the ambiguous connection between art and history. 'The explanation that history brings to the conquests of art deepens their meaning, without, however, taking it altogether into account, because time in art is not historical duration. . . . History tries to transform destiny into awareness, and art to transform it into freedom.'[55] Art filters whatever is most troubled in the past, and transmits only the pure water of time, so well indeed that 'the imaginary museum is the song of history, but not its illustration',[56] and more surely than any other creation of mankind 'art stands up to fate'.[57]

In May 1952, at the Congrès de l'Oeuvre du XXe siècle in Paris,

Malraux proclaimed that 'there is something more important than history, and that is the constancy of genius'.[58] The arts of primitive and prehistoric societies, now to be seen in the museums, attest the range and power of artistic creation – 'it is not so much that the artist creates to express himself as that he expresses himself in order to create'[59] – and the permanence of genius at the heart of the human race. After publishing, in homage to Valéry, *Tout l'oeuvre peint de Léonard de Vinci* (1950) and then, in 1952, *Tout Vermeer de Delft*, detaching pages out of Proust from the critical anthology included in this sumptuous album, Malraux undertook the publication in three volumes of *Le Musée imaginaire de la sculpture mondiale* (1952–1954). 'Painting is the art that belongs to us, and sculpture is the art that we have resurrected.'[60] Out of the tens of thousands of photographs collected, fifteen hundred were kept. These composed the 'Treasury', and Malraux was certain, on the whole, that his choice would be approved by contemporary artists, because it was dedicated by the intrinsic appeal of the works themselves rather than by his own preference. The collation and identification of documents, and the verification of fact on the spot, obliged him to undertake several fresh journeys. In Egypt the Sphinx was now cleared of sand, and when he found himself in front of it for the second time the experience was decisive. He was gripped by a lightning intuition which gave a new impetus and regulation to his thought.

It was then that I distinguished two languages which had been speaking to me in unison for thirty years. The language of appearance, of a crowd similar no doubt to that which I saw in Cairo, the voice of the ephemeral; and the language of Truth, the voice of the sacred and the eternal . . . and I discovered that art is not an adjunct of ephemeral populations, of their houses and their furniture, but of the Truth which they have created, one after another.[61]

Mallarmé made the same distinction between current speech and the essential word; and Hölderlin, witnessing to a time when the Gods had taken leave of absence, and when Being had been split in two, enjoined upon thought the task of distinguishing between this sphere and that. 'Man, as a power capable of knowledge, must distinguish worlds that are different, because knowledge is only possible through the opposition of contraries.'[62]

Les metamorphoses d'Apollon – the chapter from *Les Voix du silence* – was revised and extended in accordance with this bipartite conception of time. It became the first volume of *La Métamorphose des Dieux* (1957); Malraux had planned to entitle it *L'Inaccessible*. This is the world where the forms of the sacred, the divine, and religious belief submit appearances to the invisible Truth. Eternity reigns over the immobility of Egyptian and Sumerian civilization; and over their hypnotic faces and hieratic duplications. When Greece arises 'in a flutter of drapery',[63] dissipating the powers of the Night, the Sacred gives way to the Divine, and wonder to prostration. Tragedy is the poem of catharsis where the City is united with the Fate it has overcome. Rome was refractory to the Infinite; it enslaved itself to the real, and practised portraiture as an industry. The furnace of inspired pages are concerned precisely with sites and monuments that defy photography – Gizeh or Santa Sophia, which divinize space from without or transmute it from within. Every sacred art has its secular and naturalistic fringe. Malraux recognized the selective tendency of his study, and its deliberately metaphysical orientation. 'The purpose of this book is neither a history of art, nor an essay in aesthetics; but the significance of man's eternal answer to the question posed by that part of him which belongs to eternity – when it rises in the mind of the first civilization aware of not knowing what is the significance of man.'[64]

The appearance of the imaginary museum with its artistic pluralism coincided with the bankruptcy of standard aesthetics and their unitary point of view. According to the theoretical critic T. W. Adorno, 'Kant and Hegel were the last – to put it shortly – who could write on aesthetics without understanding anything about art'[65] – without reference, that is to say, to the special quality of the works in question. On the other hand archaeology and the history of art have greatly extended their range since then, but their traditional methods are generally confined to philology and the composition of a catalogue. Attempts at systematic interpretation by sociology or psycho-analysis have not yielded the expected results; they do no more than describe the conditions under which the works were executed. The approaches by way of iconology or semiology are still indirect or embryonic. The Faith was relit beneath the vaults of Byzantium in the gold of their mosaic, and invigilated by the faithful statues in the Romanesque churches. Meanwhile illuminated manuscripts had preserved a secret register of the sacred. Romanesque art achieved a perfect unity between the sacred and the human. Gothic transposed symbol into spectacle, liturgy into piety, and painting was from now onwards the privileged medium for a power of invention, undisclosed till then. The preaching of the Franciscans and the Christian mystery of the Incarnation – of the God-Man – found their supreme interpreter in Giotto, and in the frescoes of Assisi, Padua, and Florence. With Jan van Eyck, in Flanders, painting came away from the wall, and discovered the technique of the easel; the religious drama came down to earth, and dwelt among men, where the vibration of light registered the passing of the hours. Eternity was conquered by time.

The rhythm became ample and solemn, with its unfoldings and fore-shortenings, less jerky than it once had been, and reached its final mastery and definitive tempo. Malraux's illustrations, most opportunely, sanction the rightness of his commentary. He is sometimes accused of wishing to subject art to what can be photographed; but as one who never stops going here, there, and everywhere to get a first-hand impression of the works, and then to examine their likenesses, he has measured better than anyone the limits of reproduction. His most promising approach is the notion of form, and the purpose behind the form. This was introduced by Riegl, and Malraux subscribes to it on the level of syntax, but it proves inadequate on the level of references and spiritual mutations, when 'the mystery is soul before it is style'.[66] Thus the mosaic of St Lawrence at Milan, where Christ appears among the apostles in a toga, 'makes us realize clearly the limits of a history of art which confines itself to a history of forms; all the apostles belong to the heritage of Antiquity, but the Roman mosaic represents the gods, and Christianity manifests the Christ'.[67] When the young amateur of *La Voie royale* asks the director of the French Institute at Saigon to choose between the Khmerian statues and those from Ham, 'How should I choose?' replied the eminent academic, 'I am an archaeologist'.[68] Malraux exercises his choice in the name of the artists, not of the scholars. 'I doubt whether a single Christian sculptor admires the *Last Judgement* at Chartres as much as the *Last Judgement* at Autun; and whether any sculptor admires the first without reservations, and even without unease.'[69]

Malraux was a minister for eleven years (1958–69), and despite the routine of administration, he tried to apply his cultural and artistic policy; 'to make accessible to the greatest possible number of Frenchmen the great works of humanity, and particularly those of France'.[70] In Paris, where he was responsible for the cleaning of the monuments, he organized impressive exhibitions of old or contemporary masters, and brought to the Louvre leading experts from all over the world. He went on missions to every continent, and made speeches in Mexico, Brasilia, Tokyo, Delhi, or New York as the circumstances and the place dictated. On 28 May 1959, from the height of the Acropolis in Athens – 'the only spot in the world haunted by the spirit of bravery and the genius of the mind' – he saluted 'a civilization that has no sacred book' and for which 'the word "intelligence" meant "interrogation" '.[71]

In 1960, with the help of Georges Salles and afterwards André Parrot, he founded the encyclopaedic collection, *L'Univers des Formes*. This was a mnemotechnic palace and a sanctuary for the eye, where the illustrations, of which he was a master, played an essential rôle. The learned texts were in the hands of the best specialists, who were sometimes disconcerted by his hypotheses, but they bowed before his certainty of vision, culture, and really universal plastic memory.

In 1965 a long sea cruise, prescribed for reasons of health, was transformed into an official journey to Pekin. Following an interview with Mao – 'the massive silhouette of the bronze emperor withdrew'[72] – Malraux asked to see once again, after twenty years, the tombs of the Ming dynasty. 'How would they have changed?'[73] he wondered anxiously, in a land which had altered more in a century than ever before. They were the work, said the poet Jean Grosjean, of one of those rare men 'who are haunted alike by the great events of their own time, and by the invisible root of everything that happens'.[74] The *Antimémoires* (1967) bring us face to face with the actual overthrow of empires, and with the remarkable metamorphosis of the witness who travels over the world once again on its tracks, at an age when he feels 'his youth disappear in the depths of time'.[75] The book then turns to India, for here is the furnace of transcendence, where the vicissitudes of history are lit up and burn themselves out. The various conversations, over different periods, with Nehru have a Platonic breadth; they give one a sense of the passage of time in history, the permanence of the Absolute, and the cyclical rhythm. Nehru speaks as a man of deep culture, responsible for a huge country, and well aware of its spiritual genius and material difficulties. 'There was no play-acting in the way he spoke; he said what he wanted to say, like all the great historical figures I have met, and like most of the painters.'[76] The comparison was significant, for it gives a profound confirmation to the unity of Malraux's enterprise.

Mao appeared to him as the heir of the great Founders, and this inspired his pilgrimage, when the interview was over, along the roads bordered with willows and hollyhocks to the tombs of the Emperors where they stood up in the unchanging fields. Nehru was linked to the sacred grottoes, and to the power they have exercised from time immemorial, like a crypt hewn out of the mountain, and, acting on the same impulse, Malraux went to visit them after his conversation with the Pandit. We see him under the galleries of Ellora, filled with floral offerings and echoing to the chant of Vedic hymns.

The dance of Siva that I was looking at might have been the dance of the Essence itself at the moment when death frees it from body, mind, and soul. And even in a museum this dance transcends the limits of art; its perfection, here, belongs to the enigmatic and persuasive order of the myth and the jungle and the orchid. It is a work of the gods. Nowhere have I felt so strongly that every sacred art presupposes in its worshippers an assurance that the world holds a secret, which art transmits but does not disclose, and in which they share. I was in the nocturnal garden of the great Indian dreams.[77]

In the spring of 1971 Malraux was still under the spell of India; by the 'most religious country in the world, and the most charged with feeling'.[78] He made a chivalrous offer to fight for Bangladesh – and he was seventy years old. How often, since his adolescence, had he returned to Krishna's song in the *Bhagavad Gita*: 'I am the death of everything, and the birth of everything. I am word and memory, constancy and compassion. And I am the silence of those things that are hidden.'[79]

Malraux's official functions were linked to the personality of General de Gaulle, and they came to an end with his government. It was the painter Balthus who remarked that the General, seen in full face, resembled Poussin's self-portrait. In Malraux's description of the General, in *Les Chênes qu'on abat ...*, after their last interview at Colombey, surrounded by the woods in their blanket of snow: 'I was not thinking about a photograph,' he said, 'I was dreaming of an El Greco, but not of an El Greco where the sitter was imaginary'.[80]

There is no mention of Spain in the *Antimémoires*, because Spain is a country to which he has always refused to return. In the sublime *Lazare* (1974), a Dostoevskian journey to the frontiers of death, memories of the Spanish struggle crowd to the bedside of the sick man with their pictures of brotherhood, 'the brotherhood that the future does not efface'.[81] Modern creation in the arts is a revolutionary battle where Braque stands side by side with Chardin, Cézanne with the sculptors of classical Rome, and Picasso with Goya.

At Nice, in the summer of 1973, Malraux was present at the opening of the Biblical Museum of his friend Chagall; and in the following week at the Fondation Maeght, in Saint-Paul-de-Vence, for his own exhibition, 'André Malraux et le Musée imaginaire'. This was embellished with exceptional loans. The dinner, at which he spoke, was held at a small hotel in Mougins, at the foot of the hill where Picasso had just died. A few days later Jacqueline, the painter's widow, summoned him to the house at Mougins, where she showed him its treasures, the château of Vauvenargues, and his tomb. The most famous pre-Columbian skull is displayed by itself, under glass, in the

Museum at Mexico City, and in front of a mirror which reflects the movement of the clouds and also of the onlookers. *La Tête d'obsidienne* (1974) is art's defiance of death, the confrontation of the imaginary museum, with metamorphosis as its guiding principle, and Picasso who is 'the Saturn of Metamorphosis',[82] at once its implacable rival and its inexhaustible source. 'It was Picasso who brought artistic creation back to the grottoes, because this was an adventure that travelled parallel with his own.'[83] Among his masks and fetishes there was an idol from Crete in the shape of a violin. He was extremely fond of it, and jokingly called the man who had made it 'the little fellow from the Cyclades'.[84] It was the millenary and brotherly symbol of the creative power with which he, in his turn, had been invested. . . .'

The second volume of *La Métamorphose des Dieux* shows the adventure of art, from Florence to Rembrandt, at the service of *L'Irréel* (1974), because it idealizes classical antiquity and chooses its themes, not only from the Bible, but just as frequently from pagan legend with the complementary figures of Venus and the hero. 'The world of God is the supreme reality; the Unreal, like the Greek divinities, takes shape in art as if art were the light that it sees by.'[85] Tuscany in the *Quattrocento* created the *strict and volumetrical style* in which we recognize *our own secret classicism*, and where the impassive Piero della Francesca joins hands with the sculptors of Olympus. At the start of the following century creative exultation turned to Rome and derived its enthusiasm from a rebellious emulation, giving life to the classical forms it had rediscovered. 'The word Renaissance entered the vocabulary of art to express the gradual discovery of the power by which the artist, in making the pagan dream the rival of the religious dream, creates the exultant *Irréel*. The dependence of the creature and the transcendence of the Creator disappear together.'[86] Art comes into its kingdom, and genius into its empire. Leonardo unveils the mystery, Raphael achieves perfection and Michelangelo, a solitary demiurge, prolongs the *grand style* which mannerism transforms into *stylization*. With him sculpture asserts its primacy. Painting celebrates its triumph in Venice, where a new poetics is born from the *magic* of colour.

The chromatic splendours of Venetian painting, and the prestige of the 'Unreal', were both questioned by Rembrandt in his 'journey to the end of night'. The religious Incarnation which he hoped to realize was no longer possible – 'there is no Incarnation in the art of the Unreal, Incarnation is only possible in an art that does not think of itself as art';[87] and his own work, at once disturbed and compassionate, goes forward in the darkness and in pursuit of a 'communion *with the*

Unknown.[88] M. J. Friedlander, the great expert on Nordic art, whose formation owed more to the painter Max Liebermann than to the universities, wrote that an understanding of Rembrandt was among the spiritual conquests of the last century. Doubtless one should add Van Gogh and Delacroix, and the Russian novelists.

Malraux foresaw that the total meaning of *L'Irréel* would only become clear with the publication of the third and last volume, *L'Intemporel*. Certain conclusions he arrived at here were already fore-shadowed in the speech at Mougins, included in *La Tête d'obsidienne*. 'The intemporal is within us', said Bergson, because our inner aware-ness of time is not chronological. Time in art is not the same thing as time in history. Art is obedient to the sense of eternity when the sacred governs its forms, and to the sense of immortality when they are inspired by the Unreal. As the art of the whole world is opened out before us, and we see it as an enigma, and as painting, from Manet onwards, becomes identified with what Braque has called 'the pictorial fact', 'the intemporal is our precarious form of immortality, and it is continually reborn'.[89] Why, then, has the imaginary Museum a meaning, and what problems does it bring up to light? The meta-morphosis of the imaginary Museum began in the Far East, and it soon became the subject of artistic dialogue between the two civilizations. In the West, after the irruption of barbaric arts and other risky adventures, has the imaginary Museum fulfilled its role? Has the audio-visual already supplanted it, where the fluidity of the screen enables art to escape from history, and where the creative process is free to unroll its sequences in a spatial frame?

'One has to have died several deaths to paint like that',[90] said Van Gogh in front of Rembrandt's *Jewish Bride*. The symbol of modern art is Harlequin, and he is also the mysterious ferry-man on the boat that is bound for the underworld. Malraux has often experienced, and recorded in his books, the orphic sensation of what he called 'the return to earth'. He felt it after a long journey, and especially in the face of death. The world appeared to him then in all its original freshness, as if he were seeing it *for the first time*.

To be the object of a fake execution is not a negligible experience. But what principally gives me this feeling is the thrilling awareness of the centuries gone by; a singular and sometimes physical awareness, which my labours on the subject of art make all the more insidious, for every imaginary museum exhibits the death of civilizations and the resurrection of what they have created. I was fascinated by the course of time, and by the way the sun trembles and changes on the stream as it flows by.[91]

Artistic creation – the familiar and enigmatic 'little fellow from the Cyclades' – is restored to the present by metamorphosis. It traverses the centuries with the constancy of dreams and the force of biological instinct. It is the surest guarantee of the unity of the human race. Thanks to its connivance with death – to its astonishing and additional sense of the passage of time, and without any rupture of its tragic humanism – other conceptions of art are made possible. These allow a large place to Schiller's notion of chance, and Batville's of festivity. Malraux finds in the haunting flux of artistic creation a question to which there is no reply, and shows each of its mutations as an epiphany. He is a classical moralist, a romantic poet, a contemporary thinker, and a musician unequalled in the management of the plastic orchestra. But his greatest gift, that our own time, with its itch for reducing everything to scale, sometimes condemns as mystifying and sometimes as melodramatic, and that antiquity placed above every other, is without question his eloquence. This is the voice of his exaltation, where the faith of the citizen and the fire of the prophet are both engaged.

C. L. SULZBERGER

*

THE HUMAN CONDITION
OF MALRAUX

Malraux's greatest literary work is his own life. A child of the century, born in 1901, he has experienced its most important waves. His enemies say he began as a revolutionary and ended as a counter-revolutionary. The touchstone of this particular definition is Marxism: it is wrong both ways. Malraux was at no time a Marxist; perhaps he isn't patient enough. Victor Serge, a deceived Leninist, wrote to him from Mexico just after World War Two that if he were French he too would be a Gaullist. But that proves nothing. Malraux never really worshipped seriously at the altar of any gods – above all those that failed.

Malraux's political outlook is, in fact, totally anti-Marxist. He believes in the influence of man in history. Long ago, in 1958, he told me: 'Communism destroys democracy but maybe democracy also destroys Communism. We will beat the Communists by doing what they didn't do. But if we don't do this, we won't beat them.' Have we done it?

Obviously, Malraux is passionately interested in politics. No other Europeans (save the Greeks) exceed the French in this respect. No other event but the bicycle Tour de France so agitates French discussion. And Malraux, with his intellect, his energy, his encyclopaedic curiosity and his courage, is the quintessence of Frenchness.

He could not, nor did he wish to, escape the violence, change and disillusion that have whelmed his time. When he was born, Alsace was German; and Alsace has no special root in his heart, his experience, his writing. When he was born, stability, as represented by the gold standard, the French and British empires, seemed permanent.

Back in March 1957 Jean Cocteau told me: 'The great tragedy of

France is that its politicians are unsuccessful writers and its writers are unsuccessful politicians.' Among the former he named de Gaulle (which was, of course, absolute nonsense) and Herriot. Among the latter he named Malraux. 'Have you ever heard of a human reading *La Condition humaine*?' he asked rhetorically. (It spoiled Cocteau's charm to answer him.)

Malraux's consuming ambition, he said, was to play a political role; he told me that Malraux had once assured him he supported de Gaulle because he thought it high time for a General Boulanger to succeed in France. This is, of course, wholly ridiculous, perhaps pleasant dinner party conversation, but wholly untrue. It comes with the coffee and goes with the cigars. In truth Malraux venerated de Gaulle and held the memory of Boulanger in contempt.

It is astonishing that the Nobel Prize for Literature, designed to be the greatest tribute to a writer but too frequently awarded to nonentities, has escaped one of this century's outstanding authors, André Malraux. Unlike so many candidates, his own 'nobelity' lies in himself. The shame is not Malraux's but that of the sometimes stodgy Swedish Academy which makes the choice. Malraux's own life, which coincides precisely with that of the Nobel Prize (both were born in 1901), is in itself a piece of literature equal to any of his books.

Despite his age, despite his continual activities on a broad horizon including warfare, politics, ministerial service under de Gaulle, the beautification of Paris, feverish attempts to rally public opinion against injustice, and despite the almost unbearable series of tragedies involving those he loved, this magnificent man has continued to write.

While the audacious, romantic and sometimes mournful tapestry of Malraux's life as the most *engagé* of authors has a quality in itself worthy of special Nobel tribute, the Swedish Academy is charged – as is proper – only with considering literary output. But here it has been woefully remiss.

To a remarkable degree, action is Malraux's special sphere. I have discussed this at various times with people who knew him during the Spanish Civil War days and also with people who knew him during World War Two, in the French Resistance. General Pierre Elie Jacquot, a professional officer and St Cyrien, was assigned as Number Two to Malraux's maquis group. Jacquot was to keep an eye on the amateur whom, as Jacquot's bosses in the French military establishment knew, he had already encountered in Spain. But Jacquot subsequently confided to me that Malraux had a positive genius for guerrilla warfare.

He would have been 'a great medieval mercenary or an adventurer in America's Wild West', the General said. 'He was a true Romantic and he was dominated by an extraordinary passion for tanks.' Another day he added: 'He has the genius of a *condottiere*. He doesn't know anything about the techniques of soldiering but he is a real *chef de guerre*. With him it is instinct and art – not knowledge.'

Malraux certainly had special soldierly talents and instincts. Only a physically courageous man, he once confided to me, could command volunteer troops. Malraux fills that bill. (He says personal courage is not necessary when commanding conscripts – 'You just put your orders into the machine – colonel to major to captain to lieutenant to sergeant.')

He does not like war, but 'it has been around me all my life.' He believes that combat nowadays is less of a human strain because soldiers don't usually see the men they're killing. The bayonet charge ended fifty years ago. When he commanded his air unit in the Spanish Civil War, there was 'a particular sense of comradeship when flying for the Republic because we knew there was a comrade in another plane on each wingtip. I suppose that feeling of personal support in a human sense was something like fighting in the cavalry in the days of Napoleon.'

This kind of tough talk is rather strange coming from Malraux who doesn't look in the least belligerent. He is of medium height (what used to be called tall), of originally delicate build (somewhat filled out by age), with pale skin, long, mobile features, and an intense gaze that makes him resemble Edgar Allen Poe more than Poe himself. He is afflicted with passionate gestures and a repertoire of tics.

I have known Malraux for years and value him as a precious friend. Having often talked with him about many things, I once wrote and asked (with this article in mind) four questions on odd matters of special interest to me. These are listed herewith, together with his written answers:

Q. Once you told me that almost all men, as they get older, develop an enormous interest either in metalworkers or woodworkers and that General de Gaulle, during his last years, became fascinated with the carpenters and foresters around Colombey-les-Deux-Eglises. Have you any explanation for this phenomenon – the passion for metalworking or woodworking? And which is your own preference of the two?

A. I have no explanation. But I do know that the question 'Wood or metal?' is included in certain tests in psychiatry. For myself, it is wood – undoubtedly because of art; wood is used in painting and sculpture.

This is a curious subject, preference for wood or metal, as he puts it. One might have thought that Malraux would surely have insisted on including stone among such elementary basics. After all, not only does stone sculpture figure extensively in his ecumenical artistic concept of the imaginary museum, but it was his search for stones, the jungle-obscured Khmer ruins scattered along the Royal Road, that launched him as a youngster along the endless path of adventure.

Q. I have always been struck by your immense sympathy for animals, both dogs and cats especially. I know that my poor beagle (who died last Christmas) seemed to find a particular friend in you when you came to our home. Nevertheless, it is my impression that your preference as between cats and dogs is definitely in favour of cats. I have watched Jessie Wood's (daughter of Louise de Vilmorin) little cat romp all over you. Am I correct in saying that cats are your favourite animals and have you any conceivable explanation for this special affection?

A. I do indeed love animals. But my liking for cats is special. We will talk about it because I believe the subject to be rather complex. Affection for dogs is quite understandable; our kinship with cats, much less so. Without any doubt a race of cat-lovers and dog-lovers exists among artists.

Malraux tells many stories about animals. For example, he has assured me that de Gaulle kept a large Alsatian for years at Colombey-les-Deux-Eglises and that (somewhat furtively) he spoiled the handsome dog, who often slept on the General's bed. Madame de Gaulle (Tante Yvonne, as the French affectionately and respectfully dubbed her) disliked this and complained from time to time. 'Yes, yes,' the General would assure her with tranquillity. But the Alsatian was never dispossessed.

However, Malraux's fund of tales on cats is endless and astonishingly varied. According to him, the first cat to appear in European history was in the seventh century, when Pope Gregory was given such a pet by Ethiopia, a congregation he especially adored. Not long afterward, the church council issued a proclamation saying that it would be better if the Pope spent more time seeing to his pontifical duties and less time caressing his cat.

He also contends that the French contingent at Agincourt outnumbered the British by five to one but were defeated for the following reason. The British had a 'captaincy' of cats who drove the rats toward the French camp, where they promptly set about eating the bowstrings of France's archers so they were not in a position to shoot back.

Q. Two days ago at lunch I remarked that Sheikh Mujibur Rahman of Bangladesh was a man of great courage and you seemed, while most definitely agreeing with this, to rate physical courage as by no means an extraordinary human trait. I know of your own great courage from people who have fought with you – for example, General Jacquot. What I wanted to ask was whether you are one of those very few people who do not know the meaning of fear in any form (he once spoke to me of de Gaulle's 'geological courage') – or whether you do indeed know its meaning but always summon up the willpower to conquer it within yourself.

A. I am aided by an irrational feeling of invulnerability.

I have already explained what those who knew him as a combatant thought of Malraux as a warrior. He clearly had an intuitive skill, a sense of dash, of audacity. He also had the plain gift of courage. No one, perhaps not even Malraux himself, will ever really know if this was based on an 'irrational' self-confidence, on faith in something that transcended himself, or on an enormous, if disguised, will-power that masked internal doubts.

Q. My final question. Do you think that the *engagé* artist (meaning any kind of creative artist including writers) becomes a better artist because he is *engagé*? Did you find in your own life that the fact you were *engagé* at a very early age helped to develop your vast literary talent perhaps more rapidly and completely than otherwise? Can you think of any writer of recent times who is not *engagé* and whose work has perhaps suffered because of this?

A. Today the problem arises in a particular way, because *engagement* cuts across history, within which we live. I do not believe that *engagement* in itself has a value but that certain artists do have need of it.

This consideration of *engagement* is a key to Malraux and his entire life. He was, indeed, 'engaged' (in his Indochinese art adventure) before he was even recognized as a creative artist; he has always been 'engaged', although his causes have certainly varied from simmering revolts in Asia, to Republican Spain, to anti-Nazism, (and, incidentally) to French Resistance, to France as an idea and, finally, to humanitarianism.

When I once asked him if he thought there were still *engagé* writers in the sense that had prevailed when he was young, especially during the Spanish Civil War, he said there had always, in one or another way, been such *engagement*. Certainly since the 1789 Revolution. Indeed (and I quote with precision because, although I was his luncheon guest, I insisted on taking notes), the tradition of the *engagé* French writer had continued in an almost theatrical fashion into the Gaullist era. Many recent *engagé* artists had been clinging to a dream. For others, St John Perse, for example, it is difficult to think in terms of *engagement*. It surely cannot act as a ferment unless the artist feels it indispensable.

Like Lamartine, Malraux himself followed this tradition. After all, Lamartine also did more than write; he became, for a brief moment, a member of the five-man executive committee that governed France in 1848. But who, to rephrase Cocteau, reads Lamartine today?

Once, over luncheon, I brought Malraux together with Régis Debray, the French left-wing revolutionist who fought beside Che Guevara. Malraux told the young guerrilla: 'There is no enemy, there is no single enemy. There are just many, and these are all symbolic. The Right no longer exists and today everybody is on the Left, which means the Left no longer exists.' Debray confided to me: 'He is more human than the heroes in his novels.'

Debray wanted to know what the International Brigade had done in Spain. Malraux told him that it had indeed saved Madrid, but – above all else – it had answered the dream element of Republican Spain. 'If they are on our side, then we know we are not so pathetic,' he said. Malraux also explained that the brigade's role was enhanced by its temporary nature. No replacement was created after its disbandment.

The conversation moved to other topics. The Resistance was brought up. Malraux admitted he had not really liked the film *Le Chagrin et la Pitié*. 'The Resistance,' he said, 'was not really like that. One day I may write the book about *la résistance française*.' Then he recounted a Resistance story. A group of maquis from the Corrèze were ordered to capture a convoy of trucks transporting German sugar. The maquis didn't see the machine guns which flanked the convoy. They attacked, and they were all killed.

All the women of that small Corrèze village, in black, went to their respective family tombs. The day after, as every woman of Corrèze, in black, stood by and watched, the Germans threw the dead bodies into a communal grave. A cross, next day, was on the grave. And every day thereafter, in this war-ravaged town, a new kilobag of sugar hung from the cross.

When the subject of capitalism came up, Malraux said: 'The matter is no longer important. One asks oneself if one is good or bad, charitable or egoist, brave or cowardly – but not: am I a capitalist?'

Because of his intense interest in politics this is a subject he delights in, and I recollect political discussions as having been spicy but mixed.

Once he insisted: 'The Fifth Republic is a masque. It can't continue. I suppose that if a Communist majority gained control of the National Assembly, Pompidou [this was December 1972] would dissolve the Assembly. Then there would no longer be a Fifth Republic. There would be a union of the Left, which would be directed by the Communists.'

In between, the French continued to dream of Napoleon – as the Spanish continued to dream of Charles V. Gaullism was impossible without de Gaulle; and it was impossible to foresee just what would come in France.

Another time I asked him if Western Europe had any future as an effective political organization. He said: 'That won't happen. It would mean a Europe governed by a parliament. But the parliamentary system as such is no longer effective. The reason the United States political system works is precisely because parliament is *not* the government.' (Like all Frenchmen, how wrong he had it! This was pre-Watergate.)

He thought 'Europe' could only be created by the menace of a non-European threat – just the way the United States was created by fear of Britain. When I asked where such a potential threat lay, he said the biggest question was commercial rivalry with Japan. (Another time he mentioned the highly theoretical danger of China.) Either could galvanize Europe, not us rivalry.

One day he sadly told me (harking back to his life-link with this century): 'The capital fact is the death of Europe. When I was twenty years old, the United States was approximately in the position of Japan today in terms of world importance. Europe was at the heart of things and the great superpower was the British Empire. But now all dominating forces in today's world are foreign to Europe.

'The great power in the world is the United States and, to the side, there is the Soviet Union. Europe has virtually disappeared as a factor and it took astonishingly little time for this change to come about. Two centuries ago, the United States was not even a nation; now it is a colossus.'

Politically Malraux stresses the legendary aspect: 'One must never overlook the Joan of Arc side of things.' He is fascinated by the individual's relationship to history. When I introduced him to Debray he produced a long monologue: Alexander and Napoleon were great, the Maréchal de Saxe (who never lost a battle) and Turenne were not. In Heaven, Saxe could say: 'You lost a battle'; but Napoleon would answer '*Vous n'avez jamais fait rêver les femmes!*'

What is Malraux, this century's punctuation point? Having been minister of culture, he once remarked to me: 'It will not be a bad monument if, when I die, I have left one hundred new museums in France behind me.' His literary testament has changed: fading novels; memoirs? Of the *Antimémoires* he assured me long ago that one won't be published until fifty years after his death; it included a talk with President Kennedy about the advisability of A-bombing China. Not to be mentioned now. But in half a century nobody would care. Anyway, what is a 'literary' testament? 'This is no time for literature.'

VICTORIA OCAMPO

*

MALRAUX'S WORLD AND OURS

In 1930, I went with Waldo Frank to Alfred Stieglitz's studio, in Madison Avenue. 'An American Place' he called it. The quality of the photos he showed me was unique. I, at least, had never seen their like. Trees, people, skies, American factories and wharfs, with nothing particularly striking about them, seemed translated into poetical terms. Through being handled by an artist the camera captured not only reality, but the overhanging dreams and visions of America that spread above it. These exchanges between the human eye, aware of beings and things, and the indifferent surrender, the precision of the instrument, submissive yet incorruptible, proved once more, I thought, that in art the most perfect mechanical medium is inefficient if it is not a mere extension of man's talent using that power for self-expression. There is no remote possibility that a work of art should not be born from an 'I' (as well as an eye), transcendent and sublimated perhaps, but nevertheless an 'I'. All the rest is idle talk. In addition, you can see at a glance that even if the field of the objective is limited (voluntary or involuntary), a fragment of a cloud, a hand, a bow, a tile with its own physiognomy, confined and singular, derive their impact from an allusion to the whole they are part of.

While reading Robert Payne's *Malraux* (1970), I found coincident observations, though they differ in their application: they aim at the possible shortcomings of a *musée imaginaire*: 'A photograph is not a simple mechanical reproduction; it depends on the eye of the operator, and so each photo of a work of art is subjected to the betrayal that comes from the inevitable presence of the photographer. It inevitably deforms.' Payne believes that reproductions of this kind are *transformations* and that the art history taught in schools is damaged by that betrayal. What seems to me interesting in Stieglitz's case, and in that of other great modern photographers, is that the transmission of the photographer's personality to a living or inert thing is imposed on the machine as if the mind had impregnated it. The machine obeys orders in a way which is almost spiritual. Perhaps *artistic* would be a more adequate word. Of course, if there is a photographer there is interference. And if this interference comes on top of an already interfered with thing (deformed, transformed as all artistic creations are), it can adulterate.

This beating about the bush brings us to the point: Malraux's statement at the very beginning of his *Antimémoires*, so rich in thought and in varied experiences. I stumbled over those lines, and shied off, but their importance does not permit them to be ignored: 'What do I care about what matters only to me? . . . Almost all the writers I know love their childhood; I hate mine.' Is it presumptuous of him to differ? And yet he must.

There is nothing important to us *exclusively*. In some way or other, good or bad, what concerns us concerns everyone else. What we are, what we do or refuse to do is part of a whole (a scheme?) and weighs on it, whatever appearances might be. All the scattered leaves bind finely in one volume.

> . . . *legato in un volume*
> *ciò che per l'universo si squaderna.*

As to whether one loves or hates one's childhood, it does not take an inch out of its influence on adult years. Nothing can alter that fact. Childhood is a key word. And when I see, in Payne's book, the thirteen-year-old Malraux photographed with Mlle Thouvenin and her pupils; when I look at the small, delicate, sensitive face, with its already concentrated expression, I feel a grudge against the great writer. I would have liked him to tell us about the tense schoolboy, with a watch (was it a watch?) in his pocket. I would have liked him to be *his own* photographer, as I am certain there is more in a child's or a man's heart than 'un miserable petit tas de secrets'. He has refused. In a few instances, the repressed emotion overflows: 'From the bottom of the rue Soufflot comes a sound I remember from my childhood: the trampling of horses, which the mounted guards are keeping at walking pace.'

Comtesse Mathieu de Noailles wrote 'Jamais le sort humain n'eut mon consentement'. How much this confession meant to the poet, I don't know, but I am sure it could be true of two men: the author of *The Seven Pillars of Wisdom*, and the author of the *Antimémoires*. Neither seems to have wholly accepted his childhood, in other words, his *condition humaine*.

In a letter I quite recently read, from Mrs Bernard Shaw to T. E. Lawrence, she dwells on her 'hellish childhood'. She must have had a hard time. But she comes to this conclusion: 'The fatal mistake is to keep these things locked up.' She is right. In the first place, because to voice them is a way of getting rid of a burden. In the second place, because we have much to learn about these 'burning questions', and only those who are capable of the more subtle analysis can bring enlightenment. These analyses are far from useless if they come from someone like Malraux. And I don't agree that the confessions of a memoir writer sound childish now, compared with the monsters exhibited by psychoanalysts' explorations. I learnt more from Dostoevsky than from Freud.

Without any special study of the extraordinary T. E. Lawrence, except for a thorough and passionate reading of his book and correspondence (which I translated and published some years ago), I dared write about the knotty subject. Guesswork. The man was elusive and formidable. Yet I felt I could not hit very far off the mark. Sixteen years after my essay was written. I met A. W. Lawrence, his brother, and gave it to him. He removed any fear I still had. My interpretation had not missed the point. I cannot attribute this to any special gift. I assume it is the result of that nearly magic communication born of the written word (if talent is behind it). And perhaps to some of those little studied perceptive faculties which modern science as yet neither accepts nor discards. Nevertheless, men who risk their lives for scientific purposes or explorations, and who cannot be accused of taking the 'uncertain' for granted, have been tempted to investigate the enigma. Edgar Mitchell, I am told, whilst flying in *Apollo 14* (not a pleasure trip) tried to transmit some telepathic message to friends (or vice versa). There might be something positive in those waves we are immersed in and that connect us with the known and the yet unknown. Why not? It took time to detect certain germs and viruses that medicine is fighting against now.

We could waste much paper discussing those problems. What happens to me with Malraux, though it matters only to me according to his theory, is what I am trying to investigate. Why am I inhibited by him and not by T. E. Lawrence? Is it really because he is alive and T. E. Lawrence is just one of my living dead? I am not certain.

Many have been Malraux's generosities with me. Once he told me: 'Something is missing in your collection.' As I don't collect things, not even first editions, I asked what he was talking about. 'Your collection of great men,' he answered, smiling. To someone else I would have replied: 'Don't be silly.' But who could use the word *silly* in connection with Malraux? It was true that having lost my faith in ordinary gods I had transferred to great writers my share of credulity (as Virginia Woolf's Orlando would say). And true that I had been lucky enough to meet the 'greatest' of my time. And musicians, and architects. No warriors, hardly any political leader had aroused my interest, except Gandhi, Nehru, Indira Gandhi and Golda Meir. The first two because they tried to graft the spiritual on to the political. The two women because they were the best exponents of feminism in the political field.

The fact is that a few days after this talk I found myself in the Elysée, eating a juicy Charolais steak at the side of de Gaulle (who graciously apologized: he was doubtful his Charolais could compete with the Argentine meat I was used to). Of course, all this was due to Malraux, to his imagination and munificence. I make a special mention of it, because I am aware of what de Gaulle meant for Malraux and Malraux for de Gaulle. That lunch was not a common courtesy and I appreciated the gesture.

But the author of the *Antimémoires* was not only popular with the powerful of this world (I suspect no single name could be added to his own collection.) A Paris taxi-driver once said to me, referring to de Gaulle's government: 'Ce qui restera de tout ceci c'est l'oeuvre de Malraux.' It was also the opinion of my concierge (whose dearest wish was to have an autograph of M. le Ministre – the wish was fulfilled). A strange popularity for one who made no concessions to what is called in our days, and in several countries, 'popular culture'. Let us pray that true culture will be given to those who have none, and not simply erased from those who have it. As Shelley wrote:

True love in this differs from gold and clay
That to divide is not to take away.

Other privileges were bestowed on me by this friend. For instance, the possibility of having talks with a very busy man. Should this not put me at ease to perform this small task: a few sketchy notes on Malraux's vast territory? Unfortunately, not at all.

For weeks I have been planning to send a cable to Baroness de Courcel asking her to relieve me of my promise. But I have now decided otherwise. To face the *impossible* is just the kind of thing Malraux is accustomed to. So be it.

I read in the *Antimémoires*: 'I think of the Glières chaplain ... of the Guatemala Indians, the queen of the Casamance, the wall against which I was to be shot, the bathroom at Toulouse, Elephanta and the tanks of 1940, Mao's trees whose bark had been eaten by the peasants, the American fleet off Da-Nang. ...' I think he thinks about all this and that his reminiscences survive and converse between them. I think of his novels, and his *Musée imaginaire*, and his intimacy with the art of the whole world and of all epochs, and of his way of transforming Paris and cleaning its marvellous face, and of his habit of risking his life for a cause or gambling with it just for the sake of flying over the Queen of Sheba's invisible town. I think of his declaration to Pierre Bockel: 'I am an agnostic: you see, I must be something, for, don't forget, I am intelligent. ... But you know better than myself that nobody can escape from God.' This continuous watchfulness of his intellect puts us under a beacon that illuminates and blinds. Valéry, an expert on those matters, did not hide his auto-diagnosis: 'La bêtise n'est pas mon fort.' Neither is it the strong point of our friend, a lover of cats like Baudelaire.

The royalty granted to cats, by Baudelaire, in the animal kingdom, and to intellect, by Malraux, in the human one, is not his only trump card. It could not be. Intelligence is a most indispensable element, but just like light it can shine only over what already exists. It can reveal, but not create. It can even illuminate emptiness, nothingness and give us awareness of what we cannot encompass. We find in Malraux, along with his intellect, a profound and omnipresent consciousness of the eternally unknown that he defines as the will to subordinate oneself to what goes beyond one. The certainty 'you'll never know what it all meant'. Here we stumble on Pascal ('le silence de ces espaces infinis') and on the kinship with T. E. Lawrence. We are getting closer to the rarefied atmosphere of the modern English monk without a church.

The two men are different but the same blood runs through their veins. They belong to the race of the Unicorn, uneasy in the thoroughbred stable. Both of them are convinced they will never live to find out what *all this* means; both race along parallel lines but on different courses towards an end they cannot reach or name.

Appearances can deceive: the two-roomed cottage, Cloud's Hill, has no resemblance to the exquisite and discreet luxury displayed in La Lanterne. The rustic place in Dorset chosen by T. E. for his retreat, with no floral ornament except rhododendrons, is the opposite of a well-groomed garden on the outskirts of the Park of Versailles. But starting with great ambitions, along different roads, both men discovered, each in his own way, 'the immense spaces of unhappiness'. Both looked at death face to face (and suffered tortures worse than death, in different circumstances). Going through these experiences undoubtedly brings deep changes in one. Which means (as these men had imagination) being ready to react, to run recklessly away or *towards* the place where their fear lurked. In Lawrence it became a kind of vertigo, 'an escape forward into peril'. Malraux must have known fear too, because without it, courage is meaningless.

I believe Malraux has said about himself all he intended to say (it matters little if he said it through a talk with Mao, Nehru, de Gaulle, looking at the ruins of Mareb, or remembering Napoleon and the big bundle of unexpected love letters in St Helena). If he has left something unsaid (and evidently he has), it is not our business to inquire why. And though in *Seven Pillars*, as in *The Mint*, there was self-censorship, and the author willed himself to set bounds and give as much as possible a bare account of facts (as he afterwards described the recruits' miseries in peacetime), I reckon that T. E. Lawrence's books are an 'exposition d'amertume' – a confession less restrained than Malraux's . . . except for one title: the *Antimémoires*. That is a kind of statement.

Of these two archangels of pride, the one who seems, at the end of his life, I would not say bowed down, but deeply moved by the *condition humaine,* is the one who never accepted anything of his sojourn on earth. Through his contradictory attitudes, through their scanty peep holes, I see him more approachable. He was already dead when I met him in his book. But my French friend is very much alive, and like the cat who roved in Baudelaire's mind:

> *Il juge, il préside, il inspire*
> *Toute chose dans son empire . . .*

Besides, I insist, he has *written himself* And let us never forget his intelligence is a powerful weapon. Intelligence does not tolerate nonsense. This archangel unsheathes his sword of light as soon as anyone draws near: it is more threatening than his bodyguard's machine-guns, when he was de Gaulle's minister.

I met him more than forty years ago, in my flat in the Avenue Malakoff. Drieu la Rochelle (a friend of both of us) had announced: 'I am going to bring with me, this afternoon, a very extraordinary fellow. You will see.'

Streets in Paris have names, not merely numbers, as in New York. Numbers are segregated from memories. They cannot absorb them. But names are their born accomplices. Names of streets and places, in Paris, stand now for Malraux as others stand for Valéry, Drieu, Camus. Avenue Malakoff, Avenue de la Bourdonnais, Avenue Victor Hugo in Neuilly, the Park of Versailles, the restaurant Lasserre. I seem to hear, if the rue de la Trémoille is named, the familiar voice of the concierge announcing that the car of M. le Ministre, with the Minister inside, was waiting (*so please, Madame, hurry up*). This now much-worshipped personality (that should not be kept waiting) was no other than 'the extraordinary fellow' Drieu brought to my home, Drieu who is dead, now, and by his own hand.

One day at noon Malraux came to fetch me, after a long absence of mine. He had left the car, and was waiting in the hall as I came out of the lift. His new office, and the *carte blanche* to do with Paris as he thought fit, had increased his courtesy. I have rarely seen so courteous a minister and never one with greater power over the arts, culture and the beautifying of this most beautiful city. How many human earthquakes the world had experienced since the 'extraordinary fellow' had been introduced to me. How many changes.

Hardly had I sat down in the car than, after mentioning jokingly that it was probably the first time I had been followed by another car with men holding machine-guns, he started talking as if we had seen each other the day before: 'Where were we? . . . China?' I smiled, remembering the abrupt beginning of *La Condition humaine*: 'Would Tchen try to lift the mosquito net? Would he strike through it?' I had always admired that opening. Tchen is going to kill a sleeping man. The idea disgusts him. He feels the beginning of nausea. In his right hand he holds a razor, in his left a dagger. But the first thing we see in the room where a murder is going to be committed is the innocent mosquito net, suggesting insects, heat, sleep . . . The atmosphere is given by the contrast: near the pale, defenceless mosquito net, death hides in a hand 'detached from anything human', or wishing to be so.

Though I have travelled, in time, longer than Malraux; though I have dimly seen, through a London window, old Queen Victoria surrounded by soldiers, and the Tzar and Tzaritsa from a balcony in the Champs Elysées, and from a South American one several South American revolutions passing by; though I have gazed with horror at the ruins of European bombed towns, and sat in the Nuremberg Trials a few yards from the Nazis sentenced to death, and discussed the *Divina Commedia* with Mussolini in an Italian palace; though I have seen San

Francisco in the blackout, and met Gandhi through Tagore, and Stravinsky through the *cataclysme apprivoisé* (in Cocteau's words) of the first performance of the *Sacre du Printemps*; though I walked in my garden of the River Plate with von Braun, listening to his explanations of an imminent landing on the Moon and thinking 'This man is raving mad'; though I bathed with relish in the unpolluted waters of Punta Mogotes in the company of Saint-John Perse; though I enjoyed the thick shade of Californian redwoods with Waldo Frank, and the stained-glass light of Notre Dame with Valéry, and looked with a wistful eye at the walls of an Argentine jail (we prisoners had the privilege of breathing in the patio twice a day); though I have discussed with Camus my translation of his *Caligula* for Broadway, and smelt, with Ortega, the scent of Guadarrama's *jaras* in the Escorial; though I held the arm of the half-blind Borges to cross the *carrefours* of our town; though I saw and heard, with Keyserling, in Darmstadt, the Hitler Youth marching and singing of future violence, and with Eisenstein, in Harlem, the Spirituals of a negroes' revivalist congregation; though I made friends again with Neruda in Lima, where I met him on his way to Machu Pichu, and gazed at the Pyramids of Teotihuacan with my unforgettable Alfonso Reyes; though Gropius confided to me his forebodings in an Italian train, and Le Corbusier described to me how he would have planned a new capital for Argentina; though I forecast, with Gabriela Mistral, a bad period for Hispanic America; though I was amused and delighted at Virginia Woolf's mistaken idea of butterflies in Buenos Aires and flooded her Tavistock Square house with their Brazilian wings; though I have introduced young Caillois to Latin American writers and he in turn introduced them to Europe; though I have done the same for South America and Graham Greene and all those who cared to take notice of this undiscovered land; though my dream of meeting Ravel came true and I lunched with him at Monfort-L'Amaury; though I went to Braque's home holding two pots of unbelievably pink hyacinths as candles to a divinity, and recited Mallarmé with Aldous Huxley while our car ran along the Hudson River; though I ate a delicious home-made cake in Eliot's flat in Chelsea whilst talking of less fleshly *gourmandises*; though Helleu made a dry-point of myself in my teens saying: 'Keep still, my child, I will sketch you just like that, *la main sur la conscience*' (I believe he threw a spell over me, because I never could get rid of my conscience); though things pile up appallingly in long lives and play tricks, and push themselves to the mountain top of memories that pine for youthful valleys without past; though all this and more is my daily bread, as soon as I open the *Antimémoires* I ascertain how little I have suffered the atmospheric turbulences of my time, if I compare my experiences and their rhythm with the staggering record of my French friend. I see him passing from one peak or abyss of history to another without faltering; from China to Russia, from Russia to India, from the Spanish Civil War to the maquis; running from the Queen of Sheba to Mao, sending as his ambassadresses to the north of our immense Continent, and to the small crowded islands of Japan, two fair ladies: one a Florentine, the other a Greek. They brought the greetings of a country whose minister was gifted with applied poetic fantasy, and capable of forgetting everything else when needed by his France as Colonel Berger, Chief of the Brigade Alsace-Lorraine.

A traveller whose omnivorous curiosity knows no end, Malraux has only left – to my knowledge – two big lumps of the world untasted: Latin America (in its extreme south) and Australia (in the same latitude). We had not the kind of charm that attracted him. No worthwhile ruins, no temples, no hanging gardens, no pyramids, no sphinxes, no statues, no glamorous dead queens, no ghost cities haunting the desert, no mosques, no gigantic Buddhas. Nothing that would stir him. We could only offer the boundless pampa, the bush, the awesome wilderness, mountains, lakes, ostriches, pumas, armadillos, penguins, any number of birds, a good choice of serpents and marsupials, rabbits with different length of front and hind legs (but all these animals can be seen in zoos). Folklore? We share that popular manner of expression with the whole earth. A handful of Artists with a capital A. But that is not enough to arouse a particular interest in Malraux, hunter of long-lived civilizations. We were born last century, with many handicaps.

Well, well, we must be patient for a number of centuries before we can entrance a new Malraux (if his breed, as I hope, survives the final earthquake our civilization seems to be heading towards). At the present stage, with no past except the tradition of nomadic tribes and rough Spanish Conquerors, our ancestors (mine at least), we cannot pretend to hold his attention. Our culture has no other legitimate inheritance but that of Europe. Europe, indifferent to our fate, though we are probably destined, by the blessing or the curse of an immense territory and every kind of climate, to a vast, as yet invisible adventure in the history of mankind. More than myself, Malraux is aware, as was Valéry, that civilizations are mortal. That Niniveh is a beautiful word. Millennia are eternity for an insect; trifles for a man already capable of stating to himself the problems that haunt Malraux.

'It was the time when, in the depths of the countryside, we strained our ears at the barking of a dog in the night. . . .' Those barkings in the night, so ominous, which Malraux remembers and evokes in his farewell speech to Jean Moulin (hero of the Resistance), we too have heard them, wondering what kind of threat they conveyed. This has happened in all latitudes. In many, they brought a burden of anxiety. Thus we live in this age. In *le temps du mépris*. In the time of Malraux.

ANDRÉ MALRAUX

*

ANTI-CRITIQUE

Translated by Robert Speaight

The concept of the individual pervades the nineteenth century and part of the twentieth. It stretches from the original to the peculiar, from the ambitious to the irreplaceable: from Rousseau to Napoleon, from Napoleon to Zarathustra, from him to Barrès and to Gide. Individualism was blown to pieces by the atom bomb and bequeathed us biography.

For the first time a civilization could assume the cultural inheritance of the planet. Even if successive civilizations were organisms, and similar ones at that, our own had two unique characteristics: it was both capable of blowing up the earth and of gathering together the achievements of art since prehistoric times. However, this civilization has no assurance that biography can account completely for artistic creations or that biography is the only way or even the best way of approaching the individual.

We have had the exemplary *lives* of the classics, and the far from exemplary ones of Vasari and many others. After that a *life* went hand in hand with an autobiography from the *Confessions* of St Augustine to those of Rousseau. Then we come to the great biographies of the nineteenth century and of our own time. These were apparently historical, yet the biographer, like the novelist, but in a subtler way, changed a passively endured destiny into a mastered one. Like all literature which matters to us, whether it is the work of the living or the dead, biography was a part of history and of evolution. When the awareness of metamorphosis comes to dominate evolution and to create its own history, will another attempt to grasp man, a new kind of biography, take shape over and above the one we already know? Under what name should this ever-increasing type of book be known? The old title *Miscellanea*

springs to mind, but they are as inconclusive as the others were affirma-
tive, even when they do not give rise to any questions. Let us therefore
call them *Colloquies*.

The birth of a literary genre makes one think, since they are few and
far between. In 1900, to read nearly always meant to read a novel. In
1945, to the question: 'What is the most important fact in literature
between the two wars?' I answered: 'The replacement of the Payot
literature by the Gallimard literature.' *Belles-lettres* being superseded by
publishing. The literary literature formerly published by the *NRF* and
doing what the *Mercure de France* had done for the Symbolists, Lemerre
for the Parnassians, and Renduel for the Romantics is no longer anything but an item in the enormous list of capitalist or communist pub-
lications – the new field, increasing daily, of books which are neither
essays, poems or novels. Colloquies fit none of these. But that book
factory – the publishing house – without suppressing *belles-lettres* engulfs
them – and Colloquies are an important part of their production.

We learn a lot by projecting a new genre into the past, such as a
nineteenth century novel into the seventeenth century, a *Phèdre* by
Balzac rivalling a *Princesse de Clèves*. Or the book that a collection such as
this would have devoted to . . . Laclos! An interesting idea: here we have
the author of *Les Liaisons Dangereuses* and of virtuous notes on the up-
bringing of young ladies, the duc d'Orleans' political agent, the inventor
of the bomb. . . .

Or better still! *Racine,* despite his fame. Chapters parallel to those of
this book: Port Royal – Conversations about the Fronde – Contacts with
the King – His early Plays – His Religion – His Work as a Historiographer – His Relation to Greek Poetry – His Travelling to Constanti-
nople at the Time of Bajazet – Dialogue with a Young Greek Writer –
Symbols and Allegories – Racine and the History of Antiquity – The
Unity of Racine's Art – the Human Condition of a Secretive Person –
Racine's World and Ours – and finally a chapter by Racine himself
summing it all up. As contributors we have: leading figures of the
Fronde, people in the confidence of the Jansenists of Port Royal and of
the King, dramatists, a priest, a historiographer, a Hellenist, some young
foreigners, a poet, an actress perhaps . . . and as a supplement to the
posthumous edition: L'Affaire des Poisons.[1]

This game makes one ponder. It shows better than an analysis the
difference between a study and a biography: particularly the life of
Racine by his son. Would a modern biography be more complete? It
would lose the irreplaceable flavour of the time shared by those people
who are ignorant not only of what we do not know but also of what we

have learnt. The fish bowl comes with the fish. Should we be able to imagine each contribution, or only its pastiche? What it all lacks is the irrational element produced by any given period in time, and which cannot be reconstructed even when the furniture is genuine and when the collected essays and the author under discussion are of that same period.

Above all, the spirit behind the Colloquy did not then exist; it would require a difficult and implausible montage to give an illusion of it. Merely to assemble its component parts is in itself a new idea. Whatever this *montage*, and even if the name of God was only to be pronounced in the chapter on religion, we should still be reading a Christian book, precluding all debate on the conception of man. Confronted with our own time even the Montesquieu of *Les Lettres Persanes*, a far more free-thinking mind than Racine, becomes as dogmatic as a nineteenth century scientist. Compared to a definitive *Racine*, this book would cry aloud what it only whispers: that it questions. And would show clearly that fundamental ambiguity whereby all biographies establish retrospectively the incidences of a man's life on his work. The biographer is writing the life of a mythical character. The statue inspires the testimony and therfore precedes it.

We know how the sculptor works. What was Rodin thinking of as he started carving his *Balzac*? He meant to separate from his biographical being that superhuman character worthy of having written *La Comédie Humaine*, just as tradition has separated from an unknown Dante that aquiline profile worthy of his *Inferno* – and just as every Greek sculptor invented his own Aphrodite. Most of Balzac's witnesses are testifying to readers who would know nothing of Honoré de Balzac but for Rodin's statue: in order sometimes to suggest the image transfigured by this statue, and sometimes the man deserving of it.

Honoré de Balzac no more resembled his demiurgic *power* than Michelangelo his *David*. But ever since the Hellenic busts invented Homer and Socrates after a lapse of five hundred years, humankind has longed for the incarnation of creative genius. Homer becomes his bust just as Aphrodite became her statue. The power to give flesh and blood to the imaginary rivalled the power to incarnate the gods. Like the *Homer* of Alexandria, the mythical Balzac, before he took shape, filled the minds of men with his nebulous symphony.

Romanticism identified the author with his genius. There was a little of this in the Greek god-makers, but the gods had a hand in it; likewise in the Renaissance, but ephemerally, for Donatello was still proud of his leather apron. Nobody takes Corneille for a Cornelian character; Louis

Racine simply considered his father as 'a fine writer'. But the heroes of Romanticism, Michelangelo, Rembrandt, Beethoven, all those whom Victor Hugo called 'The Equals', from Aeschylus, that Shakespeare of Antiquity, down to Shakespeare himself, these are the heroes in the Hellenistic sense, effigies of their genuis.

They owe a great deal to the disintegration of the Christian soul. *Phèdre* has strayed a long way from Racine's sinfulness – from Jean's sinful soul, as the curé said over his coffin. For Victor Hugo the *Oresteia* was written by Aeschylus' soul and shared in the same mystery. Art became an appendage of genius. Even in the Renaissance one had genius but one was not a genius. Particularly in literature, Petrarch and Ariosto were just better ordinary poets; for the Romantics the worst poet was a bad Shakespeare. The artist has ceased to be a man who 'makes' poems, pictures or statues: the verb 'to make' – so important to the Greeks – has ceased to apply to him. A god of art was made manifest through his prophets, but although Olympio was not quite Victor Hugo and Balzac not quite Honoré the effigy had been created. The Romanticism which refused to admit the existence of both Balzac and Honoré also declined to admit that Honoré was an individual who could change his skin and become Balzac when his extrasensory powers were working at their full stretch. Just as Romanticism carries its own realism from which all future realism will be derived, so the myth of the artist claims his biography. The same contradictory force impels the reader to create his own *Balzac* by Rodin and to make it more tractable by reading *Balzac en Pantoufles*.[2]

From the very first lines, whether he realizes it or not (and why should he not realize it?), Gozlan writes about the Balzac whom the characters of the real Balzac have created in the imagination of his readers: an image rendered familiar by Madame Hanska's early letters and other correspondence of the period, and to which Rodin gave shape with genius. Honoré has no slippers because the slippers of Monsieur Dupont or Mr Smith would be of no interest whatsoever. Slippers, in the eyes of a Romantic, only exist if the feet are made of bronze.

We learn from the Key to the Dreams of Mesopotamia that in Babylon they constantly dreamed about octopus-like creatures, although, doubtless, they had never seen any octopuses. The mythical Balzac sleeps on in every one of his readers like those octopuses in the Babylonian night. Every book devoted to an artist partially deals with this symbolic character linked to his time by his mythology, his biography and his work, because that part of him which is made of bronze sleeps in the irrational awareness which unites him with the reader.

It would be difficult, but in no way impossible, to replace this book by its synthesis. It would have been done in an earlier time. In the eighteenth century it would have been treated as the raw material from which a single author would have spun a continuous story. In the nineteenth century the separate studies would have been accepted inasmuch as they would have produced a collective work with a single theme such as a continuous story in a biography. Achieving an elaborate perspective, as in painting, implied a system of values as in biography. The Colloquies break with this system as resolutely as Cubism broke with the perspective of Leonardo.

No biography escapes from the unity it owes to its author and none claims to do so. Only when it tries to imitate Cubism does a biography lose its perspective; when using fictitious characters it expounds an apparently fictitious thesis. So why not imagine this book in a similar light? Why not suppose that Messrs Mookerjee, Takemoto and Chang Mei Yuan are no more real than Messrs John Lehmann, Cyrus Sulzberger (and myself), that Professors Gombrich and Langlois are colleagues of Doctor Tar and Professor Feather?[3] Here is a situation in which the Colloquy turns its back on the methods which claim to grasp a creative artist in the name of an intelligibility which, by his very nature, he eludes.

Biography is obedient to the flow of time with a submission oddly contemporary with the novel's attack on chronology. But the novel no longer tries to wear out its characters as it did in the nineteenth century. Flaubert knew Madame Bovary better than Faulkner knew Popeye. The revolution of the novel in no way alters our attitude nor even our feeling towards man. The biographical novel coincides with the substitution of personality for character. Anna Karenina is a personality, Père Goriot is a character; the Princesse de Clèves is neither: born of a genre now vanished and to which the novel was akin – the portrait.

What does not exist in our seventeenth-century literary portraits is the correlation between the individual and what modifies his individuality, as first propounded by Goethe and then pushed as far as it would go by Proust in the wake of Meredith. But when Faulkner syncopates time it is not time that he challenges (he will not wake up as a child the next morning), it is the story. The writer sets up between himself and the subject of his biography the same distance that he establishes between himself and his living contemporaries; no historical character is intelligible where the characters of fiction are not intelligible. Unlike Hinduism and Buddhism, no modern civilization has worked out a conception of man that was not to some extent linked to the idea of his continuity. Nevermind where or when reincarnation claims its subjects, since in any case metempsychosis or deliverance are the fundamental propositions. Since man is not annihilated by his growing planetary consciousness, he questions it.

The Colloquy originated at the same time as this planetary perspective whose pluralism was in direct opposition to the limited perspectives of the biographer, the director of the Encyclopédie, the nineteenth century itself. It substitutes not another causality but the questioning which causalities and conditionings must submit to. The artist's aura is different to what they used to call his fame, even the fame of a thinker like Freud or Jung, whose claims were not exclusively scientific. This is particularly true of an artist who does not touch on fundamental feelings. The success of *Les Misérables* in India was predictable; not so that *The Possessed* would appear in paperback in the United States.

The American youth discovering the author of *The Possessed* submits to his myth and his breathless questioning. He admires the book and the author, but his feeling for Stavrogin is more complex, like his feeling for Charlus or Vautrin; quite different from the way an Indian youth night feel towards Jean Valjean, for exemplary heroes are not startling, and *Les Misérables* is a *Ramayana*. But myth is not necessarily exemplary, hence the recourse to aesthetic values. These values were and still are the yard stick by which the lifespan of a work, its reincarnation and metamorphosis are calculated. Racine was immortal because he followed immortal rules to perfection, and Shakespeare was equally immortal because he did not follow them at all. But we do not admire *Phèdre* according to the rules set out by Aristotle, but in spite of him. What distinguishes *The Possessed* not only from a mediocre novel but also from *Anna Karenina* obviously does not depend solely on the genius of the narrator. The immediacy of the great enigmatic plays such as *Hamlet* or *Le Misanthrope* is not entirely due to their great literary merit.

In what was the age of the novel let us not see only what can be translated and easily transmitted. There is a whole world of the novel in which the Princesse de Clèves lives with Camus' *Etranger* and La Sanseverina with the heroine of *A Farewell to Arms*, Faulker with Tolstoy, Balzac with Dostoevsky (he actually translated *Eugénie Grandet*). But Balzac's prestige followed in the lead of fashion in Paris or power in London. Whereas the whole of contemporary literature comes to be in a world as vast as that of Shakespeare.

The supreme temptation for the philosopher of art, said Paul Valéry, is to discover the laws which will make it possible to know with *absolute certainty* (and it was he who underlined the words) which paintings and sculptures will be admired in a hundred years' time. To which Picasso replied that art philosophers had the souls of picture dealers. In a civilization which regards posterity as hazardous, Valéry's 'absolute certainty', the fight against chance, becomes as absurd and as invincible as the desire to escape from death.

Which of us does not dream of catching posterity red-handed? ...

II

We know the Classical Imaginary Museum just as well as the Romantic. In poetry it ranges from Malherbe to Chénier in opposition to antiquity, but it failed to see that antiquity had invented *literature as an object*. Our anthologies changed when the object of poetry changed. What its readers expected from the *Booz endormi* bears no relation to what Dorat's readers[4] expected from the *Baisers*. And with Ronsard poetry had changed its role even more radically than with Victor Hugo.

In the Middle Ages, up to St Louis, neither the poets nor their listeners perceived the world of poetry as a world of forms. Apart from the verbal checkerboards which the Great Rhetoricians display at their most complicated, true medieval poetry is the legend of chivalry. It is Tristan. The Chartres sculptor made a statue before which one was to pray, the poet invented a new episode to the story of Tristan in which one was to believe. Printing allowed the poet to possess his sonnet just as the sculptor of bronze possesses his statue. So the sonnet, unlike the Ballads of the rhetoricians, ceased to be a trifle, a curiosity, but became the rival of an object of literature brought back to life, in other words – immortal.

In literature and above all in culture, France inherited the Italian primacy in painting. Classical tragedy owed its prestige much more to its high degree of civilization than to Aristotle's canons. According to Voltaire, Shakespeare was a barbarian. Valéry even wrote (in his *Cahiers*, admittedly): 'It may be that Racine ridded us of two or three monsters of a Shakespearian nature.' Classicism considered itself to be not a style but *the* style. In order to come out on top, Romanticism had to destroy the myth of perfection in favour of the myth of genius.

Victor Hugo left us a list of his elect. Homer and Aeschylus, Job, Isaiah and Ezekiel; Lucretius and Tacitus, St John and St Paul, Dante, Rabelais; Cervantes and Shakespeare. Full stop. None of these elect has been put on the shelf. We might add Sophocles, Virgil and possibly St Francis. One might have expected more Great Discoveries. This Imaginary Museum is Israel, Antiquity and the Renaissance. We can associate Tristan with Dante, not Béroul[5]; symbols rather than works. Can we link Homer with the epics of Asia and the ancient East? No. The training we owe to the combined influence of Israel and Antiquity only just survives the barrier of language, whereas in the West the Baghavad Gita remains closed to all but specialists, even in Gandhi's translation. No Indian or Chinese myth – not even the life of Buddha, sublime as it is – comes alive for us like the life of Tristan. We think of Saadi as a rival to Keats, whereas he was a rival of La Fontaine; he owes his fame to our poets, not to his own poems. In the post-Romantic era, our Imaginary Museum of sculpture had the whole earth to choose from, but our Imaginary Museum of literature did not.

For the museum of poetry symbolized by Baudelaire is as distinct from Victor Hugo's as Hugo's was distinct from Ronsard's. It is up to the reader to reach the poet who no longer imposes himself. The best translation of Höderlin, of Keats, of Pushkin, does not give us the shock that we get from Rimbaud. Beauty had given place to genius, and genius to art. So each kind of literature mingles its two Imaginary Museums. The one inspired by the experience of mankind and what is noble in the world, the other by what we call art. Both founded on the will to create something enduring. But in literature, as in painting, a form of art which derives its values from itself no longer gives rise to an aesthetic, it gives birth to a whole set of problems.

Just as genius had replaced beauty, so the library of the eighteenth century replaced that of Romanticism; each was governed by recognized values and each proclaimed its own aesthetic, more modest in its scope than the museums of music and plastic arts, for these are polyglot. The *hautes époques* and the primitive arts have no literary equivalents. But if poetry is a stranger to the invincible proliferation which invades our museums, it nevertheless knew the Renaissance. In spite of Dante and the monastic copyists, Virgil emerged from the night like a cathedral. The revolution which our own arts brought to all the other arts was the substitution for dogmatic concepts of an irrational and unconquerable empiricism.

No new aesthetic is accepted, each of us imagines his own anthology, the collection, and these, put together though refuted are admitted and form our Bibliothèque de la Pléiade. 'If those who come after us – and who will most probably read our writings in the light of metamorphosis – find in them the values which give them a sequential meaning: let them be sure that it is a thing which escaped us.

The next poet of genius will change the function that poetry assumed under the reign of Baudelaire, Rimbaud or Mallarmé. The profound change is not in the procession of schools which led from Baudelaire to Mallarmé or from Apollinaire to Verlaine, but in the replacement of Victor Hugo's utterances by Baudelaire's reverie, even if we later rediscover the ineffability of Victor Hugo. In order for this metamorphosis to take place, our very conception of poetry and the value given to it had to be erased, as was the conception of Greek tragedy, in fact the concept of literature itself. Challenge does not kill an art; what destroys it is the question: 'So what?'

Our time has known an unprecedented development in biography, in everything that is biographical in history. It seems to see in it a literary genre as eternal as the fantastic, and to consider the relationship of a writer to his work as manifestly privileged. 'The lives of exemplary or exceptional men' have been widely studied and recorded: the richness and the scope of what we call the Great Biography dominate; it becomes clearly one of the major literary expressions of individualism – André Maurois' *Balzac*, Thomas Mann's treatment of Goethe, bear no relation to the anecdotic records of Tallemant des Réaux. This development does not of course anticipate the Colloquy. But let us substitute a traditional 'procession' to the vague idea suggested by the word 'Lives'. Plutarch, Suetonius, Vasari, Tallemant[7], Saint Simon. Chateaubriand's Rancé and one of the recent biographies of Napoleon. It would appear that the Colloquy is meant to replace this procession or at least to develop side by side with it rather as modernbiography developed alongside the 'Lives' and the 'Studies'. The time is coming when people will say: 'In the days of biography. . . .'

Besides, the Colloquy has at its disposal a much wider field, its methods applying to more than the individual life. It selects events as well as people: Mao's Long March, Hiroshima, the assassination of President Kennedy, all follow one another like the acts of tragedy conceived on a planetary scale. The Colloquy will tackle in the same way a Gandhi or Day of Indian Independence, a De Gaulle and an eighteenth of June.[8] Its methods of doing this increase daily and will continue to do so in the near future. How can one fail to see that we are working out a new method of grasping the individual which is not that of individualism? Its method seems to be to substitute for well regulated lighting a vast number of snapshots, bits of film, shadow images. It owes much to journalism and audio-visual aids. Its values are not those of biography. A biographer's dream is to exhaust all the possibilities offered by his model. Even if individualism cannot hope to get everything out of the individual, it considers this effort to be a fruitful one and endows it with a certain validity in biography as well as in autobiography. The biographer tackles the obsessive problem of getting to know the man which the Colloquy seems to put aside or at any rate to postpone. Founded on the traditional psychological concept: 'know a man to be able to act upon him', the Colloquy nevertheless has to pursue the knowledge of the dead. At least it is logical: individualism takes the individual both for its subject and its object. It is subject to a postulate: the best way to know man is to know the individual. (This method meets obstruction in the end when it seeks for essential differences.) The Colloquy, being rather like a hunter on the scent, escapes those who use it as a method. Less superficial than it might appear, it regards its pluralistic approach as important, and is careful not to confuse it with electicism.

The pluralism of a Colloquy surrounds its subject, picks him out, loses him, like the beams of an anti-aircraft searchlight on the track of an aeroplane. The provisional element introduced by matamorphosis meets the element of chance introduced by the Colloquy. So it is hardly surprising that the list of the Colloquies develops concurrently with the awareness of metamorphosis. One must choose, as the seventeenth century would have put it, between knowledge and ignorance. But our own time displays a lively taste for its doubtful sciences where history and psychoanalysis meet Marxism and biography. Here the United States have an important part to play, because there writers are not as paramount as they are in Europe. Faulkner is on a par with Picasso rather than with Voltaire or Goethe. A colloquy devoted to Hemingway is more suited to his character than a biography or study that would concentrate only on his art. The link between today's literature, and particularly American literature, and the audio-visual leads us today to the Colloquy; television is and will continue to be more suited to it than to 'Lives'. In these, critical studies can only be transmitted by a monologue. It is the actors who prevent a biography from being a documentary, and at the price of a constant instability it turns the subject of a biography into the hero of a fiction. Whether it is dealing with a biography or a novel, the television screen abandons analysis in favour of narration. It cannot cope with the Colloquy even in its crudest form, that of people gathered in front of a camera. It does not answer the questions asked by biography, it asks those that biography does not ask.

The image disappears. Individualism – biography – novel composed a figure. But it is only fairly recently that the novel was taken to be inspired by the life of the novelist, the theatre, which preceded it as a major genre, did not lead itself so easily to this illusion: the approaches to the work were different. A play was judged according to what it should have been, by the rules which shaped it, almost sculpted it. The novel saw itself as a river at the very time when the myth of genius was about to dominate the myth of perfection, which the vast literature surrounding the novel today cares as little about as the novel itself. When the book takes an event for a hero (*The Longest Day*, *The Independence of India*, etc.) the characters, and even more the author, are subordinate to it: that author's biography is now as uninteresting as that of a violinist or a geometrician. The work no longer calls the writer before the curtain like a triumphant actor; he no longer has to conform to the formal pattern of the dance. Novels had converged on biography as intensely as what succeeded them diverged from it. Publishing, of which *belles-lettres* was only a part, abandons the image as well as biography. But it does not abandon literature, it discovers it. It transforms the all-enveloping into the all-enveloped, isolating its particular character, and shows by its place in the front rank how little 'evolution and conditioning' have counted for in its history. The Colloquy is no longer challenging biography nor even man himself, at least not directly. It is challenging the world of the written word, whose new organization and basic metamorphosis it senses, as not long ago it sensed those of the world of art.

III

Before the war I had the idea of inviting a number of authors to set down what they thought of whatever writers of the past they might wish to discuss. This collection of essays, published with a preface by André Gide, extended only from Corneille to Chénier. But it showed the metamorphosis of literature. I had designed this book with the notion that it would be done all over again in a hundred years' time; that even if it were not done again we would have found readers then as passionately interested as we could be ourselves in such a *Tableau de la Littérature Française* written by authors of 1850. Gide, in part of his preface, described what this would have meant in the face of academic criticism. The strength of the university lay in teaching literature primarily as literary history, which supposedly obeyed the traditional cycle of crudeness, perfection and decadence. But it became clear that literature tends to turn things upside down rather than bring them to perfection, that its history is neither a history of improvements nor a procession of 'those who have left their landmarks'. Moreover the student sensitive to poetry does not discover the poets 'from the origins to the present time', he discovers them in a non-chronological order according to the affinities they share. He does not begin at the beginning but today. He goes from Verlaine to Villon, and not from Villon to Verlaine. Already the conflict between academic values and those cherished by the writers of the past disappeared before the strange imperialism of any history of literature. This collection modestly entitled *Tableau* showed that a general view of the subject could be only incidentally obedient to history, and yet, even more than a history written by a single author, it would avoid subjective or impressionistic criticism. The book was no more opposed to the academic histories of literature than it was to Thibaudet's[9]; it was opposed to its hypothetical rivals of the last century and the century to come. Where a system was expected, a sphere was discovered, and literary metamorphosis at work.

I had asked *all* the contributors to speak of what they liked. In this respect the *Tableau* was radically different from what had gone before. On the assumption that art has no cognizance of anything but talent and mere emptiness, the book was concerned only to make the writers it dealt with better, or differently loved, and thus to bring them before the reader; each author became the stage director of the writer he had chosen.

We did not realize that the decisive metamorphosis was to be found there, and not in the transmutation of literary values for so long established and which the *Tableau* did no more than take into account. This 'criticism', like its contemporary in painting, did not attempt to convince by argument but by contagion.

Our dialogue with the past recognized as supreme value, as immeasurable value, the *presence* of a work. It is of no interest to a poet that Gérard de Nerval author of *Chimères* is a lesser artist than Victor Hugo author of *La Légende des Siècles* – presence cannot be measured. A resurrected dwarf is no less astonishing than a giant, and he is more like a resurrected giant than a dead one.

In dealing with each poet according to his own standards, be it Louise Labé or Corneille, that book broke with the perspective that anthologies had always imposed on poetry. Reducing a long poem to a short play makes what I have called a literary object or ornament. Musset's *Souvenir*, Hugo's *Olympio*, read like extracts from Racine. Just as the enlargement of a photograph gives an 'expressionist' element to details, quotations in an anthology give a poem a classical resonance. And so Villon became 'La Vieille qui fut heaulmière', Maynard 'La Belle vieille', Racan 'Sur la retraite', Musset 'Souvenir', and similarly Hugo became 'Olympio', Vigny the end of 'La Maison du berger', Baudelaire 'Recueillement' and so on to Apollinaire the 'Mal Aimé'. Nevertheless although our anthologies lend a classical presentation to our poetry, the feeling they give to it is Romantic in spite of all that separates us from Romanticism. What will ever take the place of nostalgia?

The total metamorphosis of a civilization nourished on anthologies is not to be brought about by its reform, but by its disappearance. St Bernard could not have cared less about the Greek Anthology.

'Understanding a work' is an expression no less vague than 'understanding a man'. What matters is not to make a work intelligible but to make the reader sensitive to its quality. Failure to understand a work of literature is not like failing to understand a lecture. In the latter case the reader understands *nothing*, in the former he blunders about. He attacks the artist's intention and attributes to him a purpose he never had. He reproaches him for having conceived or badly carried out this imaginary purpose. The endless and deliberate accusations hurled at innovators proves it. But is the purpose of a creative artist strictly formulated or are we victims of a prejudice when we believe that a biblical scene by Rembrandt *reproduces* a scene that he had designed in his imagination and thus becomes a *tableau vivant*? Gide wondered whether Baudelaire was not mistaken as to what constituted his own genius. But did Baudelaire really think that *Une Charogne* was a finer poem than *Recueillement*? No doubt the gap between the initial purpose and the finished work is part of a work of art. Having read Rimbaud and Mallarmé, *Recueillement* appears differently to us than it did to Baudelaire. It is by using the creations that succeeded a genius that metamorphosis first separates us from it.

Gide clings to this misunderstanding, because those who considered art as an object of knowledge believed that a 'truth' existed in a work independently of successive judgments. The truth of Giotto's frescoes in the chapel of Padua lay in what Giotto thought of them. Unfortunately he thought that they copied nature, which accounts badly for our admiration of their sovereign gentleness. It would be asking too much of the artist that he should hold the secret of his own genius.

There were many secret geniuses amongst artists recognized by their contemporaries: Baudelaire, Nerval, Diderot, Molière, Cervantes, Shakespeare. But what contemporary of Cervantes or Shakespeare considered either of them to be a colossus? The following conversation is well known: 'Monsieur Despréaux,[10] which is the greatest writer of my reign?' – 'Molière, Sir,' – 'Really,' I should never have thought so, but I expect you know better than I do.' The court thought as Louis XIV did, and so did Molière quite often. Balzac on the other hand knows he is Balzac, but he only received a single vote at the Académie (Victor Hugo's). By 'what constitutes Baudelaire's genius' André Gide means what *we* admire him for. It is time to add the element still unknown to us, whereby the next century will admire him differently. The need to discover in a work of art the promise of survival seems to me, in spite of what Picasso has said, to require the talent of a medium rather than that of a picture dealer. A work of art survives by its own double time, the time of its author and our own. A 1660 Rembrandt cannot be confined to that date, like any other picture painted that year, nor to 1976 when we gaze at it. The statue on the portico at Chartres belongs to the twelfth century as well as to our own, and possibly to the whole time span of art, just as the saint prayed before in the cathedral belongs both to the time of the sculptor and to divine enternity, as well as to the time of the man praying. A contemporary work of art assured of its posterity would also belong to a double moment in time – our own and the future.

We first started to think of posterity as the durability of fame. Victor Hugo 'had entered immortality while he was still alive', he remained there. Posterity rendered a belated justice to *poétes maudits*, but fame, once acquired, cannot be erased. No doubt for centuries antiquity was forgotten, but the Enlightenment dispelled the darkness for ever. The French classicists, narrow in outlook, had despised the cathedrals, but they have been admired for a long time – Boileau was not needed for Villon to be admired. The posthumuous life of a work of art was then predictable. Not so for us. Sophocles, like Corneille, was admired by his contemporaries. By the Hellenists and the Romans, as one of the Fathers of Tragedy still admired but no longer imitated. He vanished for a thousand years. He reappeared with a fame equal to Plato's, but the Father of Tragedy became the Father of a restrained art shy of the screams and gouged out eyes of Oedipus and even of Tiresias. Equally, Phidias became the Father of classical statuary, of the *Laocoön* and the *Apollo Belvedere* – London looked at the Elgin marbles with stupefaction and dismay; they bore no resemblance to the carvings of Canova.

Finally a Severe style emerged from the taste of the great periods, from the discovery of the *Kores* on the Acropolis and from the resurrection of Olympia. Phidias was admired not as the precursor of classical sculpture (about which we care very little) but as the last and most lyrical genius of the Severe period. Placed face to face with the Lapiths of Olympia and the Herakles of Aegina but not with the Venus of the Medicis and the statuary of the Père Lachaise cemetery which were left us by Alexandria and Rome. At the time of the discovery of the real Sophocles, Racine, who knew Greek, appears to have seen in the heroes of Euripides the statues of the Belvedere.

Conversely one could easily trace Gislebertus of Autun or the tympanum of Moissac, as well as Homer, Virgil, Villon and even Shakespeare or Racine. None of our great styles has escaped metamorphosis since the Renaissance had to resurrect a buried past and Romanticism a despised one.

Let us no more confuse metamorphosis and immortality. Is it the genius of Sophocles, Phidias or Racine that the centuries have admired each in the same way as its predecessors? But their reasons have nothing in common; the lines by Racine that we know by heart are not even those that Boileau would have chosen, and medieval sculpture came back to life as a sort of Expressionism. Metamorphosis is more visible in the plastic arts for, apart from translations, we oppose five centuries of literature to five millennia of sculpture. But the metamorphosis is the same, because our grasp of a work from the past is commanded by our Imaginary Museum, our field of reference. What we see in the frieze of the Parthenon is there; no one could invent it. But did Phidias see his friezes as we see them? This absurd idea arose from the belief that painting and sculpture were imitative arts and lasted as they were judged in relation to visible objects, real or imaginary, which they depicted. The friezes of the Parthenon which we admire have spoken the language of their own time and that of the nineteenth century, and also that which the Great Monarchies thought they understood. Goya was not admired by Picasso in the same way as he was admired by Baudelaire, Victor Hugo or Goya himself. We admire the Romanesque Virgins on the pilgrims' ways as fetishes; they were admired differently a century ago, and those who made them did not admire them at all – they prayed to them. Sophocles admired *Antigone*, but not as we do.

Few civilizations will have known so little about their reasons for admiration as ours. We have seen many masterpieces come to light, a quantity of medieval bas-reliefs freed from their baroque mouldings. We know only too well that it was a mistake to put the tales of the *argonauts* on a par with the Iliad, and that Hellenistic literature has sunk with all hands. Our knowledge of Dostoevsky began through elementary translations, whole sections of his works amputated, with prefaces which highlighted him as being a Russian Dickens. He went through a fifty-year purgatory in Russia, understandable from a Soviet point of view. Victor Hugo has hardly emerged from his own. Let us not forget that the library is a relatively new invention.

IV

Contemporary civilization, even in Russia and in China, considers itself to be the heir to the questions and the answers according to different metamorphosis. But neither the metamorphosis nor the Colloquy needs an answer. Let us imagine a book, like this one, devoted to Engels by Marxist writers. Its unity would spotlight the multiplicity and inter-rogative character of the West, where a dialectic questioning often replaces the answers. In these Colloquies there is no discussion, because most of the authors don't know what the others have written. This is contrary to *entretiens* such as those held at Pontigny.[11] Colloquies rather than leading to value-judgments, open up perspectives suggested by the occasion and not by the interpretation which is put upon it. A fact of culture the consequences of which are both sure and predictable is that a writer can now be spoken of in a planetary perspective, not because he is gifted, but because this perspective exists and because his works appear simultaneously in the great capitals of the world. The fruitful-ness of comparing photographs in the study of plastic art is well known. A fetish placed side by side with a pre-Romanesque idol is more fascin-ating to us than any theory as to how similar or different they are.

Dostoevsky could not speak of Julien Sorel in the way we do. The substitution of the Colloquy for the dialogue is less concerned with establishing the kinship between Julien and Raskolnikov than with illustrating the difference between the two novels as it is shown in the working of these two parallel ambitions. It is tempting to compare the methods by which the two writers convey an identical feeling. This is an illusion. The comparison does not illustrate different ways of expression, but a radically different field of operation. It may or may not be ambition, but what Dostoevsky selects from the shapeless fabric of life is not what Stendhal selects. They wear differently coloured spectacles. This analysis can be extended to the production of a play, to psychology and even to style. (The change in the narrative allowed Flaubert to use first the direct and then the indirect past tense in the same sentence.) This analysis is less instructive than that first impression so easily expressed by saying: 'After seeing Raskolnikov, Julien looks different.'

'The most important thing in a picture,' wrote Braque when he was eighty years old, 'is always what it cannot say.' When there will be an extensive Colloquy – devoted to Baudelaire (how surprising that there isn't one, but how can a poet be translated? . . .) we will find ourselves wondering, faced with an art which has become a Declaration of the Rights of the Unformulable, if the specific quality of every art, what used to be described as its essence, will not always consist of 'what it cannot say'.

This is not beyond an explanation, simply alongside it. To compare it with music is suggestive but no more; an art is always its own language and no work can be confused with the sum of its component parts. Nevertheless let us remember that every great work is like the libretto of its own music and the expression 'stricken dumb with admiration' is not fortuitous. But genius was believed to have escaped its concept by virtue of its strength, not that art escaped genius by its very nature. The limits of what can be formulated are clearly defined in music but less so in the other arts. Because a painting can also reproduce a stage production, a novel can also convey a special human experience. Sonnets are made with words said Mallarmé to Degas; the words can also make a lot of other things, but scales are seldom used except in music. This approach to a work of art gives the illusion of capturing it. Literature, as a form of art, escapes without a doubt logical thought to the same extent as music or as poetry when it becomes music. We regard Baudelaire as one of the greatest critical minds of his century. What has he taught us? The same genius inspired him to write *Les Phares* and to discover Manet. Do the essays of the *Curiosités esthétiques* owe more to the strength of the argumentation than to the imagery of *Les Phares*? Baudelaire is careful not to formulate a theory of art; his perspicacity is such that he can simultaneously admire in their lifetime Delacroix, Ingres, Corot, Daumier, Manet and others. In a civilization where the *presence* of a work of art is regarded as a pre-eminent sign of its value the great critic is necessarily a prophet. But would Baudelaire have refused to apply Braque's dictum to *le Balcon*? In France Jean Paulhan was the most successful explorer of his time, but nothing he wrote would allow the reader to discover writers as different as Jouhandeau, Supervielle, Saint-John Perse (the list could stretch to the bottom of the page). No philosophy of art has survived, unless one takes into account mere discussions on art, because philosophies require a mental articulation no more applicable to art than to music. If the essence of every art is linked to the inexpressible, 'what it cannot say' follows the work through its metamorphosis to the point where it sometimes becomes what can be said. Manet and Picasso revered in Goya what, for Goya, was his secret genius. Cézanne resurrected both Piero della Francesca and El Greco; literary Romanticism resurrected French sixteenth-century poetry – not only the poets of La Pléiade[12] – for Victor Hugo praised Agrippa d'Aubigné, from whom Baudelaire took his first epigraph for *Les Fleurs du Mal*. The *Rouge et le Noir* that we admire is obviously not the one of Janin[13] and Viennet[14]; was it the one of Taine and Bourget who unearthed it? Or even of Barrès and Valéry? The smell of violets now suggested by *La Chartreuse de Parme*, the Lucien Leuwen as understood by Valéry, the Julien Sorel who was first Janin and Henri Brûlard's

'monster' and then 'Napoleonic' and then 'class conscious', all these
have come to light because of literary awareness, but it did not invent
them, like the interpretations of the novel itself. It was all in the *Rouge
et le Noir* of 1830, and the stricken Beyle[15] of 1842. Like the butterfly in
its chrysalis. Time did not just polish *La Chartreuse* to change it from the
book that Balzac talks about so well into the *Chartreuse* admired by
Proust, it transformed it from a drama into an opera. Stendhal, in his
lifetime, probably did not feel his way towards this music as we do; but
what gave birth to Fabrice as seen by Proust, to Lucien Leuwen as seen
by Valéry, if not the combination in these masterpieces and even simply
in the arts in general of elements at least heterogeneous and sometimes
contradictory, of what Braque has called 'what cannot be said'?

DIGRESSION

I want to explain how the metamorphosis of Stendhal's work began. A
feeling has grown that he lived the life of the 'happy few' like a Valéry
Larbaud[16] of his time, forgetting that this metamorphosis is more than
just aesthetic. After the book was published in the *Journal des Débats* of
1830: Jules Janin wrote:

> He takes his hero, his monster, with an admirable coolness, through a
> thousand disgraceful actions and through a thousand stupidities which are
> worse. . . . Julien's stay in the seminary is the remarkable part of this novel.
> Here the author is doubly enraging and horrific, it is impossible to give a
> glimpse of this hideous picture; it struck me like the first ghost story that I
> heard from my nurse. An author such as this in body and soul goes his way
> untroubled and remorseless, casting his venom on everything he meets –
> youth, beauty, the graces and illusions of life; even the fields, the forests and
> the flowers are disfigured and crushed.

The traitor is hiding behind the curtains! which immediately shows us
that the *nature* of the critic's relationship to the novel has changed.
Janin evidently read *Le Rouge et le Noir* in the light of what a novel ought
to be; then in the light of the seminarian Berthet; and then in the light
of novels of his own time which have almost all lapsed into oblivion.
Finally he judged it in the light of what were regarded as established
fictions – and not many of these as yet were novels – but hardly as a way
of life, as a human experience to oppose to Stendhal's own. He judges
the book according to convention. He wants the equivalent of a Salon
painting, a book for his library. We can take our cue from Berthet or
pretend to, he obviously cannot refer to our library.

Memoirs and essays affect us in almost opposite ways. We shall never
know Henri Beyle, but we know the *Ecrits intimes*. The Colloquy brings

us without judgment the testimonies of hate, it shows us how the myth binds us to the past where anything contradictory is too abruptly erased. Viennet, academician and *pair de France* wrote in the *Journal* which he intended to have published after his death:

This adventurer thrown on the streets of Paris, without a penny to his name, and with a very doubtful character chose to provide a reputable journal with his literary anecdotes; and when he ran out of them he invented some in order to eat. He borrowed a name and chose Stendhal. Its Germanic ring proved the kind of literary sect which had adopted him. He ended up by writing books; the one entitled *La Charteuse de Parme* earned him a reputation of sorts among the fairly numerous mediocrities in the world of contemporary literature. I was speaking about him one day – I forget when – to Monsieur Guizot[17] who had a number of fairly close acquaintances in those circles, and was likely therefore to have known the scoundrel! 'He was a rascal', he told me, 'and that's all I could say about him, a fit of apoplexy rid us of him on March 24th'.

Henri Brûlard comes to mind, and so do *Souvenirs d'Egotisme*.
End of digression.

It would be an illusion to hope to recover the *Chartreuse* of 1840 from which time alone would have erased the varnish and the graffiti and the medley of colours. It is not enough to scratch Janin in order to find Stendhal.

Let us also forget the usual metamorphosis of fame which is a patina instead of a medley of colours. If we take refuge in wondering 'what Stendhal thought' we will find Giotto. Great artists rarely do what they think they are doing and we hardly detect in the *Chartreuse* 'a mirror scanning along the path.'[18]

So let us pause instead and consider the relationship between the elements, what painters call the palette. They mean by this the choice of colours, and their relatively constant connection which is often governed by a special correlation: sepia and claret in the case of Rembrandt, ashen blue and yellow in the case of Vermeer, etc ... If we apply it to literature, which has no equivalent, we should call it style, if style did not also mean a way of writing. The elements in a literary work – plot, character, confrontations, analysis and atmosphere – are assembled in the same way as colours. Dostoevsky and Stendhal, like Rembrandt and Vermeer, each have their own particular palette (I omit Tolstoy because he conceals his just as Velasquez often does). The world of Julien and Fabrice, that we call the world of the novel, is not confined to fiction. In itself fiction has no particular colours. The relationship between a character and its novel has changed since 1840 almost as much as novels themselves. The character of Fabrice belonged to a story and to his author's talent. His original relationship with the story is replaced by his relationship with the author, just as the atmosphere of Milan in 1796, of Waterloo, of the little courts of Italy, have been rubbed out by Stendhal's universe. The road along which that famous mirror is carried by Mozartian masks does not run through 1820 Italy but through the Italy of Henri Beyle. It is an arbitrary and musical place, and the characters are immersed in it, impregnated by a timeless past, a pure creation of memory. If we turned the *Chartreuse* into a modern film we should lose the Italy of the past and, not withstanding the director's talent, the atmosphere that no film can reproduce; you might as well try to reconstruct a still life by Cézanne with real fruits. But why should this be so?

When a film from a masterpiece is notably successful, the publishers of novels from films do not publish the masterpiece but a book 'extracted from the film', a story of the film faithful to its narrative and to its sentimental and dramatic values. Let's imagine this exercise applied to the greatest novels. In painting it would consist in replacing *Le Concert Champetre* by a *tableau vivant*. We are implying that Stendhal and the specialist of the film-novel extracted from the *Chartreuse* have both told the story of Fabrice and La Sanseverina, with Stendhal showing the greater talent. But it is by no means certain that a clever film director, like Hitchcock, should not be able to tell the story better, for the narrative power of pictures is much greater than that of words. Equally some rival of Simenon could turn Hitchcock's film into a better novel. Stendhal's genius is not purely narrative, nevertheless genius is decanted when you take away the story, even Dostoevsky's or Victor Hugo's. Of course *Crime and Punishment* cannot be separated from Raskolnikov, but from time to time the cinema shows us Raskolnikov without Dostoevsky. The difference between the masterpiece and the film-novel, or even the film itself, is not one of degree but of nature. And the author's 'palette' does not survive the casting of his characters.

Maria Casarès as La Sanseverina and Gérard Philipe as Fabrice show how the transformation of the characters and the metamorphosis that time imposes on them make them resemble their originals and yet remain irreducibly different. The cinema is quite used to turning an 1840 Fabrice into a 1976 Fabrice with the help of 1820 costumes. But beware, it is not Stendhal's Fabrice that is being transformed but a Fabrice reduced to his own biography. There is no identity between the novel and the film but between the story that the novel seems to tell and the one told by the film. One can no more confine the character in a novel to his biography than a novel to its plot. The cinema attempts to find equivalents for every element in the novel and even for the plot. Assembling these elements does not make the film equal to the novel; the gap between them is as great as that between the novel and real life.

These films stand condemned, sooner or later. Like those taken from *The Brothers Karamazov* and *Moby Dick*, from Balzac and Victor Hugo. Sometimes a great novel has been adapted with respectful fidelity. So what do we miss in the best film of *Anna Karenina* when we compare it with the novel? Tolstoy. How can we fail to apply this epigraph to him: 'Vengence is mine, saith the Lord'? Moving pictures of a love story are not enough to give the novel its eternal resonance. The real Tolstoy is what you cannot transpose when everything has been transposed. *Anna Karenina* is indivisible.

This indivisible whole includes more than the story, it includes what neither the cinema nor the theatre possess because an actor is not a character and because a great novel is a highly finished product. The vital point that it exists only in the imagination is what separates it from the cinema and the theatre. This is where an optical illusion comes in. We are talking about that specific element of a masterpiece which is part of its whole, called either music or perfume or palette or any other allusive word as if it were transcribed and had a model: somewhere a Parma would have existed, if only in Stendhal's imagination, and he would have reproduced it. If he had died without ever having written anything, Beyle would have taken with him *La Chartreuse de Parme*, his funeral violets. However there is no such thing as an unwritten *Chartreuse*, just as there is no model for a Cubist painting. The book is the result of a literary *labour*, a series of manoeuvres, sometimes of the mind and sometimes of instinct, which echo one another, to which the great novelist gives a particular coherence; manoeuvres which cannot be separated either from him or from the fictitious pattern they apply to. Stendhal or Tolstoy do not tell a story or invent a plot better than other novelists. These criteria apply to narrative novels and to detective fiction and these books are not expected to survive. Were posterity even to abandon Stendhal on the shore, it would forget the stories of Fabrice and of Julien, but it would remember *La Chartreuse de Parme* and *Le Rouge et le Noir*. It would forget Prince Andrey's story but remember *War and Peace*. That which makes Tolstoy Tolstoy and Stendhal Stendhal.

The adaptation of novels for the screen becomes even more instructive when you add what we know of the author's intentions and when you compare a masterpiece with the novels competing with it at the time of its publication. In the literary world of 1857 Feydeau's *Fanny* competed with *Madame Bovary*. *Fanny* is not a bad book, just a dead one. Flaubert's letters tell us what he meant to do and how he did it. Here we come back to Gide: was Flaubert mistaken about his own genius? Did he not confuse genius and work? Did he think he could master his work by knowing what he wanted to write and even more, what he did not want to write? He was to use the same methods in *Salammbô*, replacing observation by research, and thereby limiting himself.

Several films have been made of *Madame Bovary*. Jean Renoir's talent does not abolish the distance between a novel and its cinematic adaptation. But the gap between this novel and Flaubert's intentions is never less wide nor less specific.

Here we have a seven-year labour not, as in *La Chartreuse*, a masterpiece dictated in a few weeks. The novel obeyed the author's intentions as faithfully as his descriptions obeyed their model; and to as little purpose. *Madame Bovary*, thanks to the scandal it caused, was a triumphant success: *L'Education sentimentale*, destined to be twenty years later an example for all naturalistic novelists, was a failure. Flaubert could not understand why. Neither do we. *Madame Bovary* and *L'Education sentimentale*, as conceived by Flaubert, do not exist – and yet what plans he had for them. Plans constructed like chairs, chairs which were meant to last for ever! The metamorphosis which couples together the two novels, both turned into films, will make of the *Education* the twin sister of *Madame Bovary*. But contrary to the public which confuses Feydeau and Flaubert, some writers are more lucid. 'If that is what literature has become,' said Alexandre Dumas, 'we have had it.' What did he mean by 'that'?

He meant neither the story of *Madame Bovary* nor that of the 'Wife of Delamare'[19] nor simply Flaubert's style (which appears in translation and the book is translated everywhere) nor its analysis, nor its atmosphere nor its descriptions. What he meant was obviously their 'constellation', including 'what cannot be said' but which one can come quite near to: that by which no book can be confused with the sum total of its parts any more than the constellation of the Great Bear can be confused with its scattered stars.

What Braque was referring to was part of or even made this constellation. The obvious superiority of Tolstoy's novel to the film of Clarence Brown with Greta Garbo is not attested by a doctrine but by the consensus of opinion which dictates the Bibliothèque de la Pléiade or the paperback classics. Tolstoy's novel is more nearly akin to Stendhal's or to Flaubert's than to the film named after its heroine. This kinship will become clearer when, fifty or a hundred years hence, the novel, no longer a major genre in literature, will lose that primacy which makes everything else gravitate around it as tragedy used to do. Corneille's Augustus in *Cinna* is not only more like Racine's Pyrrhus from *Andromaque* or like any other emperor in a film: he is nearer to them than history, even than Octavius. To see the specific and deliberate character of all creative fiction set out clearly we have only to take any novel and compare it with the story that comes closest to it; the life story of a patient told by his psychoanalyst. The day will come when it will be as odd to think of the novel as an imitation of real life as it is now to regard painting as an imitation of real sights.

It is the constellation of its qualities which gives *Madame Bovary* access to the metamorphosis which is denied to *Fanny*. The same applies to *La Chartreuse de Parme* and to *Anna Karenina* – the novel changes through this accession as radically as when it is turned into a film, but in the opposite direction. The film destroys the 'constellation' by arranging the stars according to the story, and by turning its characters into real people. But the Great Bear that Flaubert thought he had established is also destroyed by its survival.

But would that informulable part of the novel, that which remain after the film has been extracted, transcend metamorphosis? It is Mallarmé's famous 'At least faithful as to himself . . .'[20] It is sometimes changed. What we find impossible to capture in Stendhal was not so for Taine, mainly because he did not consider it impossible to capture. Fashion is quick to destroy what belongs to it, the accessories and tone of a period, the macabre in Baudelaire, the eloquence in Victor Hugo. But what about the things that have nothing to do with eloquence, the finest verses of *Booz* and Baudelaire's *Tombeau de Théophile Gauthier*? Nevertheless, for about a thousand years, nobody cared about the elusive in Virgil. We apprehend the ground common to Virgil, Racine, Hugo, Baudelaire and Mallarmé. This has not been reshaped, the liquid has been poured from Racine's to Hugo's flask. It is not to be expected that a different school will follow as the Symbolists followed the Parnassians. It is this common ground that we call poetry when speaking of poetry and not of its history. It is equally difficult to define what links Stendhal and Dostoevsky in our admiration. But literature is beyond melody and narration, just as painting is beyond harmony and subject. But the 'constellation' and the elusive, far from transcending metamorphosis are its main purpose, in literature as in painting.

We cannot separate an important work from its metamorphosis, a *Night-Watch* independent from what the centuries that followed believed they were seeing. It only exists within the framework of a dialogue, and it cannot be for us what it was for Rembrandt, as he had no knowledge of the works of art that were to follow his own. This picture carries the so-called 'corporation' label, yet if the characters are substituted and it is replaced by a 'corporation painting' of the mediocre Dutch brand it will age like the costumes of its characters: it will belong to the past and it will not enter into metamorphosis. So metamorphosis introduces its own pictures into the world of painting and abandons the mediocre ones in the ordinary world which they depict. Far from pushing masterpieces into the past it brings them out of it, it takes Rembrandt from the limbo where he was ageing and grants him access to the timeless world of art.

The process is less obvious in novels, because they are more hemmed in by time. The illusion is common to both arts. In painting and sculpture it served spirituality and idealism while in the novel its reference was to realism. First of all in its choice of subjects. What in Balzac do we call subject? Everything that would necessarily be included in a film – just as the models are what a mediocre painter would preserve in *The Night-Watch*, so Blazac's models are precisely what move away from us and fall into the common past from which the 'visionary' escapes. This 'visionary' that no adaptation can express, for in metamorphosis it meets the timeless world of literature, which does not imitate the everyday world in which the logical-illusionists of the nineteenth century believed.

For them, a work of art was the execution of a plan which was expected to pass its examination (grades: success, glory, promise of survival) before a jury vaguely called the public and theoretically the critics. Novel or painting, it was then supposed to have been introduced into the world of its particular art with the rank that the critics or the academies conferred upon it. Which eradicated illusion, even a logical one. The cultured public, formerly a caste, became a crowd. Throughout the West the media withdrew from the necessarily undogmatic critics the authority they exercised. In 1857 they ranked Feydeau's *Fanny* with *Madame Bovary*, and virtually ignored *Les Fleurs du Mal*. When was *Madame Bovary* no longer compared to *Fanny* but with *La Cousine Bette*, and Baudelaire no longer to Petrus Borel[21] but to Racine? When was a literary work freed from the everyday world and allowed to enter the specific world where it need not pass any examination, and join the works 'which have survived'? Sometimes suddenly: it was Surrealism that allowed Lautréamont, neglected in spite of the efforts of Léon Bloy[22] and Rémy de Gourmont,[23] to be published in paperback. Sometimes slowly: Baudelaire's crowning seems to have had a penetrating effect. A great novel and a human being appear to have parallel lives, if the novel is set in time. Man's life goes from conception to birth and then to biography; the book's from a faint outline to its publication and then to its metamorphosis. Set in time, the life of a masterpiece and that of man are equally irreversible. The finished book can no more go back to its origins than the adult to his childhood.

Nothing is more obscure than this initial stage of the work of art once metamorphosis has taken it over. We can imagine (in vain) a stereotype of *The Night Watch*, but not believe in its existence, and that each successive century has distorted it in its own particular way: it only exists because of these distortions, just as Vermeer's subjects only exist in his paintings. The fear of losing one's depth provoked by the idea of an endless metamorphosis leads us to mistake one kind of originality – which cannot be isolated – for another kind which can be both isolated and defined. Rembrandt however existed, he painted this picture, he looked at it when he had finished it. If the completion of a work of art can be taken absolutely for its birth, its initial stage, genetics has a say in the matter. And we know enough of what great painters have written to realize that what we admire in their work was seldom what they were consciously aiming at. Baudelaire was not the only one to be mistaken about 'what made his genius' (as we see it of course). Giotto was just as mistaken in a different way. The metamorphosis of *Les Fleurs du Mal* since the book was published is not less complex than its making, and this was indeed complex. The hazy intention of *Madame Bovary* was rooted in the world of letters and was carried forward in the same world where it joined its surviving predecessors. Balzac was not competing with the Registry but with Walter Scott and the *Thousand and One Nights*.

The most complete metamorphosis that art has known was birth. That one should be able to admire the statue of the saint before which one prays, *Tristan* for its music rather than its story, a great novel in spite of its plot ... Unpredictable, the next metamorphosis is not unimaginable. Enough that it should subordinate aesthetic values to functional ones. This subordination was almost always to be found in anonymous art, and ranging from *Tristan* to Chartres they are not minor arts. Has functional art disappeared from social-realism – with its imposed subjects and 'positive heroes'. Has it disappeared as well from films where the style of an Eisenstein, a René Clair or a Sternberg is almost tolerated – or does it only dominate the story for the specialists? Has it disappeared from detective stories even, simply, from the vast majority of readers and spectators? How many centuries separate

Joyce's admirer and the serialized story reader? It can also be imagined
that the relationship between Sophocles and *Oedipus Rex* was closer than
that of Eisenstein and *Potemkin* or that of Mallarmé with *Hérodiade*. What
is at stake in total metamorphosis would not be a form of novel or of
poetry: it would be literature itself.

V

It has been predicted – not without some apparent logic – that the
awareness of metamorphosis implied an indictment of art. I am afraid
that to say there is 'no art without standards' is as misguiding as to say
there is 'no morality withour religion', and thus by confusing cause and
effect, metamorphosis and fashion are also confused. The empiricism
that the life of literature opposes to dogma is not a value and it is more
than an experience, it is the acquarium in which we live; take our
libraries and museums. Paul Valéry was already bewildered to find that
he admired both Shakespeare and Racine. As to death, what matters is
not that Sophocles or Phidias should be immortal, but that they should
be capable of rebirth. The Copernican revolution as a result of which
the arts now gravitate around us implies neither eclecticism nor rejection. Classical sculpture after Phidias attracts little attention: the rele-
vant rooms in the museums are deserted. Neither the major nor the
minor poetry of our own eighteenth century has been revived – neither
Dorat nor Lebrun-Pindare. It does not occur to us – and this is indeed
surprising – that a popular democracy might more willingly accept
Janin's virtuous judgment on Stendhal than Gide's hedonistic opinion;
nor that the judgments of the year 2176 might not be the same as our
own. Although we are not sure what successive values the future will
attribute to works of art, we believe that our own relationship to them
will hold its own. We place ourselves outside history: a disconcerting
privilege. We shall never know what *The Wounded Lioness* meant to a
King of Nimrod, nor even to its sculptor, but we admire it as much as
Goya's *The Execution of 3rd May*, and Picasso's *Guernica*. Bergotte eludes
Proust, but not his affinity with *La Vue de Delft*. We know little about
Cervantes and Dostoevsky themselves, and even less about Shakespeare.
We scarcely have an idea of how they felt about their own works: but
our individual relationship to *Don Quixote*, *The Brothers Karamazov* and
Macbeth is less ambiguous to each of us than is our individual relation-
ship with ourselves; our connection with the arts is more aggressive
than sceptical.

   Our provisional immortalities would have astonished our forebears.
This astonishment is instructive, for it reveals one of the strongest

girders in the rubble of values amongst which we live. Almost every civilization preceding our own has been concerned with the *training* of man. They have been less interested in knowing what he is, than in laying down what he ought to be. A civilization capable of moulding man does not ask too many questions about him.

To these questions the nineteenth century replied: tomorrow science will tell. Today science answers that its discoveries can destroy men but cannot make one.

I once wrote that: 'Men have always been fashioned by other means: religion, family, example and imagination. Of these, the last was not the least important. Spain and Great Britain, who founded the two greatest empires, both had a word for the exemplary man: *caballero* and *gentleman*. For Rome, it sufficed to be called a Roman. Culture became known as the Humanities. Yet our own civilization, differing in many respects from *all* the others, is the first not to hold any ultimate values. The human animal, at its most powerful, is also the first to mistake exemplarity and success. Less and less do we imagine the man that we should like to be.'

The concepts which governed the development of man are gradually disappearing. Our civilization is ebbing – in every sense of the word. A Christian of the thirteenth century, or an atheist from the middle of the nineteenth, would say that we have made problems of their certainties. Dante was not disconcerted by man, nor Balzac by the individual, nor Michelangelo by art.

But our own civilization, perhaps because it is so powerful, seems to us secretive rather than shapeless. 'What is so extraordinary,' said Einstein, 'is that somehow it probably all makes sense.' Hence the surge of questioning thought today; delving more and more into time and into the shadows of our very being is increasingly wide-ranging. By widespread questioning we hope to reach out to the fringes of posterity and to perceive the ferment which saves the work of art from oblivion. Every international Colloquy gambles with its immediate posterity, just as Queen Nefertari, at the entrance to her tomb, plays a game of chess in which the stake is her afterlife, with the invisible deity of the Dead. We are as puzzled when we behold the Picasso exhibition in Tokyo as we are when African sculpture is on show at the Grand Palais, and our very curiosity seems to guide us towards the 'highway' which will keep the work of art afloat. Like the biologists who first scanned a cell through the microscope, we are fascinated to watch the precarious fireflies of survival haphazardly flitting in the darkness. Immortality was less surprising than this.

Who believes in unchanging literary values? In a literature supplied by the various periods and their authors, like apples from apple trees? In a novel as an image of life or a mirror along the way? People still cherish a faint belief that the great works are reproductions of real or imaginary models, but they are wrong. From hackney cabs to moon rockets, the generation born with the century is in a state of metamorphosis; so are the teenagers who, in the world of today, are politely invited to sit on chairs which have been removed. Who is unaware of the existence of audio-visual aids? Who looks at an aeroplane without mentally boarding it?

However, the metamorphosis which we owe to our own aeroplane, the great leeway of the past, the challenge to literary forms, the whole adventure of writing in our day and age – all this, the Colloquy can grasp more effectively than its rival literary forms. It can juggle with the camera because the multi-sided approach is achieved. It realizes that to pool knowledge for the sake of a single work, as some specialists used to do, is not its line. The authors who write in the Colloquy know little (if anything) of each other, nothing of the work that each is engaged upon, and the general layout is mapped like the underground, not like a logical demonstration. The point is to give the greatest possible scope to chance, chance being kept under remote control – acrobatics without a safety net – but every year we see it more decisively breaking away from essays, studies and biographies. Like other new forms, the Colloquy conspires with hazard to be on the lookout for the irrational aspects of the world. Since the advent of television, its progress has not been towards perfection, for it is like a shooting range – more and more shots hit the bull's eye and the others miss the target. In many respects this book marks the end of a tradition to which it did not seem to belong: international but contemporary, its contributors are offering us Plutarch's last metamorphosis.

VI

Just as man has lived within a circumscribed *world of art* – from the gods to the cathedrals, from the cathedrals to the collections, from the collections to the museums and thence to the Imaginary Museum – in the same way we dwell in a *world of literature* which is both circumscribed and changeable.

We are living at the end of the reign of printing, between the period of the word and the period of images – already close at hand – in the age of the novel set between theatre and television. The media have now taken over story-telling: story and stage have been abandoned by painting; painting itself has increasingly specific problems and all this simultaneously challenges the very nature of the literary work.

The novel is undergoing a dual optical illusion: on the one hand the story is assimilated to letters. (The aura of epistolary novels from *La Nouvelle Héloise* to *Les Liaisons dangereuses* is widely acknowledged.) The novel relates a tale – just as a letter recounts anecdotes – and shifts from the living model to the literary transcription by way of the narrative. The other illusion does not concern time. It is the illusion of photographic accuracy applied particularly to settings. It is not as strong as in painting because a strict sense of realism would require, as Flaubert had foreseen, the narrative to be dropped altogether. But in literature as in the plastic arts, the illusion rests on the assumption that the work reproduces the model. Yet sculpture first began with the gods, and literature likewise. The model in any realistic art is only one of the means by which the artist reacts against the idealizing style or the religious style which precedes his own. The realism of the Flemish, Spanish, French and Italian schools is still linked by shadows to the Italian idealization. The naturalists, in literature, are still connected with the Romantics by way of the narrative. *L'Assommoir* was held to be the symbol of realism – the very ordinary story of Gervaise and Coupeau. But this story and this atmosphere are not in the least ordinary: in the literary context of the time, they are exotic. Our habit of considering Zola as Balzac's successor is deceptive. This successor is the author of *Nana*. But *L'Assommoir* happened in order to oppose *Les Misérables*.

Zola was not misled by this, since in spite of his debt to Flaubert, he claimed that naturalism would succeed Romanticism: chapters, not life-episodes. No novelist would ever have written *L'Assommoir* just by looking at Coupeau, just as no shepherd ever became Giotto by looking at his sheep. It has been thought that *L'Assommoir* is Coupeau plus Zola. We are beginning to understand, thanks to the metamorphosis, that in order to shift from a scenic element to a novel, a change of reference is required. Coupeau and Gervaise only refer to life, but Zola cannot refer to them without referring to the fictitious worlds created by writers. Everyone seems prepared to agree that the library – the world of literature – cannot be a constant reference, but they will only admit – without it being very clear to them – that the world of writing, like the world of art, is formed by adjunctions. The world of Zola would be our own were it not for what has been written since; just as the Louvre of Cézanne would be ours were it not for what has been painted since. In spite of the fact that in the Louvre, for instance, the public desert the antiquities in favour of the Great Period rooms, and that the difference between the literary worlds of two periods is like the difference between the Paris of Balzac and the Paris we know today. The burning of the Tuileries opened up the perspective of the Champs-Elysées, but razed the palace to the ground. We know this, yet we are not fully aware of it because we do not differentiate between the world of literature – in any given period – and that of its writers. It seems to us that the seventeenth century was thriving on Racine, but in fact as late as 1830 the real or imaginary library was still stocked with the ancient classics. Victor Hugo's plays react against the classics and in so doing take them into account; this he does in the name of Shakespeare, with the help of melodrama, but not to relate the story of Hernani. French literature became a subordinate affair when our revered French classics held the limelight. What did Ronsard mean to Racine? What did Malherbe mean to him? His master had not been a French poet, it had been Euripides. The concept of the unbroken line of French literature which made the ancient classics gradually appear archeological – it was the Goncourt's view – was established as late as modern painting. In order to assess the importance of the metamorphosis brought about by the gradual fading out of antiquity – not unconnected with the phasing out of latin studies – we need to imagine what it would be like if, in one or two centuries from now, all our poetry from Chénier to Saint John Perse, and all Western fiction from Blazac to Faulkner were to go by the board.

One no more writes *L'Assommoir* because one has been moved to tears by Coupeau than one paints like Corot because one has been stirred by the morning mist. The novel stems from the novelist's intention. Rather than take my cue from Valéry, who wanted to detect that intention and then form his own opinion of the author's merits, I will take it from Picasso: 'One always has to have a subject, a purpose, before one starts on a painting, but that subject must not be too precise.' I do in fact believe that the novelist's initial intention is but hazy and that it acts as a ferment rather than as a plan.

This intention is not to be mistaken for the first stage of the plot. A story confined to merely recording the facts would be a short one indeed. Besides a true novelist thinks of his plot in relation to factors which have nothing to do with the story – Flaubert's: 'I wanted to write a puce-coloured novel' bears this out; so do Dostoevsky's confrontations. Cézanne painting from nature is not bent on imitating it; he tries to find a way of making it look like a Cézanne. Naturally he does not think up a mental model: pictures may be deliberate but they are not imagined – they are actually made. So is a novel. But nature is not the painter's field of reference: 'If I were to choose a larger tree, if the river were bluer, etc ...' No: Cézanne was haunted by the Imaginary Museum, by the picture he was trying to achieve. Its elements find co-ordination in the world of painting, shapes and colours, and not in the world of trees and bathing soldiers.[24] They are born in the Imaginary Museum, not in real life where the relationship of one thing to another is specifically different. An artist's initial design, the major part of his work, belong to the world of art not to the world of matter: through repulsion as much as through admiration.

It was the partial influence of individualism and Impressionism which – to Degas' indignation – made painters labour for half a century under the misapprehension that the artist transcribed his individual vision, yet it would have been hard to believe that the Cubists saw their fruit dishes in pieces.

Tintoretto and Poussin undeniably worked using small wax figures as models. They did not paint these figures, but they used them to paint saints floating in the air and scenes from antiquity. Where is the difference with Cézanne's apples, or his soldiers bathing, which he called *Les Baigneuses*?

We have detailed knowledge of Flaubert's outline-plans. I am inclined to think that he used them as reminders or guides more than anything else. But whatever the case may be, no one has attempted to write, dramatize or film those chapters of *Bouvard*[25] *et Pécuchet* that we only possess in outline.

And then there is *Madame Bovary*. Flaubert read to his friends the first version of *La Tentation de Saint Antoine*. They thought it bad and suggested: 'Why don't you set to write the story of Delamare's wife.' This referred to a local incident which was to bear the same relation to *Madame Bovary* as the trial of the seminarian Berthet bore to *Le Rouge et le Noir*. But it is very peculiar that Bouilhet[26], Maxime du Camp[27] and other professional writers should have decided that Flaubert had actually devised this story. The illusion is based on the idea that a novel can be identified with its story. We are beginning to understand that the story of Madame Delamare, even if it is the seed of the plot, is not the seed of the novel; this is because 'the novel' is the sum of all the factors which make of the plot the coat-hanger on which *Madame Bovary* is the dress. As in painting, the work and the model do not belong to the same world. If we can find in local incidents the source of many plots, but not the ferment of a great book, it is because the novelist's true initial outline comes to birth in the *world of writing*, not in the world outside. It matters more that the *Mona Lisa* belongs to the world of painting more than it resembles its original model. The ferment acts as a filter. It inhales and it exhales. It brings Coupeau to light or casts him into the shadows depending on the requirements of *L'Assommoir* in progress and not according to the dictates of a hypothetical model. The *presence* of a novel in our mental library – specific universe of literary creation – is as linked to the world of novels as the *presence* of Corneille's *Cinna* would be linked to the world of tragedies.

The initial design of a great novel delivers real life from its endless confusion. Life undergoes a change in character as meadows cease to be shapeless in the eyes of the hunter. The creative will neither involves nor suggests a world architecture. It filters the world. This is done in successive stages because the filtering process varies according to he progress of the work in hand, as the pupils of a cat will vary according to the darkness. Nevertheless the creative will becomes what Delacroix calls the dictionary: a catalogue. The novelist draws from it the elements he needs – including those required for his characters – as the painter draws from it the complementary items which the voids left in his still-life call for. But the elements thus drawn are assimilated rather than inserted. A work of art develops as an organism rather than as a game of chess. For in spite of the secret or recognized rules of the game the assimilation is responsible for direction and hierarchy: from the supposed imitation of models to the independence allowed to the characters. But because this assimilation is subject to the hazards of life and creation, not to a genetic future, moulting for instance remains unforseeable, and likewise certain chrysalids may wonder that they have not turned into butterflies. Should, sometime in the future, metamorphosis adopt the novel, it will adopt it as a whole, but will essentially be concerned with the rise of the ferment, the germination: the writing and not what the writing 'represents', just as it is concerned with a painting and not its subject. The work of art is transformed within the specific world in which it was born.

Since the elements of reality penetrate the world of art by a process of assimilation, the world of the novel does not feature a vast reverie or photograph, it features a world whose likeness with life and the world we know is *subordinated* to its own coherence. This coherence is as strict as the one to which the world of music subordinates its ballets or libretti. We become more aware of this through the development of audio-visual narration than through the evolution of the novel. This coherence does not only establish the novel as a genre (it was that already) but also as a convention similar to that of the theatre or the *chanson de geste*. We do not compare Bizet's *Carmen* to Mérimée's hypothetical model.

What existence does an opera character have outside the world of opera?

If the initial design is not conceived in a specific world, there is ground for believing that it is simply lack of training which prevents an artist from expressing himself equally well in painting, literature or music; even the advocates of art as an expression of the individual accept this so long as it is not stated explicitly. Madame Delamare would not have inspired Flaubert to produce a picture, however brilliant a draughtsman he might have been. All Victor Hugo's skill would not have led him to paint the equivalent of *Booz*. One might wonder what that good Lady's death would have produced from Géricault. Not because Géricault was a better artist than Flaubert, but because neither the design nor the subject have any existence in themselves: only outlines of works exist. Géricault would have drawn his creative inspiration from a dialogue with the museum, not with the library; with the *world of art*, not the *world of writing*. Could that be what a painter is, first and foremost? Art begins when life ceases to be a model and becomes raw material, and that raw material includes the very life of the artist himself.

If the *presence* of works of art is guaranteed by a creative *fact* which is not subject to analytical thinking, if *Le Rouge et le Noir* does not derive its presence from its genius, but its genius from its *presence*, to what then does it owe its presence? No doubt from the interaction which takes place between happenings or surroundings and the *world of writing* – a dialogue akin to Stendhal's – from creation itself. What is this world? The age in which we live believes itself to be the first to have some intuition of its nature.

The coordination of language, as of forms, appears subject to the coordination of life, though we find it to be secretly related to the harmony of music. Yet the coordination of art is not subject to time: the only human coordination that is stronger than death.

The literature that exists for us as a 'presence' is in our imaginary Pléiade, not in our life memory. Heirs to the Olympus of unshakable masterpieces, variable literary successions carry like a current the works attracted by the unsteady magnetism of forthcoming creations . . . But metamorphosis is the ultimate law, because everything that is present falls into the past just as surely as it drifts towards death. This would be taken for granted if metamorphosis with its padded footsteps were not imperceptibly at work. A work of art, whether famous or ignored, does not gain access to metamorphosis on the death of the artist. Death seldom coincides with demise. But however late metamorphosis occurs, herding the transient residents of the present, it turns the defendent into a judge as inexorably as fate itself.

And starts again . . . .

If posterity no longer believes in honours lists, metamorphosis still believes in cooptions. The Imaginary Museum and the Bibliothèque de la Plèiade appear to be immobile; so does the firmament.

NOTES

1 A scandal in the reign of Louis xiv, in which several prominent personalities, including Racine and Madame de Montespan, were suspected of being involved with the Marquise de Brinvilliers and La Voisin, who were eventually condemned to death for poisoning and practising black magic.

2 A very well-known book of *souvenirs* on Balzac by a minor novelist, Léon Gozlan (1803–66) who was, at one time, Balzac's secretary.

3 Characters in a short story by Edgar Allan Poe.

4 Claude-Joseph, Chevalier Dorat (1738–80), author of indifferent and pretentious plays and verse, including *Les Baisers*.

5 A medieval poet, probably Norman, author of a long poem in octosyllabic verse based on the Tristan story.

6 Before the Second World War the publishing house of Gallimard established the Bibliothèque de la Pléïade, a unique collection of books which grew to include the complete works of all established authors.

7 Gédéon Tallement des Réaux (1619–92), author of *Les Historiettes*, a collection of anecdotal memoirs.

8 Date on which General de Gaulle launched his 'Appeal' to the French from London.

9 Albert Thibaudet (1874–1936), literary critic and member of the *NRF*, who had a great influence on French literature between the two world wars.

10 Nicolas Boileau, called Boileau-Despréaux, the best-known of seventeenth-century French critics, and author of *L'Art poétique*.

11 The Association For International Intellectual Cooperation, founded in 1910, used to held its meetings at the Abbey of Pontigny: they were known as *décades* or *entretiens*. Between the two wars, Gide, Maurois, Mauriac, Martin du Gard, Malraux, Cursius, Presolini, and Heidegger, took part in them.

12 Not the Gallimard collection, but the sixteenth-century school of poetry headed by Ronsard.

13 Jules-Gabriel Janin (1804–74), minor literary critic and novelist.

14 Jean-Pons-Guillaume Viennet (1777–1868), author of *La Françiade* and other neo-classical fables and verse, now largely forgotten.

15 Henri Beyle: Stendhal's real name.

16 Valéry Larbaud (1881–1957), author and traveller, and member of the *NRF*.

17 François Guizot (1787–1874), politician and historian.

18 A stock phrase taken from Baudelaire's 'Propos sur le roman'.

19 The victim of a real murder which inspired the story of the novel.

20 A quotation from Mallermé's *Tombeau d'Edgar Poe*: 'Tel qu'en lui-même enfin l'éternité le change'.

21 Petrus Borel (1809–59), poet and novelist, and translator of *Robinson Crusoe*.

22 Léon Bloy (1846–1917), Catholic polemical journalist.

23 Rémy de Gourmont (1858–1915), playwright and essayist.

24 As is well-known, the actual models for Cézanne's *Baigneuses* were soldiers bathing in a river.

25 A satirical book by Flaubert.

26 Louis Bouilhet (1822–69), minor poet and dramatist, and lifelong friend of Flaubert.

27 Maxime du Camp (1822–94), journalist and novelist, and friend of Flaubert.

CHRONOLOGY

compiled by Philippe and François de Saint-Cheron

1901 3 November: birth, in Paris, of Georges André Malraux. Lives in Bondy during his childhood.

1909 November: tragic death of his grandfather at Dunkirk.

1914–18 Malraux's father is conscripted.

Autumn 1915: Malraux is a pupil at the Ecole Turgot until July 1918.

1919 Attends lectures at the Musée Guimet and the Ecole du Louvre. Works for the bookseller-publisher René-Louis Doyon. Meets François Mauriac. Studies Sanskrit.

1920 Publication, in *La Connaissance*, a review edited by Doyon, of Malraux's first article, 'Des origines de la poésie cubiste'; then in the review *Action*, of articles on Lautréamont and André Salmon. Malraux publishes little-known texts by Jules Laforgue. Becomes artistic director of the publisher Simon Kra, where he publishes works by Baudelaire, Rémy de Gourmont and Max Jacob, Ensor, Léger and Derain. 'La Genèse des *Chants de Maldoror*' published in *Action*.

1921 Friendship with Kahnweiler who publishes Malraux's *Lunes en papier*, dedicated to Max Jacob, illustrated by Léger and limited to 100 copies. Publication also, in *Signaux de France et de Belgique*, of 'Les Hérissons apprivoisés' and in *Action* of 'Journal d'un pompier du jeu de massacre'. Visits Venice and Florence 21 October: Marries Clara Goldschmidt.

1922 Meets Picasso. Publication, in *Action* and the *NRF* (*Nouvelle Revue Française*), of articles on Gide, Jacob; his first article for the *NRF* is on *L'Abbaye de Typhaines* by Gobineau. Writes for *Dés* 'Des lapins pneumatiques dans un jardin français'. Writes a preface to the catalogue of the Demetrios Galanis exhibition. Travels. Unsuccessful ventures in the Stock Exchange.

1923 Writes a preface to Maurras's *Mademoiselle Monk*. Goes to Indochina with Clara and Louis Chevasson. After their expedition to the temple of Banteaï-Srey in Cambodia (from which they brought back statues and reliefs), they are accused of theft and arrested in Pnom-Penh.

1924 Trial at Pnom-Penh. Alerted by Clara who alone managed to reach Marseilles, Doyon launches in *L'Eclair* an appeal for Malraux's release. A similar appeal is launched by *Les Nouvelles Littéraires* with the signature of twenty-three well-known writers, among whom Mauriac, Gide, Breton, etc. Malraux, reprieved, returns to France. Publication, in *Accords*, 'Ecrit pour une idole à trompe'.

1925 Malraux goes back to Indochina. Organizes, with Nguyen Pho, the 'Young Annam' ('Jeune Annam') movement and launches, with Paul Monin, the newspaper *L'Indochine* (which will cease to be published in August as no printer dares to print it). Publishes in *L'Indochine*, under the pseudonym of Maurice Sainte-Rose, 'L'Expédition d'Ispahan'. November *L'Indochine* is again published under the new title of *L'Indochine enchaînée*. Possible illness of Malraux. Leaves Saigon.

1926 Back in Paris Malraux heads *A la sphère* which publishes works by Mauriac, Gide, Samain, Morand, Giraudoux, etc. August: Grasset publishes Malraux's *La Tentation de l'Occident* (of which extracts had been published in April by the *NRF* under the title 'Lettres d'un Chinois').

1927 Publication, in the review 600, of 'Ecrit pour un ours en peluche' and in *Commerce* (run by Paul Valéry, Léon Paul Fargue and Valéry Larbaud) of 'Le Voyage aux Iles Fortunées'. Publication in *Ecrits* of an essay, 'D'une jeunesse européenne'.

1928 Malraux's *Les Conquérants* and *Royaume farfelu* are published respectively by Grasset and Gallimard. Malraux visits Persia. Takes part in the Décades de Pontigny. Member of the Comité de Lecture and Artistic Director at Gallimard's until the Spanish Civil War. Responsible, in particular, for an edition of Valéry's poems annotated by Alain.

1929 One of Malraux's first public speeches, about *Les Conquérants*.

1930 *La Voie royale*, volume 1 of *Puissances du désert*, published by Grasset. Visits Afghanistan, India, Japan and the United States. 20 December: Malraux's father commits suicide.

1931 Exhibitions of Gothic-Buddhist, Greco-Buddhist and Hindu-hellenistic art at the *NRF*. Debate, at the *NRF*, between Trotsky and Malraux about *Les Conquérants*. Malraux goes to China. Writes a preface to Charles Clément's *Méditerranée*.

1932 Exhibitions: Gothic-Buddhist art of Pamir (*NRF*); 'Jeune Chine' (*NRF*); and Semirani (*NRF*). Writes a preface to D. H. Lawrence's *Lady Chatterley's Lover*. Meets Claudel at the NRF for the publication of *Le Livre de Cristophe Colomb*. Meets Heidegger in Cologne.

1933 Fautrier exhibition (*NRF*). Writes a preface to Faulkner's *Sanctuary*. *La Condition humaine* published by Gallimard. A huge success. Malraux awarded the Prix Goncourt for it in December. Birth of Florence Malraux.

1934 February: With Edouard Corniglion-Molinier flies over the Desert of Dhana, in the Yemen, in search of the 'kingdom of the Queen of Sheba'. Describes this in *L'Intransigeant*. 'Face-to-face meeting' (Malraux's own description) with the Sphinx of Gizeh. March: Meeting with Trotsky at Royan. April: Malraux describes this meeting in *Marianne*. Becomes president of the World Committee for the Liberation of Dimitrov and Thaelmann. Goes to Berlin with Gide and they present a letter to Goebbels who receives them. Member of the Presidium of the ILAA (International League against Antisemitism). President of the World Committee against War and Fascism. August: Speech at the first Congress of Soviet Writers in Moscow (which he is later to describe in a speech at the Mutualité). Meets Meyerhold and Eisenstein (whose plans to film *La Condition humaine* are stopped by Stalin). Meets Pasternak in Moscow, Gorky in the Crimea and, at Gorky's, meets Stalin. Meeting with T. E. Lawrence. Often sees Alain between 1934 and 1936.

1935 *Le Temps du mépris* published by Gallimard (the original edition does not include the Preface). Writes a preface to Andrée Viollis's *Indochine SOS*. Speech at the International Congress of Writers for the Defence of Culture in Paris, to which Pasternak is invited.

1936 June: Speech at the International Congress of Writers for the Defence of Culture in London. July: In the Spanish Civil War, organizes and heads the Escuadrilla España. Takes part in sixty-five air missions and is wounded twice. Fights at Medellin, Madrid, Toledo and Teruel. Is made a Colonel of the Spanish Republic. Meets Nehru for the first time in Spain. Meets Léon Blum. Camus adapts *Le Temps du mépris* for the Théâtre du Travail in Algiers.

1937 Takes part in the International Congress of Writers for the Defence of Culture in Madrid and Valencia. Propaganda trip to the USA on behalf of the Spanish Republican cause. Meets Hemingway. Stays with Einstein at Princeton and there meets Robert Oppenheimer. *L'Espoir* published by Gallimard. 'La Psychologie de l'Art' published before official publication in *Verve*. Meets George Bernanos.

1938 Starts filming *Sierra de Teruel* in Barcelona, with music by Darius Milhaud. 'La Psychologie des Renaissances' and 'De la Représentation en Occident et en Extrême-Orient' published in *Verve*.

1939 'Etude sur Laclos' (written in 1938) published by Gallimard in their *Tableau de la Littérature Française*; 'Esquisse d'une Psychologie du Cinéma' published in *Verve* (*see also* 1946). After many mishaps Malraux's film is finished in April and shown privately in July (*see also* 1945). Address on André Gide. At Provins Malraux volunteers as a private in the tanks.

1940 June: Taken prisoner in Sens during an attack. Five months later he escapes into the *zone libre*. 18 June: General de Gaulle's *Appeal*; Malraux writes him a letter which was never to reach him.

1941 Working on *Les Noyers de l'Altenburg*. 'La Fosse à tanks' published in *Lettres Françaises* of Buenos Aires. At Roquebrune Malraux is visited by Gide and Sartre.

1942 Starts working on a book on T. E. Lawrence (*see also* 1934), *Le Démon de* *l'Absolu (see also* 1946). The Gestapo burns the MS of *La Lutte avec l'Ange* of which only the first chapter (*Les Noyers de l'Altenburg*) remains. Responsible for Gallimard's publication of Camus's *L'Etranger*. Leaves for Corrèze with Josette Clotis.

1943 *Les Noyers de l'Altenburg* published in pre-publication in *La Semaine Littéraire*, in Geneva, and simultaneously in Lausanne by the Editions du Haut-Pays. 'Le Camp de Chartres', first part of *Les Noyers de l'Altenburg*, published in Algiers in *Fontaine*. From Beaulieu-en-Dorogne Malraux makes contact with the resistance groups in Corrèze and Dordogne.

1944 Under the name of 'Colonel Berger' Malraux heads the FFI of the Lot, Dordogne and Corrèze areas. His mission is to slow down, with 1500 men, the progress of the Das Reich division. During a raid he is wounded, then captured. The Germans at Gramat threaten him with execution, but it is only a ploy. Sent to Saint-Michel prison in Toulouse, where he is interrogated by the Gestapo but not tortured. When the Germans flee from Toulouse Malraux/Berger takes over the prison. His two half-brothers, Roland and Claude, die in deportation and Josette Clotis, by whom Malraux has had two sons, dies in an accident. Malraux founds the Brigade Alsace-Lorraine. Commands the French Forces in the battle of Dannemarie which he liberates, as well as Sainte-Odile and Mulhouse; defends Strasbourg. December: Meets General Leclerc at Erstein. Saves Grünewald's Issenheim altarpiece from the Germans.

1945 Meeting with Koestler. One of the first to enter Nuremberg and Stuttgart where De Lattre presents him with the Legion of Honour. Speech at the first national congress of the MLN, Hiroshima. Conversation with Picasso. Meets De Gaulle for the first time. Towards the end of the year meets Léon Blum again, through De Gaulle. His film, *Espoir* (originally entitled *Sierra de Teruel*) is given public showing and is awarded the Prix Louis Delluc. Writes the preface for the catalogue of Fautrier's paintings and sculptures. Becomes General de Gaulle's *conseiller technique*, then Minister of Information (Nov. 45 – Jan. 46).

1946 The first chapter of *Le Démon de l'Absolu*, 'N'était-ce donc que cela?' published by the Editions du Pavois. *Scènes choisies* and *Esquisse d'une Psychologie du Cinéma* published by Gallimard. Malraux gives an important lecture at the Sorbonne, under the sponsorship of Unesco: 'L'Homme et la Culture artistique'.

1947 RPF (Rassemblement du People Français) founded; Malraux in charge of propaganda for it. Numerous speeches for the RPF until 1952. Speech at the Gaumont-Palace after a showing of *Espoir*. Address to teachers. Writes a preface to *Les Dessins de Goya au Musée du Prado*, published by Skira. Malraux's *Le Musée imaginaire*, first volume of *La Psychologie de l'Art* also published by Skira. Independence of India.

1948 With Albert Ollivier and Pascal Pia, founds *Le Rassemblement*. Launches an 'Appel aux Intellectuels' at the Salle Pleyel, the text of which was to be added as a postscript to *Les Conquérants*. Marries Madeleine Lioux, widow of his half-brother Roland. *La Création Artistique*, volume II of *La Psychologie de l'Art*, published by Skira. *Les Noyers de L'Altenburg* published by Gallimard (*see also* 1942, 1943).

1949 Founds *La Liberté de l'Esprit*, a magazine run by Claude Mauriac. *La Monnaie de l'Absolu*, volume III of *La Psychologie de l'Art*, published by Skira.

1950 *Saturne, Essai sur Goya* published by Gallimard. Malraux very ill during the summer.

1951 Member of the Conseil des Musées de France where he is Gide's successor. *Les Voix du Silence* (i.e. *La Psychologie de l'Art*) revised, corrected and published by Gallimard.

1952 Writes a preface to *Van Gogh et les peintres d'Auvers* and to *Qu'une larme dans l'océan* by Manés Sperber. In charge of *Tout l'oeuvre peint de Léonard de Vinci* and *Tout Vermeer de Delft*. Contributes to Pierre de Boisdeffre's *Barrès parmi nous*. Speech at the Congrès de l'oeuvre du XXe siècle. Last speech by Malraux on behalf of the RPF (Saint-Maur). Volume I of *Le Musee Imaginaire de la Sculpture Mondiale* (*La Statuaire*) published by Gallimard. Visits Egypt and Persia.

1953 Writes a letter-preface to General Jacquot's *Chimères ou Réalités*, an essay on Western strategy. He had fought, in the *maquis* and in Alsace, with Jacquot, who was Commander-in-Chief in Indochina and Commander-in-chief of the Allied Forces in Europe, 1961–3.

1954 Speech at the Congress of Art and Archeology in New York for the re-opening of the Metropolitan Museum and the bicentenary of Columbia University. A pre-publication version of *La Métamorphose des Dieux* published by the *NRF*. Writes a preface to Albert Ollivier's *Saint-Just ou la force des choses*. Volumes II and III of *Le Musée Imaginaire de la Sculpture Mondiale* (*Des Bas-reliefs aux grottes sacrées* and *Le Monde chrétien*) published by Gallimard. *La Condition humaine* adapted for the theatre by Thierry Maulnier.

1955 With Georges Salles, founds the series 'L'Univers des Formes', published by Gallimard. Writes a preface to *Les Manuscrits à Peintures en France du XIIIe au XVIe siècle*, to Louis Guilloux's *Sang noir* and Nicolas Lazar and Izis's *Israël* (with jacket and frontispiece by Chagall).

1956 Speech at the 350th anniversary of Rembrandt's birth, Stockholm. Takes part in the development of the Caisse Nationale des Lettres.

1957 Volume I of *La Métamorphose des Dieux* (*L'Inaccesible*) published by Gallimard (later to be re-titled *Le Surnaturel*, see also 1977).

1958 With Martin du Gard, Mauriac and Sartre, signs an *Adresse solennelle* to the French President, condemning torture. Speeches and lectures on art in Venice: 'Le secret des Grands Vénitiens'. De Gaulle comes back into power and Malraux is made Ministre Délégué à la Présidence du Conseil, then Minister for Information. Very important press conference. 14 July: speech on the Place de l'Hôtel de Ville. 24 August: speech for the fourteenth anniversary of the liberation of Paris. 4 September: speech on Place de la

République. Numerous speeches and addresses in Martinique, Guadeloupe, Guyana, Iran and Japan and a *Message d'Adieu* to India. Meetings with Nehru and the Japanese Emperor, Hiro-Hito.

1959 First Ministry for Cultural Affairs set up. Malraux is made Minister of State in charge of Cultural Affairs (from 15 April 1962 until 1969 he is to be first in the hierarchy of Ministers of State). *La Gangrène* banned by the government. Addresses at the Biennale de Paris, Tamanrasset, Edjelé, Hassi-Messaoud. Speech at Ouargla. Addresses at the Cannes Festival and in Brazil. Speeches in Athens and Brasilia. Presents Saint-John Perse with the Grand Prix National des Lettres.

1960 Welcomes on behalf of France the President of the Peruvian Republic at Bordeaux. Visits Mexico. First to answer the appeal of the Director-General of Unesco for the preservation of the Nubian monuments. With General de Gaulle and Nehru, opens the exhibition 'Les Trésors de l'Inde' at the Petit Palais (for which both he and Nehru wrote the catalogue prefaces). Speech for the centenary of the Alliance Juive Universelle (Unesco). Unveils in Paris the statue of General José de San Martin. Opens in Tokyo the Maison Franco-Japonaise. Proclaims the independence of Tchad in Fort-Lamy; speech in Brazzaville. Proclaims the independence of Gabon, Congo and the Central African Republic. Meets Dr Schweitzer in Lambarene. Writes a preface to André Parrot's *Sumer*.

1961 Writes the preface for the catalogue of the exhibition '7000 ans d'art en Iran' at the Petit Palais. Reacts violently against the generals' revolt in Algiers. Ready to fight for the Republic. Speech at the Joan d'Arc celebrations in Orléans. Inaugurates the Place de la Brigade Alsace-Lorraine at Metz. His sons, Vincent and Pierre-Gauthier are killed in a car crash in Burgundy.

1962 OAS attempt to blow up Malraux's house; Malraux unharmed. Trip to the United States, meeting with Kennedy; speech at the White House; speech for the fiftieth anniversary of the New York French Institute. Opens, with General de Gaulle, the exhibition 'Chefs d'oeuvre de l'art mexicain'. Lunches at Orly with Nehru on a state visit to France. Founds the association 'Pour la Ve République'.

1963 Speech in Washington on the occasion of the *Mona Lisa*'s trip to the United States; Kennedy present. Funeral oration for Braque before the Louvre Colonnade. Speech in Finland. Trip to Japan. Speech and press conference in Canada. Speech in Nice.

1964 Inaugural speech at the Maison de la Culture at Bourges, in the presence of General de Gaulle. The *Venus de Milo* sent and exhibited in Japan on Malraux's order. Unveiling of the ceiling of the Paris opera house, which he had commissioned from Chagall. Speech for the Joan d'Arc celebrations in Rouen. Opens the Fondation Maeght at Saint-Paul-de-Vence. Orders nineteen statues of women by Maillol to be displayed in the Jardin du Carrousel. Funeral oration for Jean Moulin on the occasion of the transfer of his ashes to the Panthéon in the presence of General de Gaulle.

1965 On doctors' orders Malraux goes on a cruise on board the *Cambodge*; starts the *Antimémoires*. Goes to China with a message from General de Gaulle. Meeting with Chen Yi and Chou-en-lai. 3 August: meets Mao-tse-tung in Peking after visiting Yenan province. Returns through India. Made Doctor *Honoris Causa* of the university of Benares (first foreign doctor); visits Gandhi's mausoleum. Goes to Aden. Funeral oration for Le Corbusier in the Cour Carrée of the Louvre. Speech at the Palais des Sports. Unveiling of the ceiling of the Théâtre de France (formerly the Odéon) commisioned from Masson. The first volume of the final edition of *Les Voix du Silence – Le Musée Imaginaire* – revised and completed, is published by Gallimard.

1966 Inaugural speech for the Maison de la Culture at Amiens. Receives Aragon at the Ministry. Opens with Leopold Senghor in Dakar the first World Festival of Negro Art; important speech on that occasion. Organizes the Picasso retrospective exhibition at the Grand and Petit Palais.

1967 Speech at the Palais des Sports. The *Antimémoires* published by Gallimard. A huge success. Tutankhamen exhibition. Trip to Great Britain. Lecture on 'Art and Time' at the Sheldonian Theatre, Oxford. Made Doctor *Honoris Causa* of Oxford University. Inaugural speech for the Maison Française at Oxford. Founds the Centre National d'Art Contemporain. With Charles Munch establishes the Paris Orchestra. Pays homage to Nehru.

1968 Inaugural speech for the Maison de la Culture at Grenoble. Opens with a speech the 'Europe Gothique' exhibition at the Louvre before the *Victory of Samothrale*. May 68: 20 June, important speech at the Parc des Expositions. Trip to the USSR; meets Kosygin. Speech on culture in Versailles.

1969 Fernand Léger Museum. Speech in Niamey. Address at Stasbourg at the sittings of the UJP. Made Doctor *Honoris Causa* of Jyvacskylae University, Finland. Founds the Inventaire National. In his last political speech, asks the French population to vote 'yes' to the referendum. 27 April: de Gaulle resigns from power. Malraux announces that he also will retire and does so in June. Signs a petition, together with Sartre and Mauriac, for the release of Régis Debray. Goes to live at Verrières-le-Buisson in the house of Louise de Vilmorin. 11 December: last meeting with General de Gaulle. 26 December: death of Louise de Vilmorin.

1970 *Le Triangle noir* (made up of the 'Etude sur Laclos', the preface on Goya at the Prado and the preface to *Saint-Just*) published by Gallimard. 9 November: death of General de Gaulle. Malraux present at the funeral at Colombey. Death of his friend and translator into Japanese, Kyoshi Komatzu (Kyo in *La Condition humaine*). Writes a preface to Louise de Vilmorin's *Poèmes*. Plans for a film based on *La Condition humaine*, directed by F. Zinneman, are abandoned.

1971 *Oraisons funèbres* and *Les Chênes qu'on abat . . .* published by Gallimard.

Writes a preface to *Le Livre du Souvenir* dedicated to de Gaulle. The film *Espoir* is often shown in cinemas and on television. Claude Santelli and Françoise Verny made a film for television with Malraux, *La Légende du Siècle*. Appeal by Malraux for the victims in East Bengal. Open letter to President Nixon (in *Le Figaro*). Meeting with Indira Gandhi at the Indian Embassy in Paris. According to the wishes of General de Gaulle, becomes president of the Institut Charles de Gaulle. Preface 'La Querelle de la Fidelite', Ed. Michelet.

1972 Nixon invites Malraux to the White House before his trip to China. Press conference in the USA. Travels in the Mediterranean. Speech in Durestal in memory of the 'first fight of the first *maquis*'. Writes a preface to Jose Bergamin's *Le Clou brûlant* and to *Les céramiques et les sculptures de Chagall*. Adds two important chapters (on Japan and on death) to the *Antimémoires*. November, seriously ill in La Salpêtriere hospital.

1973 Writes a preface to volume 4 of the *Cahiers André Gide* and to Pierre Bockel's *L'Enfant du rire*. *La Revue des Lettres Modernes* starts a series edited by Walter Langlois: 'Du farfelu aux *Antimémoires*'. 'Paroles et écrits politiques de 47 à 72' published in *L'Espoir*. For the first time Malraux discusses with Tadao Takemoto the fundamental questions posed by the *seppuku*. *Roi, je t'attends à Babylone . . .*, with illustrations by Dali, is published in a very luxurious limited edition by Skira, first version of the second part of *Hôtes de passage*. Goes to India. Made Doctor *Honoris Causa* of Rajshahi University, Bangladesh. Speeches and addresses during this trip in Dakka and Chitta-gong. Meeting with the King of Nepal and Mrs Gandhi. July: A very important exhibition devoted to Malraux by the Fondation Maeght – 'André Malraux et le Musée Imaginaire' – which Malraux opens. Opens the 'Message Biblique Chagall' in Nice. Funeral oration for the *résistants* who died at Les Glières. Witness for the defence of Jean Kay in Versailles Assizes. Opens (but no speech) the Charles de Gaulle exhibition in Vincennes. Makes three films on art which are awarded first prize at the Asolo inter-national festival of films on art: *Les Métamorphoses du Regard*.

1974 *La tête d'obsidienne, Lazare* and *L'Irréel* (volume II of *La Métamorphose des Dieux*) published by Gallimard. During the presidential elections, Malraux proposes reform in education by means of audio-visual methods. Trip to Japan. Meets Emperor Hiro-Hito and Prime Minister Tanaka. Press con-ference, addresses and a lecture on art in Tokyo where he is sent as Special Ambassador of the French Government on the occasion of the loan of the *Mona Lisa*. Symposium in Kyoto: 'What is Asia?' Speech on audio-visual methods in Asnières. Funeral oration for the thirtieth anniversary of the Brigade Alsace-Lorraine at Créteil. Writes a preface to a new edition of Bernaḍo's *Journal d'un curé de campagne*. In new Delhi receives the Nehru prize for peace. Speech on the 'survival of our civilization' in which he suggests that the prize he has been awarded should be used as a starting fund for a new institute of international 'action methods'. Address on biology in Paris. Bestows the Academician's sword to Professor Hamburger. Supports Israel publicly.

1975 Lecture on civilization at the Ecole Polytechnique in Paris. Speech before Chartres cathedral for the thirtieth anniversary of the liberation of concentration camps. *Hôtes de passage* published by Gallimard. Writes a preface to *L'Indépendance de l'Esprit* (correspondence between Guéhenno and Rolland). Long speech in memory of General de Gaulle. Condemns Franco's regime. Trip to Haïti devoted to 'primitive' painters.

1976 Malraux announces a future book on 'the evolution of literature'. March: *La Corde et les Souris* (volume II of *Le Miroir des Limbes*, of which *Antimémoires* is the first volume) published by Gallimard. It contains I *Hôtes de Passage,* II *Les Chênes qu'on abat . . .,* III *La tête d'obsidienne* and IV *Lazare.* The first volume of *Oeuvres Complètes* (containing *Le Miroir des Limbes* and *Oraisons funèbras* brought up to date) to be published in October by La Pléiade. Also in October, *L'Intemporel,* volume III of *La Métamorphose des Dieux,* containing some very important chapters on Asia, the *arts sauvages* and audio-visual methods.

1977 An unpublished chapter of *L'Espoir,* 'Et sur la terre . . .', now completed by Malraux, is to be published by Editions Maeght, Illustrated with fifteen original dry prints by Chagall. *Le Surnaturel* (first volume of *La Métamorphose des dieux* and now revised) to be published by Gallimard. It had been published in 1957 under the title, *L'Inaccessible.*

NOTES

HUGH THOMAS
THE LYRICAL ILLUSION: SPAIN 1936

1 André Malraux, *L'Espoir*, p. 547. All references are to the Pléiade edition, Paris 1947.
2 ibid., p. 465.
3 For Malraux's timetable in July, see W. G. Langlois, 'Aux sources de L'Espoir, *La Revue des Lettres Modernes*, 1973 (5), nos. 355–9.
4 David Caute, *The Fellow Travellers*, London 1973, p. 179.
5 *L'Espoir*, p. 476.
6 ibid., p. 491.
7 ibid., p. 458.
8 Hidalgo de Cisneros, *Memorias*, Paris 1964, vol. II, p. 323 ff.
9 Letter of Colonel Garcia Lacalle to Hugh Thomas, July 1964.
10 Pietro Nenni, *La Guerre d'Espagne*, Paris 1959, p. 196.
11 Miguel Koltzov, *Diario de la Guerra de España*, Paris 1963, p. 93.
12 As quoted in Jean Lacouture, *André Malraux*, Paris 1973, p. 230.
13 Lacouture, p. 259.
14 François Mauriac, *Mémoires Politiques*, Paris 1967, p. 79.
15 *Time*, quoted in Stanley Weintraub, *The Last Great Cause*, London 1968, p. 289.
16 Alfred Kazin, *Starting out in the Thirties*, New York 1965, p. 108.
17 Remark quoted in Lacouture, p. 256.
18 *L'Espoir*, p. 529.
19 Gerald Brenan, *Personal Record 1920–1972*, London 1974, p. 335.
20 *L'Espoir*, p. 580.
21 ibid., p. 581.
22 ibid., p. 508.
23 ibid., p. 781.
24 ibid., p. 652.
25 ibid., p. 493.
26 Koltzov, p. 469.
27 *L'Espoir*, p. 479.
28 ibid., p. 489.
29 ibid., p. 491.
30 ibid., p. 529.
31 ibid., p. 533.
32 ibid., p. 542.
33 ibid., p. 532.
34 ibid., p. 642.
35 ibid., p. 780.
36 ibid., p. 757.
37 ibid., p. 781.
38 ibid., p. 526.
39 ibid., p. 440.
40 ibid., p. 501.
41 Manuel Azaña, dairy entry 7 November 1937, *O-bras Completas*, Mexico 1969, vol. IV, p. 85.
42 *L'Espoir*, p. 505.

CHANG MAI YUAN
MALRAUX AND CHINESE THINKING
André Malraux, *La Tentation de l'Occident*, Paris 1926 (republished 1956), p. 198.

2 ibid.
3 Confucius, *The Conversations*, Book I, Chapter II, section 7.
4 *Tentation*, p. 112.
5 *Conversations*, Book VI, Chapter XII, section 4.
6 *Tentation*, pp. 70–1.
7 ibid., p. 39.
8 ibid., pp. 38–9.
9 ibid., pp. 197–8.
10 ibid., p. 112.
11 ibid., p. 151.
12 ibid., p. 110.
13 André Malraux, *Antimémoires*, Paris 1967, p. 517.
14 *Tentation*, p. 162.
15 André Malraux, 'Jeune Chine: Présentation de documents', *Nouvelle Revue Française*, XXVIII, January 1932, p. 6.
16 André Malraux, *Les Conquérants*, Paris 1928. Livre de poche edition, p. 91.
17 Mencius, *Meng-tseu-Chou*, Book IV, section 26.
18 *Les Conquérants*, p. 148.
19 *Conversations*, Chapter XV.
20 *Tentation*, pp. 182–3.
21 ibid., p. 182.
22 ibid., p. 198.
23 ibid.
24 André Malraux, *Les Voix du silence*, Paris 1951, p. 556.
25 Through a burning desire to rebuild a ruined China, the young Chinese intellectuals set about acquiring the culture of the West (particularly science and the practice of democracy). They cried 'Down with Confucianism!' during the cultural revolution of the 'May the Fourth Movement' in 1919.
26 The cruel and inhuman laws, so called, were promulgated by the Confucians under the Sung Dynasty (960–1280).
27 'Jeune Chine', p. 6.
28 *Tentation*, p. 187.
29 ibid.
30 Feng Yu-lan, *A Short History of Chinese Philosophy*, ed. Derk Bodde, New York 1961, p. 99.
31 *Tentation*, p. 160.

32 ibid.
33 ibid., p. 161.
34 ibid.
35 ibid., p. 155.
36 ibid., p. 67.
37 ibid., p. 183.
38 Lao-tse, *Tao-te-king*, tr. Lion Kia-Hway, Paris 1967.
39 *Tentation*, p. 159.
40 ibid., p. 96.
41 ibid., p. 161.
42 Feng, p. 241.
43 *Tentation*, p. 161.
44 ibid., p. 162.
45 *Tao-te-king*, Chapter III.
46 *Tentation*, p. 187.
47 ibid.
48 ibid., p. 184.
49 ibid., p. 108.
50 *Les Conquérants*, p. 19.
51 ibid., p. 92.
52 David Wilkinson, *Malraux: An Essay in Political Criticism*, Cambridge, Mass. 1967, p. 171.
53 *Tao-te-king*, Chapter XXXIII: 'He who conquers another is strong, but he who conquers himself has strength of soul.'
54 *Les Conquérants*, p. 110.
55 *Tao-te-king*, Chapter XXXVI: 'The soft gets the better of the hard, the weak gets the better of the strong.'
56 *Les Conquérants*, p. 111.

FRANÇOISE DORENLOT
UNITY OF PURPOSE
THROUGH ART
AND ACTION

1 André Malraux, *Antimémoires*, tr. Terence Kilmartin, New York 1968, p. 7. 'It' refers to the collection of novels which Malraux would have published if the Gestapo had not destroyed too many pages. The first volume of this series, *Les Noyers de l'Altenburg*, was fortunately published in Switzerland in 1943.
2 André Malraux, *The Walnut Trees of Altenburg*, tr. A. W. Fielding, London 1952, p. 114.
3 Letter from Malraux to Gaëtan Picon, reproduced in Picon's *Malraux par lui-même*, Paris 1953, p. 2.

4 André Malraux, *Man's Hope*, tr. Stuart Gilbert and Alastair Macdonald, New York 1938, p. 396.

5 After the title of Walter G. Langlois' book, which treats this question fully. *André Malraux – The Indo-China Adventure*, New York/Washington 1966, London 1966.

6 One has only to read the *Antimémoires* to realize that this book is inspired by much else besides (pp. 6–7).

7 In *Verve*, No. 1, December 1937, pp. 41–3.

8 André Malraux, *Man's Fate*, tr. Haakon Chevalier, New York 1934, p. 241.

9 'Révolte et revolution', *Magazine Littéraire*, No. 11, October 1967, p. 28.

10 André Malraux, *Lazare*, Paris 1974, pp. 237–8. 'Men always hear their voice through their throat, and the voice of others through their ears. . . . I had written that every man hears *his life* through his throat, others' through his ears, but in fraternity or love. The book was called *Man's Fate*.'

11 *Antimémoires*, p. 405.

12 It is not difficult to establish a link between Malraux's own life and the recurrence of this theme in his writings. Also perhaps a reminiscence of Pascal.

13 'Sur l'Héritage culturel', *Commune*, September 1936, p. 1.

14 Manès Sperber, *Qu'une larme dans l'océan* . . ., Paris 1952.

15 André Malraux, *The Royal Way*, tr. Stuart Gilbert, New York, 1935 pp. 165–6.

16 'D'une jeunesse européenne' in *Ecrits*, Collection 'Les Cahiers Verts', No. 70. Paris 1927, p. 149.

17 *Man's Fate*, p. 242.

18 *The Royal Way*, p. 87.

19 *The Walnut Trees of Altenburg*, p. 107.

20 An hypothesis implied by certain passages of *Le Musée Imaginaire de la Sculpture Mondiale*, vol. 1, Paris 1952. One finds here, italicized in the text, '. . . the key to the cosmos is not

the key to man', p. 57. See also the *Antimémoires*, 1972 edition. Gallimard, 'Folio' pp. 471–8, and the whole very strange conversation between Malraux and Méry.

21 André Malraux, *The Conquerors*, tr. Winifred Stephens Whale, Boston 1962, p. 164.

22 *Man's Hope*, p. 325. In *Lazare*, facing his possible death, Malraux develops this theme at length, even quoting his character.

23 *Man's Hope*, p. 323.

24 *Man's Fate*, p. 352.

25 See especially the speech of 2 July 1947 in *Espoir*, review of the Institut Charles de Gaulle, No. 2, January 1973, p. 5.

26 Speech of 24 November 1963 in *Espoir*, p. 53. Italicized in the text. An observation which recurs in the speeches for the RPF and the *Antimémoires*, ed. 1972, pp. 437–8.

27 *Man's Hope*, p. 159.

28 'L'Art est une conquête', *Commune*, September–October 1934, p. 68.

29 *Antimémoires*, ed. 1972, p. 427.

30 'Appel aux Intellectuels' of 5 March 1948. Published as an appendix to *Les Conquérants. The Conquerors*, p. 187.

31 'Man's Quest', *Time*, 18 July 1955.

32 'La Révolution étranglée', NRF, April 1931, pp. 488–500.

33 *The Conquerors*, p. 126.

34 In *Fin d'une jeunesse*, Paris 1954, p. 41.

35 'L'Homme et la culture artistique', lecture for UNESCO in *Les Conférences de l'UNESCO*, Paris, p. 77.

36 The expression is Malraux's, applied to Communism, in 'L'attitude de l'artiste', *Commune*, November 1934, p. 173.

37 André Malraux, *The Temptation of the West*, tr. Robert Hollander, New York 1961, p. 117.

38 *The Walnut Trees of Altenburg*, pp. 24 and 22–3.

39 *Man's Fate*, p. 156, italicized in the text.

40 *Man's Fate*, p. 69.

41 'D'une jeunesse européenne', p. 133: 'In face of its dead gods, the whole of the West, having exhausted the joy

of its triumph, prepares to vanquish its own enigmas.'

42 ibid., p. 133.

43 UNESCO lecture already quoted, p. 75.

44 In *Espoir*, p. 97.

45 In *Fin d'une jeunesse*, p. 63.

46 De la française, de la culture, des hommes – interview with Fanny Deschamps, *Elle*, 9 March 1967, p. 111.

47 André Malraux, *La Tête d'obsidienne*, Paris 1974, p. 213.

48 *The Walnut Trees of Altenburg*, p. 107.

49 To judge from the importance it is given in *Lazare*, this episode seems to have impressed Malraux tremendously.

50 See especially the speech of 12 February 1949 in *Espoir*, p. 22, and the *Antimémoires*.

51 Speech in Brasilia, 25 August 1955.

52 *The Temptation of the West*, p. 121.

53 Preface to *Israël* by Lazare Izis, Lausanne 1955, p. 11.

54 Speech in Brasilia already quoted.

55 *Man's Fate*, p. 220, italicized in the text.

56 *Antimémoires*, p. 407.

57 *Man's Hope*, p. 511.

58 *Antimémoires*, p. 2.

59 *Fin d'une jeunesse*, p. 63.

60 *Antimémoires*, p. 233.

61 ibid., p. 6.

62 *Malraux par lui-même*, p. 41, note 10.

63 *Qu'une larme dans l'océan* . . .

64 'D'une jeunesse européenne', p. 148.

65 *The Walnut Trees of Altenburg*, p. 107.

66 *Antimémoires*, p. 3.

67 ibid., p. 221.

68 Preface to André Malraux, *Days of Wrath*, tr. Haakon Chevalier, New York 1936, pp. 4–5.

69 *Antimémoires*, p. 83.

70 ibid., p. 84.

71 André Malraux, *The Voices of Silence*, tr. Stuart Gilbert, New York 1953, p. 642.

72 *La Tête d'obsidienne*, p. 1.

73 'N'était-ce donc que cela?', the only fragment to be published from *Le Démon de l'absolu*, which was to have been a study of T. E. Lawrence. In *Saisons III*, 1946–7, p. 22.

E. H. GOMBRICH
MALRAUX'S PHILOSOPHY OF ART IN HISTORICAL PERSPECTIVE

1 André Malraux, *Les Voix du silence*, synopsis of p. 309.

2 Qunitillan, *Institutio Oratoria*, x 1. 88.

3 André Malraux, *Les Noyers de L'Altenburg*, Paris 1948, pp. 151–2. I should like to thank Enid McLeod for her expert help in translating this and subsequent passages.

4 André Malraux, *Antimémoires*, p. 78.

5 André Malraux, *La Tête d'obsidienne*, Paris 1974, p. 158.

6 André Malraux, *Saturne*, Paris 1950, p. 31.

7 *Antimémoires*, pp. 51, 52.

8 André Malraux, *Le Musée imaginaire*, Paris 1965, p. 161.

9 Johann Gottfried Herder, *Über Ossian und die Lieder alter Völker*, *Sämmtliche Werke*, Stuttgart 1828, vol. 7.

10 J. W. Goethe, *Von deutscher Baukunst*, *Sämmtliche Werke*, Stuttgart 1872, vol. 13.

11 W. H. Wackenroder, *Werke und Briefe*, Jena 1910, pp. 47–50.

12 Alf Boe, *From Gothic Revival to Functionalism*, Oslo 1957.

13 *La Tête d'obsidienne*, p. 159.

14 *Le Musée imaginaire*, p. 110.

15 See my review of the English edition of *The Voices of Silence*, 'André Malraux and the Crisis of Expressionism', reprinted in *Meditations on a Hobby Horse*, London 1963, pp. 78–85.

16 *Musée*, p. 33; *Saturne*, p. 113, *La Métamorphose des dieux*; Paris 1957, especially the conclusion of Part 1, and *La Tête d'obsidienne*, p. 185.

17 Reprinted in *Meditations on a Hobby. Horse*, pp. 30–44.

18 *La Tête d'obsidienne*, p. 94.

19 ibid., p. 56.

20 *Les Voix du silence*, summary of p. 637 of English edition.

21 *Musée*, p. 136.

22 Peter J. Ucko, 'The interpretation of prehistoric anthropomorphic figurines', *Journal of the Royal Anthropological Institute* 1962, pp. 38–54.

23 See my essay 'On Physiognomic

Perception' in *Meditations on a Hobby Horse*, p. 45 with further bibliography.

24 *Les Noyers de L'Altenburg*, p. 122.

25 *Musée*, p. 234.

26 ibid., p. 222.

JEAN LEYMARIE
MALRAUX AND THE CREATIVE PROCESS

1 *Antimémoires*, Paris 1972, p. 41.

2 *L'Intemporel* (unpublished).

3 *Antimémoires*, p. 63.

4 *Oraisons funèbres*, Paris 1971, p. 81.

5 'La peinture de Galanis': *Dictionnaire biographique des artistes contemporains*, vol. II, Paris 1931, p. 90.

6 G. Picon, *Malraux par lui-même*, Paris 1931, p. 18.

7 *Antimémoires*, p. 100.

8 *La Tentation de l'Occident*, Paris 1926, p. 141.

9 ibid., p. 143.

10 ibid., p. 218.

11 'D'une jeunesse européenne', *Ecrits*, Paris 1927.

12 *Les Conquérants*, in *Romans*, Paris 1947 (Pléiade edition), p. 153.

13 ibid., p. 138.

14 Drieu la Rochelle, *Malraux, l'homme nouveau*. NRF, December 1930.

15 *La Voie royale*, Paris 1930, p. 36.

16 ibid., p. 41.

17 ibid., p. 42.

18 ibid., p. 53.

19 ibid., p. 85.

20 *La Condition humaine*, in *Romans*, p. 430.

21 *Antimémoires*, p. 12.

22 *Les Voix du silence*, Paris 1951, p. 628.

23 Notes on the tragic expression in painting (*Rouault*) in *Formes*, December 1929.

24 *Le Temps du mépris*, Paris 1935, p. 12.

25 *Antimémoires*, p. 63.

26 *L'Espoir*; in *Romans*, p. 472.

27 ibid., p. 764.

28 ibid., p. 572.

29 ibid., p. 500.

30 ibid., p. 858.

31 *La Tête d'obsidienne*, Paris 1974, p. 147.

32 ibid., p. 270.

33 *Antimémoires*, p. 302.

34 ibid., p. 44.

35 R. Stéphane, *Fin d'une jeunesse*, Paris 1954, p. 69.

36 Baudelaire, *Oeuvres*, Paris 1952 (Pléiade edition), p. 1219.

37 ibid., p. 1215.

38 'L'homme et la culture artistique', in *Carrefour*, 7, XI, 1946.

39 M. Blanchot, *L'Amitié*, Paris 1971, pp. 21–51.

40 *Sumer*, introduction, 1960, p. XLVIII (*L'Univers des Formes*).

41 *Le Musée imaginaire*, Paris 1965 (Idées-Arts).

42 *Saturne, essai sur Goya*, Paris 1950.

43 *Les Voix du silence*, p. 14.

44 ibid., p. 44.

45 ibid., p. 446.

46 *L'Intemporel* (unpublished).

47 H. Peyre, 'Malraux le romantique', in *Revue des Lettres modernes*, 1973, p. 18.

48 *Les Voix du silence*, p. 371.

49 ibid., p. 604.

50 M. Dvoràk, *Kunstgeschichte als Geistgeschichte*, Munich 1924, p. 276.

51 J. Thuillier, 'La Tour, Enigmes et hypothèses', in cat. exposition Orangerie, Paris 1972, p. 27.

52 *Les Voix du silence*, p. 44.

53 ibid., pp. 50–1.

54 ibid., p. 605.

55 ibid., p. 621.

56 ibid., p. 622.

57 ibid., p. 637.

58 Ce que avons à défendre', in *Arts*, 5–11 June 1952, p. 11.

59 *Le Musée imaginaire de la sculpture mondiale*, 1, Paris 1952, p. 11.

60 ibid., p. 9.

61 *Antimémoires*, pp. 56–7.

62 M. Blanchot, *L'espace littéraire*, Paris 1955, p. 374.

63 *La Métamorphose des Dieux*, Paris 1957, p. 56.

64 ibid., p. 127.

65 T. W. Adorno, 'Introduction première a la théorie esthétique', in *Revue d'Esthetique*, Paris 1975, I, p. 15.

66 *La Métamorphose des Dieux*, p. 136.

67 *La Voie royale*, p. 44.

68 *La Métamorphose des Dieux*, p. 136.

69 *Journal Officiel*, Paris, 9, I, 1959.

70 *Oraisons funèbres*, pp. 37 and 38.

71 *Antimémoires*, p. 562.

72 ibid., p. 563.

73 J. Grosjean, 'Les Antimémoires d'André Malraux', NRF, October 1967, p. 659.

74 *Antimémoires*, p. 437.

75 ibid., p. 212.

76 ibid., p. 287.

77 ibid., p. 300.

78 ibid., p. 278.

79 *Les Chênes qu'on abat . . .*, Paris 1971, p. 11.

80 *Lazare*, Paris 1974, p. 196.

81 *La Tête d'obsidienne*, p. 279.

82 ibid., p. 102.

83 ibid., p. 118.

84 *L'Irréel*, Paris 1974, p. 131.

85 ibid., p. 168.

86 ibid., p. 278.

87 ibid., p. 283.

88 *L'Intemporel* (unpublished).

89 *Complete correspondence of Vincent van Gogh*, Paris 1960, vol. II, p. 485.

90 *Antimémoires*, p. 16–17.

91 J. Schlumberger, *Jalons*, Paris 1941.

BIBLIOGRAPHY

WORKS BY ANDRÉ MALRAUX (LISTED CHRONOLOGICALLY)

French:

Lunes en papier, Editions des Galeries Simon, 1921.

La Tentation de l'Occident, Grasset, 1926.

Les Conquérants, Grasset, 1928.

Royaume Farfelu, Gallimard, 1928

Les puissances du désert, I: *La Voie Royale*, Grasset, 1930. (Ier Prix Interallie.)

La Condition humaine, Gallimard nrf, 1933. (Prix Goncourt.)

Le Temps du Mépris, Gallimard nrf, 1935.

L'Espoir, Gallimard nrf, 1937.

La Lutte avec l'ange, I: *Les Noyers de l'Altenburg*, Editions du Haut-Pays, 1943.

Le Démon de l'Absolu, I: *N'était-de donc que cela?*, Editions du Pavois, 1946.

Scènes Choisies, Gallimard nrf, 1946.

Les Noyers de l'Altenburg, Gallimard nrf, 1948.

La Psychologie de l'Art, I: *Le Musée Imaginaire*, Editions Skira, 1947.

La Psychologie de l'Art, II: *La Création artistique*, Editions Skira, 1948.

La Psychologie de l'Art, III: *La Monnaie de l'Absolu*, Editions Skira, 1949.

Saturne, Essai sur Goya, Gallimard nrf, 1950.

Les Voix du Silence, I: *Le Musée Imaginaire*, Gallimard nrf, 1951.

Les Voix du Silence, II: *Les Métamorphoses d'Apollon*. Gallimard nrf, 1951.

Les Voix du Silence, III: *La Création Artistique*, Gallimard nrf, 1951.

Les Voix du Silence, IV: *La Monnaie de l'Absolu*, Gallimard nrf, 1951.

Le Musée Imaginaire de la Sculpture Mondiale, I: *La statuaire*, Gallimard nrf, 1952.

Le Musée Imaginaire de la Scultpure Mondiale, II: *Des Bas-reliefs aux grottes sacrées*, Gallimard nrf, 1954.

Le Musée Imaginaire de la Sculpture Mondiale, III: *Le monde chrétien*, Gallimard nrf, 1954.

La Métamorphose des dieux, Gallimard nrf, 1957.

L'Inaccessible, Gallimard nrf, 1957. To be published in 1977 under the title: *Le Surnaturel*.

Le Musée Imaginaire, Gallimard Idées/Art, 1965.

Antimémories I, Gallimard nrf, 1967.

Le Triangle noir, Gallimard nrf, 1970.
Les chênes qu'on abat . . ., Gallimard nrf, 1971.
Oraisons funèbres, Gallimard nrf, 1971.
Roi je t'attends à Babylone . . ., Editions Skira, 1973. Later published in *Les Hotes de Passage*.
La Tête d'obsidienne, Gallimard nrf, 1974.
Lazare, Gallimard nrf, 1974.
L'Irreél, Gallimard nrf, 1974.
L'Intemporel, Gallimard nrf. To be published in 1976.
Le Miroir des Limbes, I: *Antimémoires* I, Gallimard Folio, 1972. Definitive version.
Le Miroir des Limbes, II: *La Corde et les Souris*, 1: *Hotes de Passage*, Gallimard Folio, 1976.
Le Miroir des Limbes, II: *La Corde et les Souris*, 2: *Les chenes qu'on abat . . .*, Gallimard Folio, 1976.
Le Miroir des Limbes, II: *La Corde et les Souris*, 3: *La Tête d'obsidienne*, Gallimard Folio, 1976.
Le Miroir des Limbes, II: *La Corde et les Souris*, 4: *Lazare*, Gallimard Folio, 1976.
Tome I des Oeuvres Completes, I: *Le Miroir des Limbes*, Pléiade/Gallimard; to be published.
Tome I des Oeuvres Completes, II: *Les Oraisons funèbres* (expanded edn.), Plèiade/Gallimard; to be published.

English:

Psychology of Art, 2 Vols., Pantheon Books, 1949.
Voices of Silence, Doubleday, 1953.
Metamorphoses of the Gods, Doubleday, 1960.
Temptation of the West, 2 vols., Vintage Books, 1961.
Museum without Walls, Doubleday, 1967; Secker and Warburg, 1967.
Antimemoirs, Hamish Hamilton, 1968.
Condition Humaine, University of London Press, 1968.
Days of Hope, Hamish Hamilton, 1968.
Man's Estate, Hamish Hamilton, 1968.
Man's Fate, Random House, 1968.
Fallen Oaks: Conversation with De Gaulle, Hamish Hamilton, 1972.
Voices of Silence, Paladin, 1974.

MAIN BOOKS ON MALRAUX

French:

Recommended as an introduction to Malraux and annotated by him:
Picon, G. *Malraux par lui-même*, Ecrivains de toujours. Seuil, 1953.

Recommended as a basis for the study of Malraux's work:
Gaillard, P. *Les Critiques de Notre Temps et Malraux*. Garnier, 1970.
Lacouture, J. *André Malraux, une vie dans le siècle*. Seuil, 1973.

Boisdeffre, P. de. *André Malraux*. Editions Universitaires, 1952.
Brincourt, A. et J. *Les Oeuvres et les lumières*. Table Ronde, 1955.
Delhomme, J. *Temps et Destin*. Gallimard, 4th edn., 1955.
Dorenlot, F. *Malraux ou l'Unite de Pensée*. Gallimard, 1970.
Duthuit, G. *Le Musée Inimaginable*, 3 vols. Jose Corti, 1956.
Erhenbourg, I. *Vus par un Ecrivain d'URSS: Gide, Malraux, Mauriac, Duhamel*. Gallimard, 1934.
Gaillard, P. *Présence Litteraire: Malraux*. Bordas, 1970.
Goldman, L. *Pour une sociologie du roman: Introduction à une étude structurale des romans de Malraux*. Gallimard, 1964.
Hoffman, J. *L'Humanisme de Malraux*. Klincksieck, 1963.
Langlois, W. G. *L'Aventure Indochinoise d'André Malraux*. Mercure de France, 1967.
  La Revue des Lettres Modernes: Série André Malraux
    'Influences et affinités', 1975.
    'Visages du Romancier', 1974.
    'Du Farfelu aux Antimémoires', 1973.
Malraux, C. *Le Bruit de nos pas*, 3 vols. Grasset, 1946.
Marion, D. *André Malraux: Cinéma d'aujourd'hui*. Seghers, 1970.
Mauriac, C. *Malraux et le Gaullisme*. Cahiers de la Fondation Nationale des Sciences Politiques. Colin, 1970.
Mounier, E. *Malraux, Camus, Sartre, Bernanos, l'Espoir des Désespérés*. Seuil. 1953.
Stéphane, R. *Proces de l'Aventurier: T. E. Lawrence, Von Salomon, Malraux* (Preface de J. P. Sartre). Sagittaire, 1968.
Vandegans, A. *La Jeunesse littéraire d'André Malraux*. Pauvert, 1964.

English:

Blend, C. D. *The Tragic Humanism of André Malraux*, Ohio State University Press, 1968.
Boak, D. *André Malraux*, Oxford, Clarendon Press, 1968.
Flanner, J. *Men and Monuments*, Harpers and Brothers, 1957; Hamish Hamilton, 1957.
Gannon, E. *The Honor of Being A Man*, Lloyola University Press, 1957.
Frohock, W. M. *André Malraux and the Tragic Imagination*, Stanford University Press, 1952.
Lacouture, J. *André Malraux*, Deutsch, 1975.
Langlois. W. G. *The Indochina Adventure*, Praeger Publishers, 1966; Pall Mall Press, 1966.
Payne, R. *A Portrait of André Malraux*, Prentice Hall, Inc., 1970.

Righter, W. *The Rhetorical Hero, An Essay on the Aesthetics of André Malraux*, Chilmark Press, 1964.

Savage, C. *Malraux, Sartre and Aragon as Political Novelists*, University of Florida Press, 1964.

Wilson, E. *The Shores of Light: A Literary Chronicle of the Twenties*, Farrar, Strauss & Giroux, pp. 566–74).

'The Bit between My Teeth: A Literary Chronicle of 1950–1965', *The Museum without Walls*, Farrar, Strauss & Giroux.

REVIEWS AND ARTICLES

Among the innumerable articles which have been written on Malraux, the following are particularly important:

French:

Grosjean, J. 'Les Antimemoires d'André Malraux', *Nouvelle Revue Francaise*, no. 178, October 1967.

Peyre, H. 'Malraux, le Romantique', *Revue des Lettres Francaises*, Mignard, pp. 355–9.

'Malraux, Paroles et Ecrits Politiques, 1947–72', *Espoir*, no. 2, revue de l'Institut Charles de Gaulle.

Le No. Special de la Revue *Esprit*, no. 10, October 1948. This issue contains articles by A. Beguin, P. Debray, G. Picon, C. E. Magny, E. Mounier, R. Stéphane.

English:

Chiaromonte, N. 'Malraux and the Demons of Action', *Partisan Review*, July 1948.

Steiner, G. 'André Malraux, a Gaul for All Seasons', *Life*, May 1968.

Wolfe, B. 'Malraux Mosaic: Reflections Seen through A Creative Prism', *Chicago Daily News*, 26 October 1968.

RECORDS

Hommage de la France a Jean Moulin, ORTF, 1965.

Les questions que posent les Antimémoires: André Malraux répond aux jeunes. (Entretien du 25 Octobre 1967 sur Europe I), Collection: Français de notre temps, 65 FT 68.

Entretien avec Pierre de Boisdeffre, ADES, ORTF, 1967.

André Malraux, Discours Politiques (1922–68), Hommes et faits du xxéme siècle, CERF.

André Malraux, Discours historiques (Institut Charles de Gaulle, Déesse DDLX 83–4.

INDEX